Strategic Planning: Readings

Compiled by:

Professor P.J. Smit
(University of South Africa)

Typeset by: Pat de Zeeuw cc, Johannesburg
Cover design by: Dallas du Toit, Cape Town
Printed and bound by: Creda Communications, Eliot Avenue,
Epping, Cape Town

Preface

Strategic planning is viewed as the concept and process that links an organisation and its environment. Today's business environment is profoundly different to any previously seen. To compound the complexity of aligning the organisation with its environment, organisations are taking on new and flexible forms. The traditional theory and practice of strategic management – which dominate textbooks on the subject – have to give way to innovative alternatives.

Strategic Planning: Readings has been compiled to give credit to conventional wisdom regarding strategic planning issues as well as contemporary views on the subject. This compilation can be seen as a flexible way of dealing with a subject that is constantly changing.

The compilation deals with all the critical components of strategic planning that have to be addressed in the 'thinking' phase of strategic management, namely strategic planning issues. To deal with these components meaningfully, these articles have been clustered into four sections:

Section One: The Nature and Value of Strategic Management

Section Two: The Business Environment

Section Three: The Vision and Mission

Section Four: Formulating Long-Term Goals

The point of departure in selecting relevant articles for this compilation was that students need to become critical thinkers. They therefore have to master the relevant knowledge, skills and attitudes and they need to apply these in different contexts. If students are able to do this, they will be regarded as competent in this field. A prescribed textbook alone cannot achieve this.

In the light of the above, each article was carefully selected on the basis of:

- its understandability for undergraduate and postgraduate students;

- its clarity and conciseness in dealing with the relevant topic;
- the extent to which it explains the theoretical concepts;
- how the concepts have been applied in practice; and
- its acceptability in terms of sound research principles.

The logical and chronological way in which *Strategic Planning: Readings* was compiled therefore lends itself to being used in conjunction with other study material or as a stand-alone guide in a course dealing with strategic planning.

Although there are many other brilliant refereed articles on the topics dealt with in this compilation, they could not be included because of space limitations. Should you come across another article or excerpt that you consider meriting placement in the next issue, you are welcome to contact me on 082 442 5707. Your contribution will be much appreciated.

To complement *Strategic Planning: Readings*, we are compiling articles dealing with the implementation of strategy and intend publishing them as *Readings in Strategy Implementation and Control.* The new text will be published early in the year 2000.

Please note that copyright permission has been obtained for the use of the articles in the text and that, as such, there is no consistency in referencing styles or language and grammar usage. We are governed by the styles used in each of the individual articles. A few terms have been changed so that the content conforms to the requirements of the southern African reader.

I trust that you will enjoy using Strategic Planning: Readings and wish you well in your studies.

Professor P.J. Smit
University of South Africa
November 1999

Contents

SECTION ONE

THE NATURE AND VALUE OF STRATEGIC MANAGEMENT

Shifting the Strategic Management Paradigm
- John Camillus

The Long and the Short of Strategic Planning
- F. Paul Carlson

Does Strategic Planning Improve Company Performance - Gordon E. Greenley

Strategic Management – Tasks and Challenges in the 1990s - Dietger Hahn

Pressures from Stakeholders Hit Japanese Companies – Mark E. Steadman, Thomas W. Zimmerer and Ronald F. Green

Shifting the Strategic Management Paradigm

By **John Camillus**, *Donald R. Beall Professor of Strategic Management, Katz Graduate School of Business, University of Pittsburgh*

European Management Journal Vol. 15, No. 1, pp 1-7, 1997

John Camillus, Katz Graduate School of Business, University of Pittsburgh, Pittsburgh, Pennsylvania 15260, USA.

John Camillus is the Donald R. Beall Professor of Strategic Management at the University of Pittsburgh's Graduate School of Business. He was formerly Professor of Management at the Indian Institute of Management, Ahmedabad. He received his doctorate from Harvard Business School. He has published extensively, both articles and books. He is on the editorial advisory boards of Long Range Planning and Strategy and Leadership, and is a columnist for Praxis.

His primary research and consulting interests lie in strategic planning processes and his clients range from fast growing, professional firms to Fortune 500 companies in chemical, energy and manufacturing industries.

He has received awards in the US and abroad for teaching excellence including the university-wide Chancellor's Distinguished Teaching Award at the University of Pittsburgh.

Traditional theory and practice of strategic management explains the behavior of organizations in their business environments. Current turbulence means traditional models of strategic management are having to give way to alternative explanations.

John Camillus reviews the 'predictive' and learning' paradigms accepted in the early evolution of strategic management, and points out their weaknesses in the face of massive discontinuous change, both external and internal to the company.

New forms of organization have arisen in the current climate of change which are better explained by a 'transformational' paradigm which is pro-active and well-suited to bridge discontinuities. The author provides corporate examples of the adoption of the new paradigm.

Business strategy and strategic management have long been viewed as the concept and process that link an organization and its environment. In these changing times with business environments far different than any previously seen and with organizations taking on new and flexible forms, it follows that traditional ways of articulating strategy and practicing strategic management have to give way to innovative alternatives. To speculate meaningfully about these innovations requires that we review the conventional wisdom regarding strategy and understand the nature of the changes that are taking place in organizations and their environments.

The Evolution of Strategic Management

Mintzberg's (1994) recent and quite premature obituary for strategic planning is an important milestone in a long tradition of management thought, initiated by Henri Fayol in the nineteenth century. Fayol's (1969) linear, unidimensional and stylized understanding of the management process (planning, organizing, staffing. directing, implementing and controlling) gave way to Anthony's (1965) more complex and realistic partitioning of the management process into strategic planning, management control and operational control. Anthony's seminal contribution was to recognize the difference in both degree and kind that exists in planning and control activities at various levels in a formal organization. For instance, to take just one of many dimensions, the CEO of a major corporation would be seen as derelict in her duties if the planning horizon considered by her was not of the order of five to ten years. On the other hand, a regional sales manager in the same firm would be viewed as impractical if he developed ten-year plans. The important distinction is not only the difference in the horizon, a *difference in degree*, but the fact that the CEO needs to look far enough into the future to go beyond the period of certainty, beyond the period for which the business can expect to maintain its current strategy. She has to plan not only the conduct of strategy as at present, but the transformation of the organization to enable it to conduct business beyond the period of viability of the current strategy. The regional sales manager would not ordinarily be expected to plan beyond the horizon of certainty, beyond the viability of the existing strategy, a *difference in kind*. Anthony's identification of the distinct, different strategic planning task of management found reinforcement, conceptual development and process delineation offered by Ansoff (1965) and Andrews (1970). The Anthony-Ansoff-Andrews paradigm came to maturity, full expression and acceptance in an international seminar on strategic planning held at the University of Pittsburgh in 1978, which was

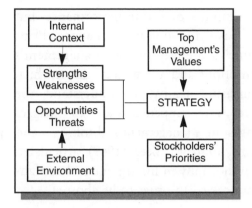

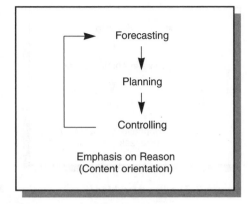

Figure 1. The Traditional Process   **Figure 2.** The Prediction Model

documented and disseminated by Schendel and Hofer (1979) in their book titled *Strategic Management*. This understanding of strategic management is still today the most widely accepted and implemented view of the process by which managers develop, define and motivate the competitive strategy, organizational architecture and long-term objectives of the organization. The traditional strategic planning process that is part of the total strategic management activity is shown in Figure 1.

Underlying this model is an emphasis on analysis and reason, very much in keeping with Fayol's view of the management function. There is a presumption that a combination of analysis, experience and insight can lead to reliable predictions regarding the future; a philosophy that the arrow of history has predetermined the course of the future. This classic 'prediction' paradigm is stylistically represented in Figure 2.

The Challenge of Uncertainty

The classic paradigm, ubiquitous though often hidden, combined with an increasingly dynamic environment, resulted in an evolution of management systems from the master budgets of the fifties, through the long range plans of the sixties, to the strategic plans of the seventies. In the eighties, the rapidity with which the business environment changed brought home the validity of Neils Bohr's tongue-in-cheek aphorism that 'prediction is very difficult, especially about the future.' With the inability to predict the future came the need to view plans differently. No longer could they be seen as predictions of the future, based on reliable forecasts, dependent only on effective managerial actions. Plans came to be seen not

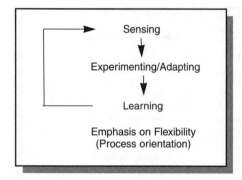

Figure 3. The Learning Model

as descriptors of future performance, but as a basis for initiating changes. Plans became a descriptor of management's assumptions and a template against which to measure reality, to understand the future as it happened and to trigger changes in management's thinking and actions. Stafford Beer (1969) articulated this philosophy in his argument that plans are conceived in order to be aborted.

Accepting this philosophy changed the focus of strategic planning and management in organizations from an attempt to adapt to a predictable future to flexible and speedy responses to a changing present. GE's Jack Welch, in the 1980s, shifted his attention from the sophisticated strategic plans prepared by his strategic business unit managers to the pressing, current, strategic issues that they faced. Honda's success in the US is commonly attributed to its willingness to modify its intended strategy to adapt on a real-time basis to signals from the market.

The top management of several leading Japanese companies such as Matshushita have explicitly adopted a philosophy that views strategic management not as a grand, immutable plan based on insight about what the future holds, but as the design of 'experiments' to provide a basis for learning and adaptation. The paradigm underlying this approach is shown in Figure 3.

This learning paradigm of sensing, experimenting, and adapting utterly transforms the nature of strategic management. As Chakravarthy (1982) phrased it, the task of strategic management is one of managing adaptation. It accepts as true, the proposition that the only sustainable competitive advantage for an organization is the ability to learn faster than its competition.

The learning paradigm changes the character of the techniques commonly utilized in strategic planning. For instance, scenario development changes its character from the science of the probable under the prediction paradigm to the art of the possible under the learning paradigm. Scenarios become important as a way of heightening managers' awareness of the unpredictable effects of the drivers of change rather than as a context for developing detailed action plans. SWOT analysis is no longer an occasional identification of strengths, weaknesses, opportunities and threats, but becomes a real-time, ongoing state of mind.

Analyses, techniques and processes that were viewed as infrequent, discrete strategic planning exercises become an integral part of the business planning, action planning, ongoing operational decision-making activity. In the learning paradigm the *process* of strategic management dominates, in contrast to the analytically based content of strategy that was the focus of the prediction paradigm.

The Predicament of Discontinuity

The learning paradigm has proved its value to many organizations. There is, however, a major problem, an inevitable context that renders the learning paradigm inadequate and ineffective. Organizations are only now becoming aware of the notion of how change occurs in living, organic and open systems contexts. In a multitude of disciplines it is demonstrated and understood that change occurs in evolutionary ways for a period of time but will inevitably, at intervals, be revolutionary in character. Economic systems, biological entities, chemical systems, organizations and in fact any open system are subject to this pattern of change. Open systems experience this pattern of initial balance, followed by gradually increasing inconsistency with the environment, leading to disintegration of the system, requiring a radical restructuring to create a new balance. In biology, evolution, episodic speciations and mutations illustrate this phenomenon. Economists expect periods of equilibrium to be interrupted by catastrophes in the context of economic systems. Greiner's (1972) classic model of organizational growth maps directly onto the process of evolutionary changes separated by brief revolutionary intervals.

The learning paradigm works well in the evolutionary periods. When revolutions occur the learning paradigm disintegrates in the face of massive, discontinuous change.

When discontinuity hits, fundamental strategic repositioning in a very short period of time is necessary. New capabilities have to be developed. A telling example is PPG's experience in several of its businesses. PPG, starting as a manufacturer of plate glass, became a corporate giant by applying low cost commodity manufacturing expertise in three business lines - glass, paint and chemicals. The saga of one of its business units - automotive replacement glass - is typical of PPG's experiences in several of its lines and is illustrative of the strategic consequences of discontinuity. PPG's ability to manufacture automotive windshields, side windows and rear windows more cost effectively than other American manufacturers gave it a dominating edge until Chinese manufacturers entered the arena with glass produced and priced more cheaply than PPG's. PPG's core competence of commodity manufacturing was inadequate to maintain its share of the market. PPG's competitive response was to shift the battle to another field. It built a state-of-the-art logistics and distribution capability. This enabled it to meet a service goal of delivering a replacement windshield for any make or model of car sold in the US from 1949 onwards, to any of over 20 000 independent installers located all over the United States within an hour!

This incredible capability helped PPG regain its dominance as no Chinese supplier could reasonably aspire to match this delivery system. Installers, competing among themselves, would promise replacement windshield service within a few hours of an order by relying on PPG's distribution system. PPG's automotive replacement glass (ARC) business explicitly redefined its original 'commodity manufactures' concept of business and described the ARC business as one of distribution with limited in-house manufacturing capability.

This strategic repositioning based on a new capability served PPG well until a competitor – Safelite – developed a novel strategy. Recognizing two factors, first that 70 per cent of replacement windshields are paid for by insurance companies, and second that it costs insurance companies over $100 in paperwork and clerical costs to process a claim, Safelite built an efficient system that took over the claim verification and processing function on behalf of the insurance companies. The resultant significant saving from the insurance company's point of view is a strong motivation to direct all policy holders to Safelite, even if it occasionally takes an extra day or so more to get the windshield replaced than if it were done by a PPG-related installer. Faced with the Safelite challenge, the ARG unit clearly again needs to reposition itself strategically and expeditiously to maintain its share of the market.

As indicated in Figure 4, discontinuities demand that businesses move from their existing businesses and capabilities to create new businesses or capabilities. Occasionally, organizations are faced with the daunting challenge of developing new businesses that demand capabilities that the organization does not possess.

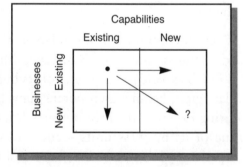

Figure 4. The Challenge of Change

When evolution gives way to revolution both the predictive and the learning paradigms are ineffective. A shift is required in the paradigm underlying strategic management when quantum changes are necessary for survival. The existing management system – organizational structure, planning processes, measurement practices, evaluation and reward systems, human resource management and cultural norms – is more a source of inertia than a proactive force for change. Prior experiences, theories of the business and formulas for success become more an impediment to the fresh thinking required than a basis for dealing with the new environment. The organization, particularly if it has been very successful in the past, is poised to become another victim of the winner's curse.

Toffler's (1970) understanding of the exponentially accelerating rate of change suggests that discontinuities will be experienced ever more frequently. In the halcyon days of the past, organizations could thrive on the predictive and learning paradigms, first because change was minimal and predictable and second because the equilibrium periods between the punctuations of discontinuity – to use Gersick's (1991) terminology – were so long. To initiate an effective paradigm shift that can cope with discontinuities requires an understanding of the causes and implications of rapid and discontinuous changes.

Origins and Managerial Implications of Discontinuity

Discontinuities occur in the environment when the drivers of change themselves change. As Toffler (1970, 1980, 1990) sees it, the drivers of societal change have shifted from agriculture, to industry, to electronics, to information. Each time the driver changes, human society goes through fundamental transformations and each subsequent occurrence takes an order of magnitude less time to happen. Thus organizations can expect to encounter environmental discontinuities every few years as opposed to the millions, thousands, hundreds and tens of years between previous discontinuities.

Competitive developments in terms of new capabilities and innovations in technology similarly create the imperative for organizations to transform themselves in order to survive and succeed. Such organizational transformations cannot be achieved through the existing organizational structure, which is just not designed to perform the transformational task. Consequently organizations set up task forces, skunk works, super teams and other collateral forms in order to effect the metamorphosis necessary for survival.

In addition to these external, societal and competitive sources of discontinuity, developments within organizations themselves create unprecedented management challenges. Three such developments are: (a) information technology, (b) professionalization and the growth of the knowledge base needed, and (c) globalization and the increase in diversity of products, markets and personnel.

The developments in *information technology* make it possible for senior managers to 'manage by walking around' electronically. The Chairman of CNG, located in Pittsburgh, can access the data bases of the exploration and production divisions located in Texas and leave email for the divisional managers regarding his observations, concerns and recommendations. Junior managers can utilize decision support technologies that empower them to make decisions with the same level of competence that previously took years of experience to reach. Communication technologies make consultation and knowledge transfer across continents as easy as across the corridor in a headquarters building. These developments in information technology create discontinuities in terms of the possible roles of senior and junior managers and offer the potential for entirely new organizational forms.

The increased *professionalization* and knowledge orientation within even the simplest businesses is also a source of quantum changes. Even a business as simple as cooking hamburgers requires extraordinary capabilities. McDonald's success, for instance, stems from its best-in-class location analysis, world-class industrial engineering and unparalleled quality management. In today's businesses, all levels within the organizational hierarchy can possess knowledge of strategic importance. The temperature at which coffee is maintained in fast food outlets is a top management decision, balancing customer preferences for very hot coffee with the risk of liability for burns caused by spilled coffee. On the other hand, GE's half-billion dollar debacle with centrifugal compressors in its refrigerators could have been avoided if the knowledge existing on the shop floor had been accessed by senior managers making the decision to shift from reciprocating compressors. These senior managers were motivated by the cost efficiencies of centrifugal compressors and were falsely reassured regarding their reliability because of their successful application in window air conditioners. Technicians on the shop floor, however, were aware of the susceptibility to failure of centrifugal compressors if heat was to build up as it would in refrigerators that are usually placed against a wall, as opposed to window air conditioners that could transfer waste heat more readily.

Globalization and diversity are developments that place the strategy development function at operating rather than the traditional senior levels. When Kentucky

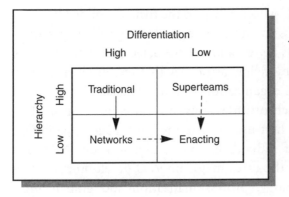

Figure 5. Emerging Organizational Forms

Fried Chicken (KFC) first entered Japan, it was only the manager on location who could make the decisions to reduce the sugar in the coleslaw, change the sizes of the portions, add fish to the menu and price the product competitively so as to cater to the tastes, preferences and pockets of the Japanese customer. Again, it was the manager on location who developed the fundamental insight that for KFC the profitable business opportunity in Japan was not 'fast-food' as in the US, but rather selling 'Americana' or the American experience to upscale Japanese customers. The implications in terms of location, pricing and promotion were totally different for each of these two concepts of business.

These internal developments in organizations, driven by information technology, professionalization and globalization, all call for what Lawler (1988) terms high involvement organizations. In these organizations all levels of management can and should impact on both operations and strategy.

Even a casual observer of the business scene cannot but be aware of the proliferating use of collateral organizations responding to external changes, and emergence of high involvement organizations resulting from the internal forces just described. The fundamental differences between traditional forms of organization and the newer forms that have been gaining popularity can be captured by examining the two basic dimensions of classic organizational structures, namely hierarchy and differentiation. Traditional organizations are characterized by the vertical dimension of *hierarchy* of management levels and the horizontal dimensions of *differentiation* of management functions. The novel forms of organization tend to de-emphasize one or the other and possibly both of these dimensions as shown in Figure 5. Naisbitt and Aburdene (1985) described the emergence of 'networks' – organizations in which formal hierarchies are substantially absent. On the other hand, the business press is rife with descriptions of organizations that integrate traditionally separate functions in what are popularly referred to as 'superteams'.

Networks recognize and indeed emphasize the varying knowledge and capabilities of individuals in an organization. With the emphasis on knowledge and the significance of individuals, hierarchy takes on less importance. In organizations like

W. L. Gore and Associates, 'associates' who newly join the firm are guided by mentors rather than superiors, have access to any other associate, regardless of seniority, who may help them do their jobs better, and are evaluated primarily by peers who assess the contributions made by fellow associates that enable them to perform more effectively in moving the organization towards its goals. Hierarchy is not a significant characteristic of such organizations, but differentiation is obvious. Networks are designed to make best use of differing knowledge, capabilities, access to resources and locations of individuals in the organization. Networks both respond to and are enabled by the three major internal developments identified earlier – information technology, professionalization and globalization /diversity.

Superteams, in contrast to networks, while acknowledging that individual members possess different points of view and competencies, subordinate these differences to the commonality of purpose, the *raison d'etre* of the superteam. Superteams may, and indeed do include experts in different disciplines such as marketing, manufacturing, engineering specialties, finance, and human resources. These differences are subsidiary to the superteam's mission of, for instance, creating a new product line, opening up a new market, reorienting strategic direction, or transforming an organization's culture. A superteam blends and directs the competencies of its members toward accomplishing its mission. In superteams the classic dimensions of differentiation identified by Lawrence and Lorsch (1967) become insignificant. Goals, interpersonal relationships, structure and time horizon are similar for members of a superteam regardless of their backgrounds, functional orientations or expertise. Thus, 'Team Taurus' in Ford, the 'skunk works' members in Lockheed and IBM, the 'LH Platform Team' in Chrysler and the 'Saturn Division' in GM were empowered by the different capabilities of their members but submerged their members' differences in their commitment to the accomplishment of a singular purpose. Hierarchy does exist in superteams. Superteams are formed and disbanded by executives with authority. Team leaders are identified and have the power to select and to transfer out individuals based on their fit with the teams' needs and characteristics.

The four-celled matrix presented in Figure 5 also suggests the intriguing possibility of organizations that minimize both hierarchy and differentiation. This 'enacting' form of organization has been speculated about for quite some time. The enacting organizational form is consistent with the self-designing tenets of Hedberg, Nystrom and Starbuck (1976) and is reflective of the interpretive system model of Daft and Weick (1984). Mills' (1991) description of 'cluster organiza-

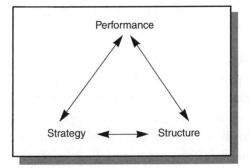

Figure 6. 'Best-in-Class' Perspective on Structure

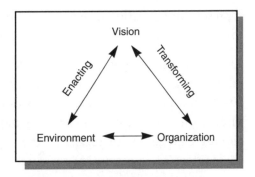

Figure 7. The Transformational Model

tions' offers a novel approach to organizational design that de-emphasizes both hierarchy and differentiation.

An instance of an enacting organization is presented in Semler's (1989) description of his organization. Enacting organizations, with their minimization of the defining structural elements of hierarchy and differentiation, are a sophisticated and perhaps even paradoxical response to the pressures and challenges of a turbulent environment.

Paradigm Shift

These three novel forms of organization represent approaches to management that are dramatically different from the traditional. It has been argued (Camillus, 1993) that each of these three structural forms require or result from unique and different approaches to conceptualizing strategy, different designs of planning and control systems, and different styles of decision-making.

There are, however, certain fundamental characteristics of all these novel forms of organization. First they represent a managerial mindset in which organizational structure is a variable rather than a given or stable element. A recent (1995) benchmarking study sponsored by the International Benchmarking Clearing house of the American Productivity and Quality Center identified the best-in-class mindset, presented in Figure 6, in which both strategy and structure are viewed as variables that are constantly manipulated to enhance performance, instead of being immutable or long-term in character. Second, these three forms of organization exist in contexts of significant internal or external change. These forms not only represent organizational redesigns to respond to changes but all three inherently, intrinsically, inevitably stimulate changes.

These two fundamental characteristics point to the key differences between this paradigm and the preceding prediction and learning models. This paradigm is based on a proactive approach. It is not about responding to unforeseen changes, or adapting to developments as they happen. Rather, it is about creating and even forcing change – with regard to the organization itself as well as with regard to the context or environment in which the organization functions. In a word, the essence of this paradigm is *transformation*.

An organization in such a mode requires a beacon or touchstone to guide its transformational efforts. With both structure and strategy being viewed as variables, it is necessary to identify a more enduring set of factors to guide transformational efforts.

Organizations that have embraced and powerfully illustrate the transformational paradigm include Federal Express, Microsoft, Bell Atlantic and Nucor. All of them are driven by a vision of the future that is based to a substantial extent on the human and managerial values espoused by their leaders and the distinctive and unique capabilities that distinguish them from other organizations. Federal Express, for instance, changed the regulatory world in which it operates. Both the then Civil Aeronautics Board and the US Postal Service modified their stances to accommodate it. Federal Express changed the way its customers did business. And, it constantly changed itself, often initiating the technological developments necessary to effect these changes. Fred Smith at the helm of Federal Express, articulated his vision even before the organization came into being. His vision embraced both a service that would change the way high value-added and professional businesses operate, and a culture that promoted unparalleled levels of reliability and performance.

This transformational paradigm is diagrammed in Figure 7. This paradigm is well suited to bridge discontinuities The values and capabilities that underlie an organization's vision can survive the metamorphosis caused by discontinuity. The organization's vision fashions the value proposition that underlies its profitable or meaningful existence in the new arena and indeed can shape the very arena itself. The transformational paradigm goes beyond predicting and away from adapting to actually creating the future.

The transformational paradigm mandates a dramatically different managerial mindset than those of the prediction and learning paradigms. For instance, in both the prediction and learning paradigms the nature and degree of competition is often a key driving force. In contrast, in the transformational context collaboration with other organizations is not uncommonly a dominant consideration. When creating new industries or new value propositions, an organization may need to complement and add to its capabilities and resources. Hence the need for alliances and collaboration. Such collaboration expresses itself through the joint ventures and consortia that typify emerging industries. Even the fiercest of competitors often find themselves acting in consort to create new opportunities. Witness Kodak and Fuji in the context of the advanced photo system, or GM and Toyota in the context of the Numi plant.

In closing, it must be recognized that adopting the transformational paradigm does not imply that the prediction and learning paradigms are entirely irrelevant. There are situations in which the prediction or learning paradigms can appropriately and effectively guide an organization's strategic management endeavors. Indeed, the challenge is not only to recognize the very different management systems and process implications that derive from a particular paradigm, but also to exercise judgment about which paradigm can best serve the organization at a given moment – when should an organization merely refine its strategic posture and when should it seek to create a new self and a new strategic domain.

References

Ansoff, I.H. (1965) *Corporate Strategy: An Analytic Approach to Business Policy for Growth and Expansion*. McGraw-Hill, New York.

Anthony, R.N. (1965) *Planning and Control Systems: A Framework for Analysis*. Harvard Business School, Boston, MA.

Andrews, K.R. (1970) *The Concept of Strategy*, Irwin, Homewood, IL.

Beer, S. (1969) The Aborting Corporate Plan. In *Perspectives of Planning*, ed. Eric Jantsch, Paris, France: OECD.

Camillus, J. C. (1993) Crafting the competitive corporation. In *Implementing Strategic Process*, ed. Peter Lorange, et. al. pp. 313-328. Blackwell, Oxford.

Chakravarthy, B. S. (1982) Adaptation; A promising metaphor for strategic management. *Academy of Management Review*, January.

Daft, R. L. and Weick, K. E. (1984) Toward a model of organizations as interpretation systems. *Academy of Management Review*, April.

Fayol, H. (1969) *General and Industrial Management*. Pitman, London.

Galbraith, J. R. (1977) Organization Design. Addison-Wesley, Reading, MA.

Gersiek, C. J. G. (1991). Revolutionary change theories: a multilevel exploration of the punctuated equilibrium paradigm. *Academy of Management Review*, January.

Greiner, L. E. (1972) Evolution and revolution as organizations grow. *Harvard Business Review*, July-August.

Hedberg, B., Nystrom, P. and Starbuck, W. (1976) Camping on seesaws. *Administrative Science Quarterly*, March.

Lawler, E. (1988) Choosing an involvement strategy. *Academy of Management Executive* August.

Lawrence P. R. and Lorsch, J. W, (1967) *Organization and Environment*. Harvard Graduate School of Business Administration, Boston, MA.

Mills, D.Q. (1991) *Rebirth of the Corporation*. John Wiley & Sons, New York.

Mintzberg, H, (1994) *The Rise and Fall of Strategic Planning*. Free Press.

Naisbitt, J. and Aburdene, P. (1985) *Re-inventing the Corporation*. New York, Warner Books.

Schendel, D.E. and Hofer, C.W. (eds) (1979) *Strategic Management*. Little Brown, Boston, MA.

Semler, R. (1989) Managing without managers. *Harvard Business Review*, September-October.

Toffler, A. (1970) *Future Shock*. Random House, New York.

Toffler, A. (1980) *The Third Wave*. Morrow, New York.

Toffler, A. (1990) *Powershift*. Bantam, New York.

The Long and Short of Strategic Planning

By F. Paul Carlson
From: *The Journal of Business Strategy* May/ June 1990. Reprinted with permission.

F. Paul Carlson is Vice President of Strategy and Business Development at Honeywell, Inc. in Minneapolis, Minnesota.

RO1 forces a corporation to measure its performance based on a short-term horizon. What is needed is a way to blend both short-term and long-term plans to achieve corporate objectives.

Long-term strategic planning faces a harsh climate in the 1990s. Publicly held companies are constantly under pressure to deliver short-term returns or face a raider acting in the name of "shareholder value." On the other hand, going private offers little refuge. Companies taken private face their own set of long-term planning constraints: Debt service reduces their ability to invest in their futures and increases their vulnerability to business cycles.

Nevertheless, strategic planning plays a key role in achieving a balance between the short and the long term. A company focused strictly on the near term is sailing a rudderless ship. Managing principally for current cash flow and quarterly earnings improvements tends to mortgage the com-pany's future. An intense focus on the near term also produces an aversion to risk that dooms a business to stagnation.

However, overemphasis on the longer term is just as inappropriate. Companies that overextend themselves betting on the future may penalize near-term prof-

Scope / Parameters	Short-Term Operational Performance	Long-Term Strategic Performance
Objective	Near-term profits	Competitive advantage
Assumption	Continuity	Change
Emphasis	Control	Creativity
Document	Budget	Plan
Framework for analysis	Accounting	Accountability through critical success factors

Exhibit 1. Measures of Organization Performance

itability and cash flow to such an extent as to make long-term planning academic.

To reconcile the conflict between long-term objectives and short-term imperatives, strategic plans for the 1990s must balance acceptable financial performance with preparation for the inevitable changes in markets, technology, and competition as well as in economic and even political factors. Expressed another way, long-term strategic plans in this new decade must deliver near-term results while at the same time providing a platform for long-term value enhancement.

Of course, achieving this result is easier said than done. Short-term issues tend to command more management attention. Measuring progress against these issues is easily done and provides a sense of achievement. In contrast to a short-term profit enhancement, consider how difficult it is to measure incremental improvements in competitive advantage, despite their obvious contributions to the longer-term strength of the business as well as their potential for improving the returns to shareholders over time.

Strategic planners need to find ways to overcome the natural bias for the short term. To do this, they must devise plans and develop measurement criteria that meld the positioning of the business for long-term value enhancement with the achievement of near-term objectives. This melding will require developing balanced strategies and implementation tactics that reconcile short- and long-term goals that may not seem to be complementary. (See Exhibit 1.)

The Planner's Juggling Act

Here are examples of how this approach can work. A company's near-term objective is to improve the control of product-development cycles and achieve shorter times to market. At the same time, the company wants to encourage creativity and interaction to stimulate thinking about new projects and new ways to satisfy customer needs. To reconcile the apparent conflict between maximum control and maximum creativity, the tactical approach might be as follows: Use firmer schedules and a better-defined budget to achieve control in a macro sense while allowing those managers and departments charged with product development free rein in solving the perceived problems.

The charge might be: "You must work within these schedule and budget boundaries. But within them, you can do whatever you need to do to get the job done."

At Honeywell, Inc., as well as at many other companies, this translation of a long-term strategy into tactics that enhance the short term has given rise to new approaches, such as team-based product development, that have shortened manufacturing cycles, improved quality, and reduced costs.

In another example, consider a company that wants to improve both near-term profitability and long-term competitive strength. Formulating the objective requires developing strategies and tactics to achieve these dual goals. Therefore, certain types of expense reductions that would only produce onetime "pops" in profits will be less attractive than a more diligent look at the basic cost structure of the business.

This examination may lead to decisions to sharpen the company's focus and allocate resources differently, thus improving performance on several fronts. As a result, the company achieves improvements in the near term while also positioning itself for long-term strength as a lower- or lowest-cost producer.

Businesses must also ensure short- and long-term balance in the measures of performance that they use. If performance is measured solely on accounting-based return on investment (ROI), management is motivated to strive for higher near-term revenues and write down the related investment at year-end. Unchecked by a longer-term view, this strategy gives rise to a cycle in which short-term dynamics, misfocused investment, and current period transactions are all that matter. The irony here is that managers will likely earn healthy bonuses while jeopardizing the future of the business.

To attack this destructive cycle, businesses must add achieving growth in shareholder value to performance measurement and to the incentive compensation system. This strategy will force a focus on longer-term management of the growth of the business and will result in a clearer investment strategy. A focus on shareholder value has an inherent tendency to bring attention to better operating profits and cash management. The ROI focus, on the other hand, favors classical "hockey stick" plans – that is, "we will get the results in a year or two, and they will be great. "

Adding shareholder value components to performance measurement ensures that accountability, not just accounting, is properly recognized. Clever actions at year-end cannot make up for a continual lack of strategic planning for the long term. Carefully detailing higher revenue expectations against investment requirements and cash flow needs over three-to-five-year periods demands a careful assessment of market and customer needs and trends.

Coupled with a focus on shareholder value is a need to produce a heightened awareness of cash management. "Cash Max", a cash management program implemented at Honeywell, focuses everyone on finding ways to unlock cash and reduce working capital requirements. Associated with this program is a stronger focus on more cost-sensitive procurement practices and material management processes.

Cost reductions in these categories go immediately to the bottom line and allow people to gain a keener sense of good business practice. The behavioral changes brought about by adding shareholder value and cash management criteria to performance measurement will have an important impact on overall business performance; thus, they represent a set of critical success factors that are ultimately more meaningful in the longer view than accounting measures.

Planning Imperatives

If achieving these links and balances is the key to reconciling long- and short-term performance issues, then what follows are imperatives for planners in the 1990s:

❏ **Strive for flexibility.** Recognize that change will occur, and plan for transitions before they become crises. Businesses must organize to anticipate the opportunities that come with change and to respond quickly to situations that need attention.

For example, manufacturing practices can be made more adaptable to shorter runs and various but similar product mixes, thus enabling quicker changes. Work practices –"people systems"– must be modified to allow for more versatility and cross-training of employee teams.

Job functions that change to meet current needs can also create a context for renewal and stimulation of long-term employees. Although change is stressful, the lessons learned from smaller entrepreneurial organizations and the associated improvements in productivity demonstrate the importance of flexibility in job functions. This strategy can also instill a culture of continual improvement.

Keep an open mind, and be responsive to organizations that have a strong union dependence. Union work-rule concepts will continue to be under assault throughout the 1990s. But the by-product of a more flexible, task-team approach will provide more effective employee involvement.

❏ **Globalize.** While markets will retain regional characteristics, serving them will require planning and organizing resources globally. For example, Honeywell

International has a long-term global distribution strategy with two major thrusts: the optimization of its mature sales and service infrastructure and the penetration of selective, developing geographic markets.

❑ **Spread information.** Use information to link operations to strategy, identify decision points, and drive decision making to the lowest practical level in the business. Honeywell is accomplishing this goal with its Cash Max program. With a proven track record at other companies, the program is already raising cash consciousness at every function and level at Honeywell.

❑ **Standardize.** Establish clear boundaries of authority and responsibility so that people know the span of control that they can exercise within their respective business units.

❑ **Measure.** Keep people accountable. Measurement must be unambiguous so that accountability does not shift up or down if performance falters. Action must follow measurement to reinforce commitment to achieving plan objectives.

❑ **Reward.** Keep people motivated. Encourage superior performance by establishing clear reward and incentive systems. To link team performance to corporate goals, make shareholder value a component of incentive plans. Once a direction is established, it is sustained by incentives that encourage long-term commitment and outstanding performance.

❑ **Reorganize.** Favor teams over hierarchies. Flexible teams and task groups will tend to replace the classical organization pyramid. This change will be driven by the pyramid's unfavorable cost structure as well as by communications problems inherent in such a hierarchical system.

Examine how products get to the customer and what costs are associated with each distribution channel. Is the customer giving more weight to support and service in making the "buy" decision? If so, the structure and skills that the organization requires will likely need to change. Be sure that the business is organized first for the customer's benefit and then for the company's.

At Honeywell, the balance between a functionally structured organization and a product structured organization is continually being examined. The conflict between the two organizational styles is rooted in many factors, some that the company controls and others that it does not. These factors include changes in technology, vertical integration of more value-added activities, and customer expectations of suppliers. Functionally designed organizations will generally have lower overhead costs, particularly when a broad spectrum of products is involved, because of the elimination of duplication across the business.

❏ **Balance the interests of all constituents.** Develop coordinated strategies, policies, and action plans with a clear commitment to balance. This balance will impose a higher standard of performance on senior management, creating an organization that is a strong contender in a very competitive marketplace.

Given these imperatives, the ideal manager of the 1990s will demonstrate these qualities:

- Comfort with strategic exploring;
- The vision to see both opportunities and dangers in crises;
- The ability to operate in higher-risk arenas; and
- The flexibility to change one's style and response, depending on the situational need.

An SBU Strategy

At Honeywell, the strategic planning team asks two basic questions: What businesses should we be in, and how shall we manage them?

Honeywell's restructuring announcements indicated that the company was going to reduce its dependence on the defense industry and focus on the core business of controls. Part of this restructuring was to develop a set of strategic business units (SBUs).

The SBU concept is not new. As the term is defined at Honeywell, SBUs are a means to align separate but interrelated business units through coordinated objectives and actions that target clearly defined markets. By strategically grouping businesses that serve common customers and have common technologies, the SBU concept will keep Honeywell's focus on customer needs, help create competitive advantages, require the company to think more strategically about its markets and competition, and shorten its management and communications links. SBUs do not replace the divisions of the current organization. Rather, they help create horizontal linkages and synergies within a traditional vertical structure. Some of these synergies might come through shared distribution channels, research and development programs, or engineering resources. Others will come through the sharing of production facilities.

At Honeywell, an SBU has the following characteristics:

- It is a single business or collection of related businesses.
- It has a distinct mission.
- It has its own competitors.
- It has its own worldwide management.
- It consists of one or more program units (such as product or market segments) and functional units (such as finance and marketing).
- It can benefit from strategic planning across its mission.
- It can plan independently but can be operated in a co-ordinated environment.

The SBU approach helps Honeywell's employees function as teams. They find themselves working across divisional lines more often than they have been accustomed to in the past. Managers may have less autonomy in some areas but greater autonomy in others. And some functions currently performed at local levels, such as marketing and human resources, may eventually be carried out at the SBU level.

The SBU model will enable Honeywell to increase its participation in joint ventures and strategic alliances, which will become increasingly common in the 1990s. The SBU structure will position Honeywell to take full advantage of the opportunities for shared risk and shared benefit within defined business areas.

Honeywell's initial set of SBU characteristics will change as the company completes its current round of restructuring moves. What Honeywell employees are learning is that initial conceptualizations are generally not as practical as originally imagined, and the understanding of what drives the business becomes clearer as the SBU concept is used in responding to global market changes.

Along with this organizational focus is a drive to improve the productivity and financial performance of the whole enterprise. These moves have demonstrated that further refinement in the sense of "how to manage the businesses" is needed and justified. Reductions in levels of management and moves to find higher levels of economies of scale in the culturally autonomous units are needed. The process is iterative and does demonstrate a few fundamental "rules":

- Not all lines of business need the same organizational structure in a large enterprise.
- Customer and market demands shape the final form in order to pull the organization closer to the customer.
- Competitive advantages will lie in different domains across the enterprise (technology and classical line structure may dominate in one line of business while

distribution channels and after-market dynamics will drive another).
- Flexibility and a willingness to experiment are crucial.
- All constituents' interests must be considered.

When an organization is changing rapidly, an enormous amount of energy is needed to keep the agendas for the future linked and focused on the same goal. Restructuring costs, reserve actions, and earnings reporting all must be factored into the planning process.

As the future is being planned at Honeywell, the new SBU approach will make us more efficient and valuable as a company by enabling us to serve customers in a more unified, consistent, and focused manner – in the short term and the long term.

Does Strategic Planning Improve Company Performance?

By Gordon E. Greenley, University of Birmingham

Long Range Planning, Vol. 19 No. 2, pp 101 to 109, 1986, with permission from Elsevier Science.

Gordon E. Greenley is in the Department of Industrial Economics and Business Studies at the University of Birmingham, P.O. Box 363, Birmingham B152TT

This article examines the current published empirical data relative to the relationship of strategic planning in manufacturing companies and their overall performance. The conclusion from this examination is that this data is far from conclusive in establishing such a relationship. The article also examines the potential advantages and intrinsic values of strategic planning, although this examination illustrates a lack of evidence to substantiate such benefits. Finally, the article suggests a range of implications as a consequence of these results.

This article is concerned with the effectiveness of strategic planning in manufacturing companies. As a function of the overall management of an organization, the literature describes planning as being effective relative to its contribution to the performance, or end results, that the planning system was initially designed to achieve. These end results are generally initially established in the strategic planning system as a range of corporate objectives. The first area of attention in this article is published reports of empirical data, which have examined such a relationship between strategic planning and company performance. However, the author concludes that the research published to date, relative to manufacturing companies, is far from conclusive in establishing a relationship between strategic planning and performance, or end results. Therefore it cannot be concluded that strategic planning is an effective, or indeed ineffective, tool for the overall management of organizations.

The problems associated with assessing effectiveness by measuring performance have been discussed by writers such as Dyson and Foster[1] and Greenley.[2] In an attempt to overcome these problems, writers such as Kotler,[3] Dyson and Foster[1] and Heroux[4] have proposed methods to assess the effectiveness of the planning system itself, as opposed to the end results that it produces. However, these methods are based upon a range of arbitrary attributes, the existence of which, in a particular planning system, is claimed to indicate that the system is likely to be effective. However, the major problem here is paradoxical when compared to a performance assessment, in that, even if the attributes are present, there is still no assurance that the required results will be achieved. However, there is still a range of potential advantages to be gained within a company due to the utilization of strategic planning, even if specific cause and effect relationships cannot, at this point in time, be established. In addition to such advantages, the article recognizes benefits which accrue from the utilization of strategic planning, which are inherent as a consequence of its utilization. These are labelled as being 'intrinsic values' of planning, which not only accrue to the organization, but also to external stakeholders. These potential advantages, plus intrinsic values, are the second area of attention in the article.

To summarize, this article examines published research into the relationship of strategic planning and company performance, but concludes that the nature of such a relationship has yet to be established. Despite this conclusion, there is still a range of potential advantages to be gained from the utilization of strategic planning, plus a range of intrinsic values which can accrue to both the company and external stakeholders, as a consequence of strategic planning. The first section of the article considers the published research, the second considers potential advantages and the third considers intrinsic values. The final section summarizes the conclusions and suggests a range of implications.

Empirical Data Relative to Strategic Planning and Company Performance

The literature search revealed nine previous studies which are appropriate to the article. All utilized sample surveys, with all but one being carried out in the U.S.A., the other had been in the U.K. All the surveys investigated strategic planning within manufacturing companies, where sample sizes ranged from 10 to 386 companies. Of the nine studies, five conclude that companies which utilize strategic planning achieve higher levels of performance or end results, than companies which do not utilize strategic planning. The five studies which claim such a relationship are: Ansoff et al.,[5] Gershefski;[6] Thune and House,[7] Herold[8] and Karger and Malik.[9,10]

The results of these surveys claimed that strategic planning is effective, in that higher levels of results have been achieved by the companies utilizing strategic planning. However, the remaining four studies do not claim such a relationship between strategic planning and end results. These four studies are: Fulmer and Rue;[11, 12] Grinyer and Norburn;[13] Kudia; [14, 15] and Leontiades and Tezel.[16]

Alternatively, from the results of these four surveys it was concluded that higher levels of end results did not necessarily relate to the utilization of strategic planning. Therefore, from this comparison of the overall results of each survey, the conflicting conclusions obviously indicate that a firm conclusion as to the relationship of strategic planning to performance cannot be arrived at. This means that further examinations of each study are necessary, relative to both the methodological rigour of the studies and their results.

Approaches to evaluate the methodological rigour of such studies have been given in the literature by writers such as Porras and Berg[17] and Terpstra.[18] The latter provides fives criteria for the evaluation, as follows:

- sampling strategy; scores 1 if sample representative, 0 if it is not.
- sample size; scores 1 if $N > 30$, or 0 if $N < 30$.
- control group; scores 1 if a control was used, or 0 if one was not used.
- measurement strategy; scores 1 it a pre-test strategy was made, or 0 if one was not made.

	Sampling strategy	Sample size	Control group	Measurement strategy	Significance level	Score for each study
Ansoff et al[5]	1	1	0	0	1	3
Gershefski[6]	0	1	0	0	0	1
Thune and House[7]	1	1	0	1	0	3
Herold[8]	1	0	0	1	0	2
Karger and Malik[9, 10]	1	1	0	1	1	4
Average score						2,6
Fulmer and Rule,[11, 12]	1	1	0	0	0	2
Grinyer and Norburn[13]	1	0	0	0	1	2
Kudla[14, 15]	1	1	1	0	1	4
Leontiades and Tezel[16]	1	1	0	0	1	3
Average score						2,75

Table 1. Comparison of Surveys

- significance levels; scores 1 if significance levels are reported to at least the $P < 0,05$ level, or 0 if no reporting, or if $P > 0,05$.

Using these criteria, the resultant comparisons of the nine studies are given in Table 1.

Consequently the average score per group is low at 2,6 and 2,75, respectively, but this falls to an average of only 2,25 and 2,33 if the scores of 4 are removed. Although Terpstra does not give any standards against which to compare such evaluating, the scores are perhaps self evident and can be interpreted by visual inspection. Hence none of the studies can be considered to be particularly rigorous in their methodology, based on these criteria, except perhaps for the studies by Karger and Malik[9, 10] and Kudla. [14, 15] As each of these studies is within a different group of studies, as the frequency of the other scores within each group shows little difference and as the average score per group is similar, then it can be concluded that there is no difference between the groups based upon methodological rigour. Therefore, from this comparison of the studies, based upon these criteria of methodological rigour, an indication as to the relationship of strategic planning and performance is not evident.

However, other criteria can also be examined in the comparison of the surveys. The nature of the questions used and survey bias would be such valuable criteria, although both of these were not available. Other valuable criteria relate to the individual sample characteristics, geographical differences and timing. In the case of sample characteristics, most studies covered both industrial and consumer firms (although several did not disclose this information), information on the personnel responding was generally not reported, although sample size was readily available. Here the sample sizes within the studies which do claim an association between strategic planning and end results ranged from $N = 10$ to $N = 323$, with an average size of 110. However, the sample sizes within the studies which do not claim such an association ranged from $N = 21$ to $N = 386$, with an average size of 200. Although this is the only criterion which indicates any difference in methodological rigour, it can only be considered to be a slight indication of a possible difference. In the case of geographical location, this can perhaps be considered to be constant in that all but one of the surveys were based in the U.S.A. However, in the case of timing there is a different situation. Within the studies which do claim an association between strategic planning and end results, four of the studies were before 1975, with the other study being reported at that time. However, within the studies which do not claim such an association, all but one are post-

1975. Again this criterion can only be taken to be an indication of a possible difference in methodological rigour.

Therefore, from the overall comparison of the two groups of studies, based upon methodological rigour, an overall conclusion as to the relationship of strategic planning and performance cannot be arrived at. This, then, leads to an examination of the nature of the results of the studies.

Nature of Results; Studies Claiming a Relationship.
The results of these studies are summarized as follows:

Ansoff et al. (N = 93)
The study used 13 separate variables of financial performance using 21 different measures within these variables. These were measured in more than one way, in order to minimize the effects of bias from any one type of measure. The 13 variables used were: sales; earnings; earnings/share; total assets; earnings/equity; dividends/share; stock price; debt/equity; common equity; earnings/total equity; P/E ratio; payout (dividends/earnings) and price/equity ratio.

The values of these variables for companies which do extensive strategic planning were compared with the values of the companies which did little planning. With the exception of equity growth and growth of assets, the companies which do extensive strategic planning outperformed the other companies, with levels of statistical significance of these differences ranging from $P < 0,1$ to $P < 0,005$.

Gershefski (N = 323)
This survey compared the growth of sales in companies over a 5-year period before strategic planning was introduced, and over a period of 5 years after planning was introduced. The results of this comparison led the author to conclude that companies with formal strategic planning outperform companies with little planning and that this indicates that strategic planning is effective. However, the statistical significance of the differences between formal and informal planners were not reported and data were not made available to calculate levels of significance.

Thune and House (N = 36)
The approach taken in this study was to examine the performance of each company both before and after formal strategic planning was initiated. Although these periods of time were equal for each company, they did vary from firm to firm. Comparisons were then made of these changes, relative to both formal and informal planners. The variables which were used to measure changes in performance

were: sales; stock prices; earnings per share; return on equity and return on capital employed.

The comparison of planners and informal planners showed that the planners outperformed the informal planners on all five measures. The authors report that these differences were statistically significant, but the actual levels of significance were not reported. In addition they found that formal planners outperformed their own performance after the introduction of formal planning.

Herold (N = 10)
This study was instigated in response to the Thune and House study, in an attempt to cross-validate and broaden the results of the latter. However, the study resulted in a survey of only 10 companies in the drugs and chemicals industry. The performance of formal and informal planners were compared over a 7-year period, using the variables of sales growth, profit growth and R & D expenditure as measures for comparison. The author concludes that formal planners outperform informal planners with respect to these measures, from the point in time when the formal strategic planning was initiated. Although it is claimed that these differences are significant they have not been statistically tested. Indeed Herold highlights that this was not done, due to the small sample size. However, he does conclude that the results support those of Thune and House.

Karger and Malik (N = 90)
The approach taken in this study was similar to that taken by Ansoff *et al.*, in that the values of a range of variables of planners were compared to the values of the same variables of non-planners. The range of variables used in this study are as follows: sales value; sales per share; cash flow per share; earnings per share; rate earned on net worth; operating margin; per cent of dividends to income; stock price; book value per share; net income; rate earned on capital; price/earning ratio and capital spending per share.

From these comparisons, the authors conclude that the planners out-performed the non-planners relative to all variables except capital spending, stock price and dividends to income. The comparison of each variable between planners and non-planners was tested for statistical significance. Here, six of the 13 comparisons were significant at the $P < 0,05$ level and a further two were significant at the $0,05 < P < 0,10$ level. The remaining five comparisons were insignificant at the 10 per cent level.

Nature of Results; Studies Claiming No Relationship
The results of these studies are summarized as follows:

Fulmer and Rue (N = 386)
The survey used in this study was firstly designed to classify the formality of the companys' strategic planning. The survey also measured the financial performance of the companies, using the following four variables to assess performance: sales growth; earnings/sales ratio; earnings growth and earnings/total capital.

In making the comparisons for each variable, the authors split the respondents into large and small firms, with the aim of making a more realistic comparison. The overall conclusion they came to is that there is no simple across the board relationship between the completeness of strategic planning and financial performance. However, they do not conclude that strategic planning does not affect end results, but that their study indicates that there is no clear relationship between strategic planning and these variables. In making these comparisons the authors did not report the use of statistical significance testing, nor do they volunteer why such testing was not applied.

Grinyr and Norbum (N = 21)
In this study a single measure of financial performance was adopted as follows:
    Return on net assets =

$$\frac{\text{Profit before interest and tax}}{\text{Fixed assets + current assets − current liabilities}}$$

The study involved correlation analysis of the relationship of financial performance with a common perception of objectives, role perception and formality of planning. In all cases they found that there was no association with financial performance, with none of the comparisons being statistically significant at the 0,05 level. As they could find no evidence, particularly none relating formality of planning to financial performance, the authors consider that their results call into question most of the basic assumptions on which strategic planning is established.

Kudla (N = 328)
The study did not use a range of financial performance measures, but restricted its assessment to comparing the payments made to shareholders. The hypothesis tested was that the shareholders of planning companies would receive higher returns than the shareholders of non-planning companies. The survey covered a

period of 5 years before the planners introduced strategic planning to their companies and a 10-year period after its introduction. The study concluded that strategic planning had a negligible affect on the level of shareholders' earnings, with this result being statistically significant at the 0,05 level. Therefore, Kudla concludes that strategic planning and performance are not related and sees his results as being consistent with those of Grinyer and Norburn.

Leontiades and Tezel (N = 61)

In this study the authors firstly claim a weakness in previous studies, which they relate to subjectivity in defining the formality of strategic planning and consequently subjectivity in defining companies as being planners or non-planners. The approach they used was to get the Chief Executive and the Chief Planning Officer, of each company to assess the importance of strategic planning on a numerical bipolar, semantic differential scale, with the aim of providing a quantified variable which could then be compared with company performance. Five variables were used to measure this performance, as follows: return on equity; return on assets; price – earnings multiples; earnings per share growth and sales growth.

The variables were measured for each company over a 6-year period. The study tested several hypotheses that would have indicated that the ratings of strategic planning and performance were related, but none of these were statistically significant at the 10 per cent level. Therefore the authors conclude that there is no evidence, from their study, of an association between the perceived importance of strategic planning and company performance.

From the examination of these studies there are five major areas of criticism, relative to the investigation of the relationship. The first is that there are many other variables which can also affect performance/end results, so that the changes detected in company performance may not have been affected by strategic planning, or may have been only partially affected by strategic planning, or indeed affected only by strategic planning (although the latter is highly unlikely). Although it can be hypothesized that a partial affect is likely, none of the studies were able to negotiate this situation. In addition, where an association between strategic planning and performance was claimed, a causal relationship would need to be established, which, due to the variation in results, cannot be asserted. In addition, the direction of the causality would need to be established. This could be that indeed strategic planning does improve company performance, but it could also be that improved performance gives the firm the capacity or ability to implement strategic planning, with improved profits yielding the resources for its utilization.

Again the direction of such a causal relationship is not apparent and therefore the relationship cannot be asserted.

The second area of criticism relates to subjectivity within the studies. In all the studies subjectivity was evident in defining formality of planning and in differentiating between planners and non-planners. Not only were these definitions subjective within each study, but the criteria of definition was not common across the studies. The studies can also be claimed to exhibit subjectivity in that only financial measures were included in determining company performance. Indeed there are other end results which are established in strategic planning objectives, which perhaps would need to be considered in such studies. These points lead on to the third area of criticism, which is concerned with bias.

Comments made in this paragraph imply the possibility of researcher bias, in that personal opinions either favouring or not favouring strategic planning, may have affected the results. However, this is merely implied. Alternatively, bias due to weak methodology has already been suggested in the previous examination of methodological rigour. The lack of utilization of tests of statistical significance is perhaps of prime consideration here, although this will be discussed further as the last criticism.

The fourth area of criticism relates to the lack of commonality in the studies, leading to difficulty in the cross validation of results. First there was the large variation in sample size, mix in type of company (between consumer and industrial products) and mix in companies by size. Here the studies not only exhibited variation in these three characteristics, but also showed lack of consideration in these variables and their possible affects on the strategic planning/performance relationship being studied. Only one study compared large and small firms, but the definition of large and small was by comparison of sales turnover to an arbitrary level. The second area of lack of commonality was concerned with the variables used throughout the studies to measure financial performance. Here there was variation in the measures used with a tendency to measure financial performance orientated towards results required by shareholders. Although this can be claimed to be a valid measure, there are other stakeholder groups and associated financial measures which are also important, which relates back to the full range of established company objectives. The final area of lack of commonality is the time periods over which the studies were carried out. This relates back to the first area of criticism. Variations in external variables are likely to have differed over the various time periods of the studies, and such affects of these variables on the planning/performance relationship are likely to have been different. This is particularly pertinent as the studies did not give any evidence of having tackled such affects and indeed the intensity of such affects on performance is likely to vary from company to company.

The fifth and final area of criticism relates to the statistical significance of the results reported within each study. Of the studies which claim a relationship between strategic planning and performance, only two studies[5,9,10] report the statistical significance of their results. Although Ansoff *et al.* report levels ranging from $P < 0,1$ to $P < 0,005$, only six of the 13 measures made by Karger and Malik were significant at the $< 0,05$ level. The Gershefski study failed to report levels of significance, as did Thune and House, although Herold did acknowledge that statistical testing had not been used due to the small sample size in his study. Of the studies which did not claim a relationship between strategic planning and performance, only the study by Fulmer and Rue failed to report levels of significance. The studies by Grinyer and Norburn and Kudla were perhaps the most stringent relative to the significance of the results, in that these were reported at the 0,05 level. However, Leontiades and Tezel used the 0,10 level for rejecting hypotheses.

These five areas of criticism are summarized as follows:

- Weakness in not identifying other variables affecting the relationship being investigated; a causal relationship and its direction was not established.
- Evidence of subjectivity across the studies in the definition of terms adopted.
- Evidence of bias in methodological rigour and also implied personal bias.
- The lack of commonality of parameters of research, across the studies.
- Wide variations in the reporting of the statistical significance of results, with four of the studies not reporting such testing.

Therefore from the assessments of both methodological rigour and the results of each study, it is concluded that the research published to date, relative to manufacturing companies, is far from conclusive in establishing a relationship between strategic planning and performance, or end results.

Potential Advantages of Strategic Planning

Regardless of whether or not strategic planning can be claimed to affect company performance, several advantages are suggested within the literature, which are claimed to arise due to the utilization of strategic planning. Within the literature these are split between those prescribed by several writers as being potential advantages, and those which are given by managers as potential advantages, as revealed by previous research and reported in the literature. The former will be discussed first.

The overall advantage of strategic planning claimed within the literature is epitomized by Godiwalla, Meinhart and Warde.[19] This is that planning results in a viable match between the changing internal organizational conditions of the firm and its external environmental variables. The purpose of this match is to ensure that the plans continuously realign the firm's objectives and strategies to the changing conditions, to improve the long run performance of the company. In addition to this overall advantage, several specific advantages are given in the literature, being classified into those being concerned with the planning process and those concerned with the personnel involved with the planning. These have been extracted from the literature as follows, from works by writers such as Stern[20] Loasby[21], Hausler[22], Walker[23] and Wilson[24] ;

Process Advantages

- The identification and exploitation of future marketing opportunities.
- An objective view of management problems.
- The provision of a framework for the review of plan execution and control of activities.
- Minimization of affects of adverse conditions and changes.
- Major decisions can be more effectively related to established objectives.
- More effective allocation of time and resources to identified opportunities.
- Provides for co-ordination of the execution of the tactics of the plan.
- Allows for the combination of all marketing functions into a combined effort.
- Less resources and time need to be devoted to correcting erroneous *ad hoc* decisions.
- Creates a framework for internal communication between personnel.
- Allows for the identification of priorities within the timing of the plan.
- The utilization of planning provides an advantage over competitors.

Personnel Advantages

- Helps to integrate the behaviour of individuals in the organization into a total effort.
- Provides a basis for the clarification of individual responsibilities, giving a contribution to motivation.
- Gives an encouragement to forward thinking on the part of personnel.

- Stimulates a co-operative, integrated and enthusiastic approach to tackling problems and opportunities.
- Encourages a favourable attitude to change.
- Gives a degree of discipline and formality to the management of a business function that would not exist without planning.

This range of prescribed advantages of strategic planning would appear to be logically self evident, being suggestive that the adoption of strategic planning would result in such advantages. However, although these benefits are claimed, none of these writers substantiate these benefits. Therefore the next stage is to examine potential advantages given by managers in previous research. Higgins and Finn[25] found that companies with the most experience of corporate planning consider that it is more successful than companies with a lesser period of experience. However, they did find that only 40 per cent of firms found corporate planning to be of limited success, although all the companies using this form of planning considered it to be worth carrying on with. Taylor and Irving[26] found that all the respondents in their survey were enthusiastic about the benefits of strategic planning, although most found difficulty in being specific in defining what it had achieved. However, they do report a selection of the advantages reported by their respondents, although they do not cite the numbers who perceive these advantages. The examples they give are as follows:

- An indication of problems before they happen.
- A change of interests and attitudes of managers.
- A discipline that identifies change and allows for consequential action.
- The identification of a need to redefine the nature of the business.
- Improves co-ordination of effort towards predetermined objectives.
- Enables managers to have a clearer understanding of the business.

The benefits of strategic planning were also investigated in two separate surveys by Al-Bazzaz and Grinyer[27] and Ang and Chua.[28] These surveys found the following percentages of respondents claiming the following advantages (see p. 37):

As with the advantages of strategic planning prescribed by writers within the literature, those claimed by respondents within the above surveys are also not substantiated. Although it is recognized that these surveys were probably not designed to investigate such evidence, and that, indeed, such evidence is likely to be difficult to reveal, it is suggested that they do need to be substantiated, as opposed to being merely implied. Although it could be argued that there is an *a priori* case

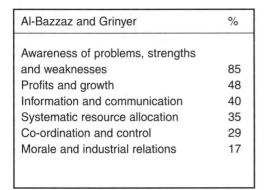

Al-Bazzaz and Grinyer	%	Ang and Chua	%
Awareness of problems, strengths		Able to explore more alternatives	66
and weaknesses	85	Faster and better quality decision	
Profits and growth	48	making	58
Information and communication	40	More timely information	49
Systematic resource allocation	35	Better understanding of the business	
Co-ordination and control	29	process	45
Morale and industrial relations	17	More accurate forecasts	43
		Cost savings	27

for such advantages, this is obviously not a sound basis for the establishment of principles within strategic management.

Intrinsic Values of Strategic Planning

The claimed advantages discussed in the previous section, whether they can be substantiated or not, are considered by the writer to be specific benefits which are intended to accrue through the actual utilization of strategic planning. However, the article also recognizes other values or qualities which accrue as a consequence of the utilization of strategic planning, which extend the intended advantages, encompassing not only the company but also its external environment. These are intrinsic in that they are inherent within the adoption of the process. However, like the claimed advantages of strategic planning, the literature does not provide evidence to substantiate such intrinsic values. Again all that can be offered is an *a priori* case that such intrinsic values are likely to accrue.

Indeed the concept of intrinsic values is not given direct treatment in the literature as a separate area of understanding. However, Camillus[29] uses the phrase 'intrinsic purposes' in explaining the benefits of planning, as the development of earlier work by Vancil.[30] Here six major purposes of planning were purported, although three are direct company advantages, being directly related to the planning process. However, the other three are more concerned with the intrinsic value of planning, in that they relate to the personal development of managers, the 'mind-stretching' nature of planning and the development of conceptual frameworks for managers to carry out the business. Another indication from the literature is from an article by Wilson.[31] Although the emphasis of this work is the integration of social responsibility and business needs, it emphasizes the broad, external social implications of company planning, based upon potential ramifications of planning within society as a whole and the consequential social responsibility that befalls the company.

The range of intrinsic values is considered to fall into three classifications. These are the general external environment, markets and the internal environment. Intrinsic values accruing from strategic planning in each of these three areas are considered to be as follows:

General External Environment
The strategic planning of the firm's business over a future time period is firstly seen to be of value to the owners/shareholders of the company. As a consequence of effective strategic planning, improved security of investment can be considered, as can future returns, as part of the role of the strategic planning process is the future assurance of such returns. These plans are also likely to give an indication of the timing of future additionally required investments, so that again the owners/shareholders can themselves plan their own future returns.

The second area of intrinsic values in this classification relates to the general public in contact with the company. One example here is that effective strategic planning allows for anticipated levels of future employment, with growth strategies likely to yield growth of employment opportunities. Another example of such an intrinsic value is a contribution to quality of life and standards of living. Effective strategic planning is likely to yield continuous product improvement, a continued understanding of the needs and wants of market segments, the establishment of justifiable prices and improved benefits to both products and related services. In addition, as the strategic planning framework requires an improved understanding of the society as part of the macro environment, it is likely that intrinsic values relative to areas such as product liability, quality control and environmental pollution control, will improve. Finally, in its widest sense, the utilization of strategic planning can be considered to be a logical exercise in the allocation of resources, which, over a long period of time, can be considered to be a contribution to efficient allocation of the world's finite resources.

The final intrinsic value of strategic planning given in this classification relates to the economy of the country in which the company is located. Long-term stability within a company provides a contribution to the stability of the GNP and companies planning for growth provide a contribution to the planned economic growth of the country's economy.

The Company's Markets
This logical organization of the firm's business over a future time period, through strategic planning, can be expected to produce several intrinsic values to its customers. The total strategic planning process focuses on customer requirements and therefore an effective strategic planning process would result in the satisfaction of these. The results of such planning could be expected to yield intrinsic values such as follows:

- Improvements to the benefits of offerings.
- Effective assessment of changes in customer requirements.
- The provision of improvements to the future product mix and the providing of future consumer benefits.
- Realistic unit prices relative to market price levels and company requirements.
- The avoidance of undue pressure from the communications output through the balancing of the elements of the marketing mix.
- The development and continuation of free competition within the marketplace, with the consequential benefits of such market conditions.

Effective strategic planning can also be considered to result in intrinsic values for suppliers of inputs to the firm's business. The demand for inputs and the required product development of such inputs will be more clearly identified at an earlier time, through the strategic planning of the company. This will have consequences for suppliers in that such requirements become part of the planning data for these companies and rationality in this data is likely to contribute to the effectiveness of the planning of suppliers.

The Internal Environment
The first area internally where strategic planning provides intrinsic values is in the co-ordination of the various business functions within the company. Although co-ordination was given previously as an advantage, the full consequences were probably not apparent. The strategic planning process *per se* obviously has value in that, if it is effective then the total company is unified and integrated towards a common aim, giving an overall framework for the co-ordination of the individual business functions. In addition, strategic marketing planning provides intrinsic values to other business functions, in that it provides inputs to other operational plans, providing a further contribution to co-ordination. Thus outputs from marketing planning provide inputs to the production plan for production scheduling, inputs to the financial plan for budgeting and other financial statements, plus inputs to the manpower plan for levels of employment needed for future levels of

sales. Following on from this, effective strategic planning also provides a basis for the internal allocation of resources. Throughout the planning process the various decisions to participate in various product/market scopes, to aim at certain growth strategies, to participate in various market segments and to pursue certain marketing opportunities, are all decisions which result in the allocation of resources.

The final intrinsic value of strategic planning given in this classification relates to the company personnel. Advantages of strategic planning to personnel were discussed previously and any split in classification between advantages and intrinsic values would be merely pedantic. However, the overall logical and rational framework given to the company by the strategic planning process is likely to contribute to a working environment in which not only is motivation, leadership and morale fostered, but in which security of operation gives a framework for overall personal development.

Conclusions and Implications

This article has examined empirical data relative to strategic planning and company performance, examined the potential advantages of strategic planning, plus its intrinsic values. The conclusion of these examinations were:

- The research published to date, relative to manufacturing companies, is far from conclusive in establishing a relationship between strategic planning and company performance.
- Although there is a strong *a priori* case that strategic planning provides a range of both advantages and intrinsic values, empirical evidence is lacking to substantiate these.

Following on from these it cannot be concluded as to whether or not strategic planning is an effective tool for the overall management of organizations.

However, despite these conclusions, several implications are apparent. The first is that, over future periods of time, additional empirical data may be reported within the literature relative to the relationship of strategic planning and company performance, which may be indicative of the effectiveness of strategic planning. The second is that empirical data may be reported relative to the substantiation of the advantages and intrinsic values of strategic planning. Also, further works may strengthen the *a priori* case for strategic planning. The third implication is that further research may indicate that company performance is not a valid basis on which to assess effectiveness. As already mentioned in the introduction, research has already started in this area, notably from the works of Dyson and Foster,[1,32] and Greenley[2] which has examined effectiveness relative to the nature of the planning process itself, as opposed to end results. The final implication is that, as a consequence of the above, the instigation of further research is obviously essential in order to consolidate the body of knowledge, with the aim of establishing the effectiveness of strategic planning as a tool for the overall management of organizations.

References

1. R.G.Dyson and M.J.Foster, Effectiveness in strategic planning, *European Journal of Operational Research.* 5 (3), 163-170 (1980).
2. G. E, Greenley. Effectiveness in marketing planning. *Strategic Management Journal.* 4 (1), 1-10 (1983).
3. P. Kotler, From sales obsession to marketing effectiveness, *Harvard Business Review.* 55 (6), 67-75 (1977).
4. R. L. Heroux, *How effective is your planning. Managerial Planning,* 30 (2). 3-16 (1981).
5. H. I. Ansoff, *et al.* Does planning pay? *Long Range Planning.* 3 (2). 2-7 (1970).
6. G. W. Gershefski, Corporate models – the state of the art, *Management Science.* 16 (6), 303-312 (1970).
7. S. S, Thune and R. J. House, Where long range planning pays off. *Business Horizons.* 29, August, 81-87 (1970).
8. D. M. Herold, Long range planning and organisational performance, *Academy of Management Journal,* 15, March, 91-102 (1972).
9. D. W. Karger and Z. A. Malik, Long range planning and organisational performance. *Long Range Planning.* 8 (6), 60-64 (1975).
10. D. W. Karger and Z. A. Malik, Does long range planning improve company performance? *Management Review.* September, 27-31 (1975).
11. R. M. Fulmer and L. W. Rue. Is long range planning profitable? *Proceedings of the Academy of Management.* 66-73 (1973).
12. R.M. Fulmer and L.W. Rue, The practice and profitability of long range planning, *Managerial Planning.* 22 (6), 1-7 (1974).
13. P. H. Grinyer and D. Norburn, Planning for existing markets, *Journal of the Royal Statistical Society.* 138 (1), 70-97 (1975).
14. R. J. Kudla, The effects of strategic planning on common stock returns. *Academy of Management Journal.* 23 (I), 5-20 (1980).
15. R. J. Kudla, Strategic planning and risk. *Review of Business and Economic Research.* 17 (1), 2-14 (1981).

16. M. Leontiades and A. Tezel, Planning perceptions and planning results. *Strategic Management Journal.* 1 (1), 65-75 (1980).
17. J. 1. Porras and P. 0. Berg, Evaluation methodology in organisational development: an analysis and critique, *Journal of Applied Behavioural Science.* 14, 151-173 (1978).
18. D. E. Terpstra, Relationship between methodological rigor and reported outcomes in organisation development evaluation research. *Journal of Applied Psychology.* 66 (5), 541-543 (1981).
19. Y. M. Godiwalla, W. A. Meinhart and W. A. Warde, General management and corporate strategy. *Managerial Planning.* 30 (2), 17-29 (1981).
20. M. E. Stern, *Marketing Planning: A Systems Approach.* McGraw-Hill, U.S.A. (1966).
21. B. J. Loasby, Long-range formal planning in perspective, *Journal of Management Studies.* 4 (3), 300-308 (1967).
22. J. Hausler, Planning: a way of shaping the future. *Management International Review.* 2 (3), 12-21 (1968).
23. K. R.Walker, How to draw up a marketing plan that will keep you on track. *Industrial Marketing.* September, 126-128 (1976).
24. R. M. S.Wilson, *Management Controls and Marketing Planning.* Heinemann, London (1979).
25. J. C. Higgins and R. Finn, The organisation and practice of corporate planning in the U.K., *Long Range Planning.* 10 (4), 88-92 (1977).
26. B. Taylor and P. lrving. Organised planning in major U.K. companies. *Long Range Planning.* 4 (3), 10-26 (1971).
27. S. Al-Bazzaz and P. M. Grinyer, How planning works in practice – a survey of 48 U.K. companies. *Long Range Planning.* 13 (4), 30-41 (1980).
28. J. S. Ang and J. H. Chua. Long range planning in large U.S. corporations. *Long Range Planning.* 12 (2), 99-102 (1979).
29. J. C. Camillus, Evaluating the benefits of formal planning systems. *Long Range Planning.* 8 (3), 33-40 (1975).
30. R. F. Vancil, The accuracy of long range planning. *Harvard Business Review.* 48 (5), 98-101 (1970).
31. I. H. Wilson, Reforming the strategic planning process: integration of social responsibility and business needs. *Long Range Planning.* 7 (5). 2-6 (1974).
32. R. G. Dyson and M. J. Foster, The relationship of participation and effectiveness in strategic planning. *Strategic Management Journal.* 3 (1), 77-88 (1982).

Strategic Management — Tasks and Challenges in the 1990s

By Dietger Hahn

Long Range Planning, Vol 24, No. 1, pp 26-39, 1991, with permission from Elsevier Science.

Dr **Dietger Hahn** is Professor of Business Administration, in Corporate Planning and Industrial Management at the Justus Liebig University, Giessen; Visiting Professor at the Technical University, Berlin and Research Director of the Institute for Corporate Planning in Giessen and Berlin.

Management in the 1990s means the management of rapid change. Changing environments create new challenges and threats, lead to new tasks and require continuous changes within companies.[1] For the management of leading German companies the major developments which are anticipated are:[2]

- increasing globalization;
- intensified competition;
- higher prices of raw materials;
- shorter product life cycles;
- difficulties in covering expenditures for research and development during commercialization;
- a need to increase flexibility within the whole company; and
- to implement new forms of inter-industry and international co-operation.

Changes within the companies will create new pressures and will require new management concepts. In particular, fundamental changes in the values of the younger generation, who will move the corporate hierarchy into senior management positions – a new familiarity with information technology and an increased commitment to the environment will require a revision of company values, policies and actions. Companies will need to resolve conflicting demands:

- to innovate and yet to maintain traditional forms and values;
- to provide scope for individual development and for participation to meet demands for employee participation and consultation;
- to decentralize and provide autonomy but also to integrate and co-ordinate activities in different parts of the organization.

To sustain successful development will require appropriate management concepts, in particular a further shift from strategic planning towards strategic management. This article describes a new concept of strategic management which is adapted to these new requirements – building on existing theory and practice.[3]

Strategic Management

Management is a process of decision making and control. On the one hand this means to delegate responsibility; on the other hand it involves that managers take responsibility, that is they are willing to justify their actions. This has to be done

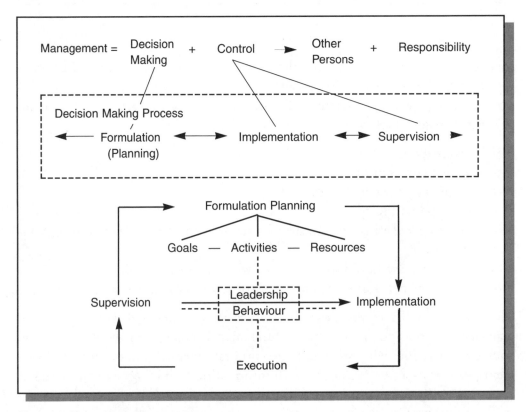

Figure 1. Management Processes

towards shareholders, employees, and other groups which are closely involved with the company. Furthermore, to take responsibility for corporate decisions and actions in the 1990s includes a broader accountability to the local community and society.[4]

Management involves complex processes of planning and control. Control activities cover implementation as well as supervision, the latter also includes the analysis of deviations of actual and planned performance. These management processes involve the formulation, implementation, and supervision of goals, activities, and resources. These responsibilities also require a specific type of leadership behavior, which has to combine emotional rational aspects as well. Increasingly, a co-operative style of leadership is needed to achieve the motivation and commitment of subordinates, to respond to the changing values of the younger generations and to foster innovation. Despite increasing pressures on time, a participative leadership style forces managers to invest more time in management processes. To make time for fuller communication with employees and for various forms of consultation and participation, managers are forced to delegate and decentralize. On the other hand a decentralized organization also needs to be integrated through systems for planning, control and co-ordination.

These conflicting demands for time-saving and motivating decentralization and simultaneously for integration raise the need for strategic management approaches; approaches for a pro-active determination of a company's future direction, its structure, and its key decision-makers while still allowing flexibility at the operational level.

Strategic management involves more than strategic planning. It is based on the fundamental ideas of 'strategy' and 'management',[5] and includes a wide range of management processes. In addition to planning it includes implementation and supervision. After thorough analysis and projection into the future, the main steps are: (1) identifying the critical issues, then (2) generation, evaluation, selection, implementation and supervision of strategic alternatives (see Figure 2).

Strategic management processes apply to 'strategies', a term which refers to fundamentally important management decision and actions. These fundamental decision affect the organization's nature and direction. Strategic decision have the following characteristics:

- they substantially affect a company's ability to generate cash and profits;

- they relate to a company as a whole;
- they are taken by the top executive team and the board of directors;
- they take affect in the long term and therefore tend to be made infrequently; and
- they reflect the values of top management and are taken in accordance with corporate philosophy and culture.

In addition to strategic planning, strategic management usually includes the definition of goals and objectives. These corporate goals need to be based on the shared values of top management, who also largely determine the corporate culture. So we can define strategic management as involving the development and communication of the corporate goals, the strategic plans, the corporate philosophy, and the corporate culture.

Based on this analysis we can define the tasks and responsibilities of strategic management as follows (see Figure 3):

1. determining the corporate philosophy;
2. defining the corporate objectives and goals;
3. formulating business strategies, functional strategies and regional strategies;

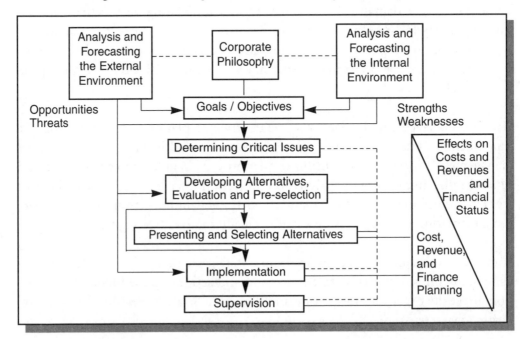

Figure 2. The process of strategic management

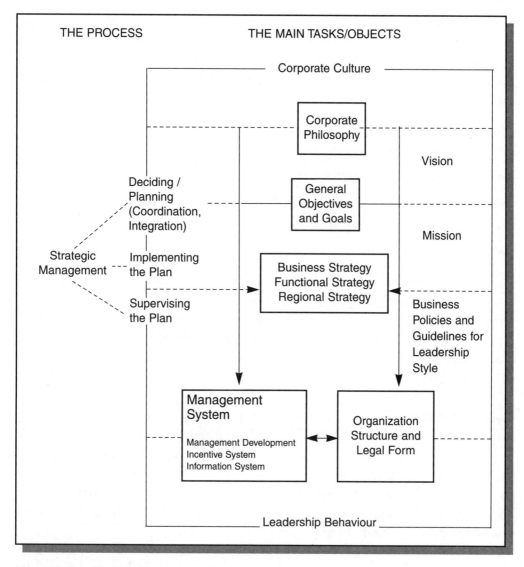

Figure 3. The Strategic Management Concept.

4. planning the company's organization structure and its legal forms;
5. planning the management system and process including:
   - management development
   - information system, and
   - management pay and incentives;
6. the processes of implementation and supervision; and
7. the design of the desired corporate culture.

These strategic management processes must reflect the top management's corporate vision i.e. the future purposes and goals of the company.[6] The vision of an entrepreneur may also influence the form of the strategic management process. Strategic management should also be reflected in the corporate mission, which sets out the strategic decision and the company's management and leadership policies in more specific terms.

Strategic Management Tasks in the 1990s

This section examines the core tasks of strategic management and ways in which they might change in response to trends in the business environment during the 1990s.

Obviously environmental changes shape corporate culture, corporate philosophy and corporate objectives and goals. Corporate culture can be defined as the patterns of thinking and behaving which emerge in a company during its historical evolution. This culture becomes visible through specific expressions and symbols. The culture is based upon a corporate philosophy which should reflect the shared values of top management.

Corporate culture shapes and reflects a company's leadership style. Of increasing importance are leadership styles which demonstrate openness, and acceptable responsibility, and the need to take initiatives and accept the different values of subordinates and foster their confidence. Leaders are expected to demonstrate enthusiasm and a desire to change, and they are required to formulate a vision and to be socially responsible.[7] Initiating changes in leadership styles also creates a need for different kinds of managers.

The basic purpose or goal of a company's management should be to develop the company successfully. Only the survival and successful development of the company can ensure the achievement of needs and goals of those groups which are closely involved with the company (see Figure 4). The success of the company can only be achieved through maximising net present value of its assets and profit and cash flow from its operations. More detailed, financial means have to be generated – on an ongoing basis – in an amount that allows for coverage of all payments to shareholders, employees, suppliers, creditors, and the government. In this context we advocate that investments are made in accordance with strategic commitments. Pressures to demonstrate higher quarterly profits in the short-run should

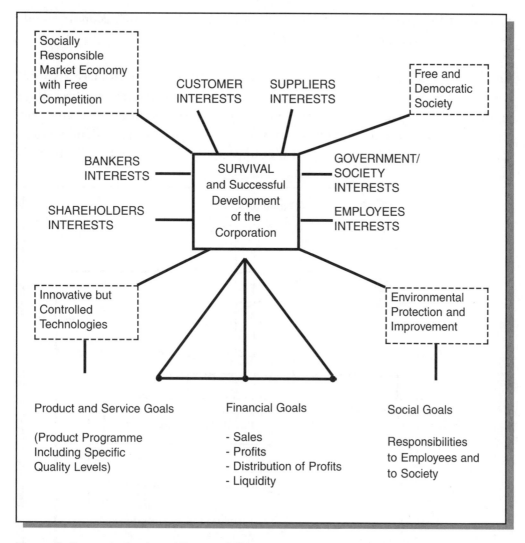

Figure 4. Corporate Goals and Responsibilities

not lead to a neglect of fundamentally necessary investments in the company's future: investments in new products, new processes, new ventures, and in people.

Corporate goals should also take account of critical environmental issues and restrictions. Important issues, which may form the basis of corporate goals and objectives include:

- environmental protection and environmental improvement;
- the development and utilization of innovative environmentally-friendly technologies;

- support for a socially responsible but competitive, free-market economy; and
- preserving a free and democratic society.

Among strategic management tasks, formulating business strategics (see Figure 5) is still central.[8] Business strategies set the production programme and variations in production capacity (including locations). Business strategies are also concerned increasingly with developing an integrated range of products and services, combined into total systems, if possible supported by system-leadership. In addi-

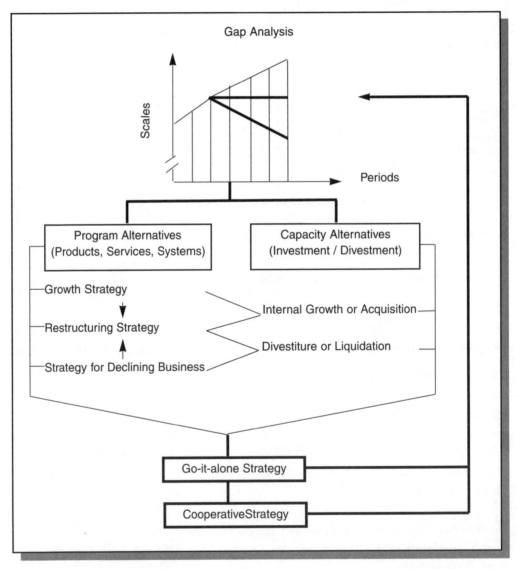

Figure 5. Formulating Business Strategy

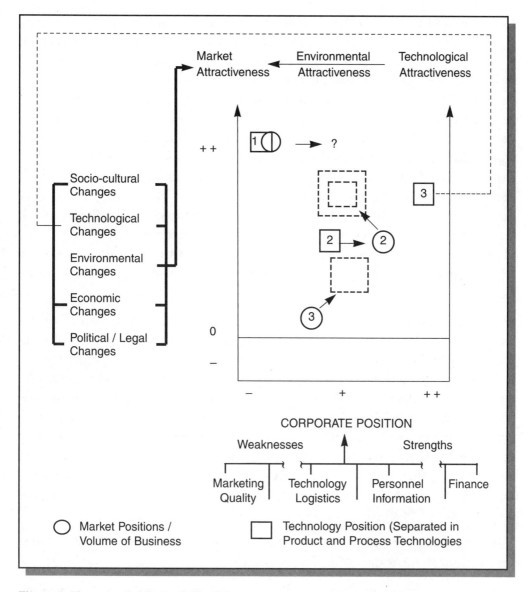

Figure 6. Managing the Strategic Portfolio

tion to 'internal growth', acquisitions often aimed at the creation of new business units, are becoming more and more important. Mergers and acquisitions are already a core activity in strategic management. The search for prospective target companies for acquisition can no longer be limited to one nation or to Europe; the search is often global. A successful external growth strategy also requires increasingly the formulation and implementation of co-operative strategies through the arrangement of joint ventures and other forms of strategic alliances.[9]

Reviewing and revising the basic product portfolio is a continuous strategic management task. On the one hand a product portfolio assesses the attractiveness of a company's products and processes from various points of view – the market, the technology and the environment. These assessments are made based on an analysis and a forecast of the business environment. On the other hand it requires an evaluation of a company's competitive position, this means its strengths and weaknesses in all of the functional areas of the company compared with the strongest competitor. Companies should exploit their opportunities while limiting their risks, through the production and marketing of products and processes with high market, technological and environmental attractiveness. Companies should have the courage to make the necessary investments to develop new technologies, which are critical for the successful growth of the national economy – for example, microelectronics or biotechnology – in order to move from positions of weakness to positions of strength – such as shown in Figure 6 in the case of Product Group 1.

To exploit opportunities which are critical for the successful expansion of a company requires more than business strategies. It also requires formulation of complementary and innovative functional strategies and strategies for specific regions or for global markets. For example, strategies for research and development, production and marketing should be closely related to the specific phase in the life-cycle of particular products (see Figure 7). R & D expenditures on designing products for recycling will make it possible to reduce payments to external recycling specialists. Products which are easier to recycle can often be sold at premium prices because they appeal to customers who wish to protect the natural environment. The extra income from these 'ecological' products often exceeds the expenditures required to develop the products.

The development of integrated functional strategies still remains a potential area for the improvement of profits. For example:

- information-based integration of R & D, production, quality and controlling tasks within the context of CIM (Computer Integrated Manufacturing);[10]
- development of logistic-systems including integrated production planning and control systems within the context of an integrated production strategy as well as information and communication strategy – possibly as a network between different companies; and
- redefinition of production and R & D structure, that is make or buy decisions (internal or external production) connected with internal or external research and development of products and processes.

Functional strategies are closely associated with business and regional strategies (see Figure 8). While large-sized companies successfully become international through the development of global strategies or specific regional strategies, the problem of internationalization of business activities constitutes one of the most difficult and critical barriers to growth for medium-sized companies. Internationalization of medium-sized companies frequently requires application of co-operative strategies.[11] This issue was emphasized by a field study which has been conducted in co-operation between Institute fur Unternehmungsplanung-

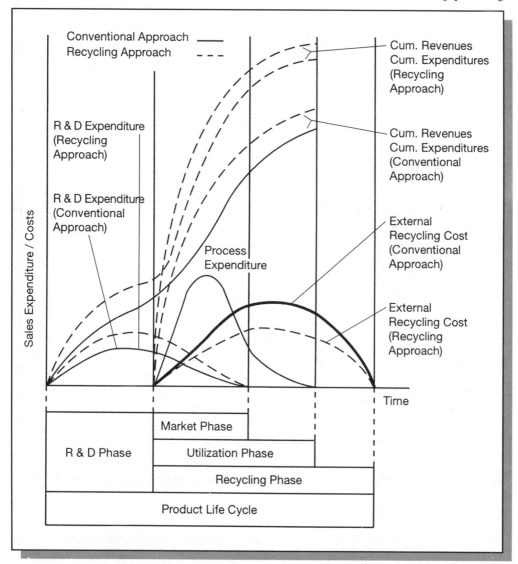

Figure 7. Integrated Planning of R & D Product Policies and Recycling

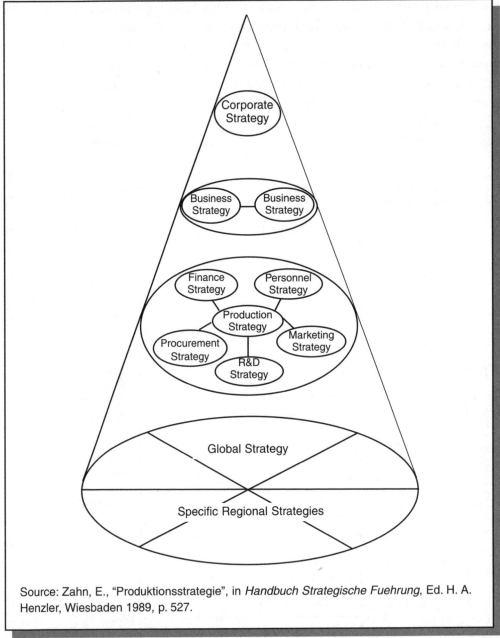

Source: Zahn, E., "Produktionsstrategie", in *Handbuch Strategische Fuehrung*, Ed. H. A. Henzler, Wiesbaden 1989, p. 527.

Figure 8. Corporate, Business, Functional and Regional Strategies

IUP Giessen/Berlin and Prof. Bernard Taylor of The Henley Management College analysing success factors and growth strategies of medium-sized companies in Germany and Great Britain.[12]

Results of this study concerning German companies can be summarized through the following basic growth strategies for successful, innovative medium-sized companies:

(1) Early entry into growing markets.
(2) Specialization – application of market niche strategies with respect to specific customer groups.
(3) Development and commercialization of innovative products in order to achieve positions of trendsetter- and price-leadership.
(4) Early application of new, flexible process technologies for comprehensive quality insurance combined with productivity improvements and cost-leadership.
(5) Flexible service orientation designed to serve specific customer needs.
(6) Extension of product programmes within existing business areas in order to use existing strengths effectively; internationalization often through co-operation with medium- and large-sized companies.
(7) Leadership supporting motivation, based on an explicit mission, applying flexible structures as well as utilizing concentrated information and, finally;
(8) Retaining qualified employees in key positions.

Structure follows strategy. Development of strategy and structure should correspond with each other (see Figure 9). In companies with primarily functional structures, extensive growth of tasks within the traditional functional areas as well as the addition of new functions – the cross-sectional or co-ordination functions – cause significant organizational and management problems. Besides personnel, finance and controlling tasks:

* product management;
* quality management;
* logistics management;
* environmental protection management and energy management;
* risk management;
* technology management; and
* information and communication management.

cause a broad variety of additional intersections among functions and require additional co-ordination. Present commercial and technological data bases, and existing software packages do not support these tasks sufficiently yet. While the managers are required to invest more and more time in line and cross-sectional tasks, the risk of neglecting the core tasks of line managers is growing.

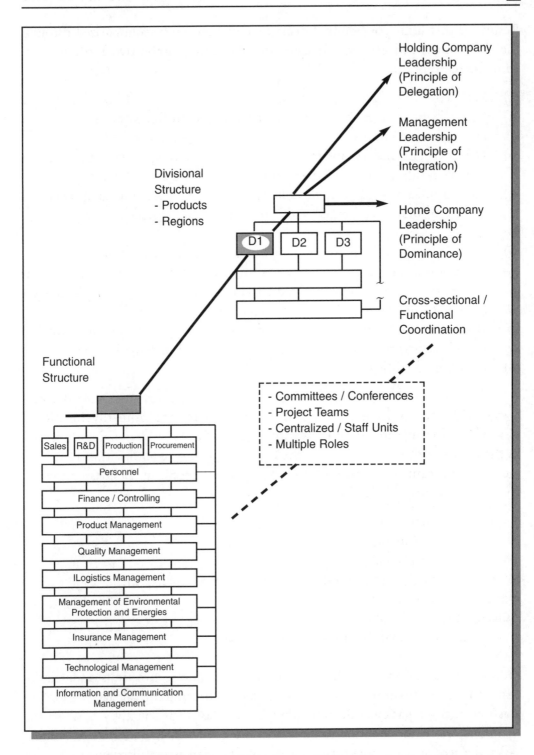

Figure 9. Development of Organizational Structure as a Strategic Management Task

Additional need for co-ordination due to added cross-sectional functions also arises in companies with a primarily divisional structure. Besides co-ordination tasks with respect to traditional functional responsible management areas new cross sectional functions also cause in these companies additional needs for integration and co-ordination. This requires additional units for integration and co-ordination such as increased use of committees, project groups, central or staff units as well as multiple mandates for top management.

Companies are exposed to pressures on time and success. They need more time for object-oriented and especially people-oriented co-ordination. Hence we recommend simple, decentralized, and distinct top management structures and management concepts – referring to all corporate levels including top management!

Regarding the development of top management structures, a tendency is becoming increasingly obvious; an evolution from the headunit-concept to the management-concept and, in parts, further to the holding-concept. This means a tendency away from the principle of dominance, to the principle of integration and further to the principle of delegation.

In particular, the management-concept is realized by an increasing number of companies such as Siemens, ABB, Thyssen and Daimler-Benz. Within this concept, top managers of important divisions also constitute the top management of the group along with managers, who are responsible for functional areas within the group. This concept necessarily includes decentralization and leads to improved market orientation and motivation throughout the company. Figure 10 shows the new structure of Daimler-Benz as an example of the management concept.

Decentralized units – subsidiaries or divisions often have autonomous product and profit responsibilities. They must be led by entrepreneurs. Having an entrepreneurial commitment is the only way to obtain the advantages of a successful medium-sized company within a large corporation. Large corporations increasingly need general managers (all round businessmen) as well as specialized managers for specific functions.

Management development which takes into account the changing requirements of organizations and individuals is becoming an important and critical strategic issue (see Figure 11). The quality of managers and the planning for management succession often determines a company's development. Systematic succession planning and individual career planning are therefore becoming tasks of high pri-

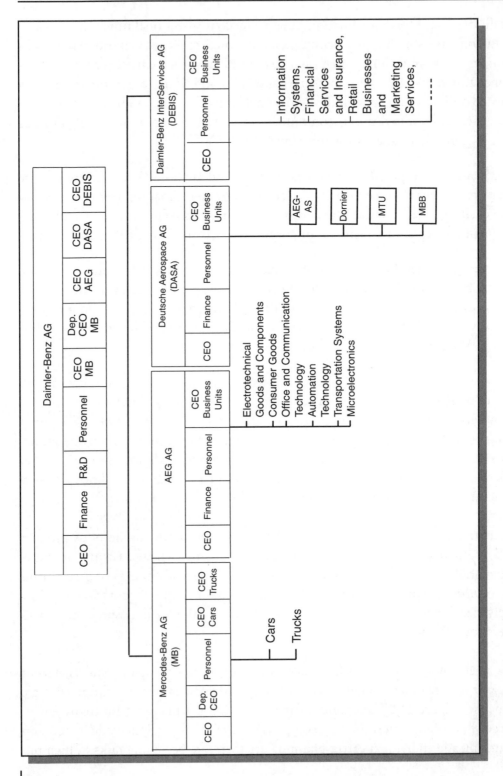

Figure 10. The new organizational structure of Daimler-Benz

ority and importance. Management development is required to cover technological, commercial, and social issues. Involvement in committees and project-teams, job rotation (from the headquarters to subsidiaries, and from the home country to a foreign country and vice versa) and mandateship are ways to acquire management and leadership know-how and to help managers to solve increasingly complex management problems.[13]

To cope with rapid changes in the business environment and the changes which are occurring within organizations, companies need managers who are not only highly qualified but are highly motivated and who use a certain style of leadership. Motivated leadership behaviour is determined by a variety of socio-psychological parameters. Among these parameters incentives, which are granted by a company, are most important in order to simultaneously achieve corporate and individual goals. Incentives which are of course differently perceived and weighted lead to motivation. Thus, we consider incentives and design of management incentive systems an important component of strategic management.

STEPS	SOURCES OF INFORMATION	
Audit of Present Management - Number and Quality	Present Organization Structure, Job Descriptions and - Personnel Records	
- Forecasting of Future Management Requirements	- Business Plans - Future Organization Structure	
- Supply of Managers - Assessment — Internal & External	Personnel Records and Job Market Information	Succession-Planning ↑
- Management Development	Management Development - Courses - Committee Work - Project Teams - Multiple Roles - Job-Rotation - Secondment	↓ Career-Planning

Figure 11. The Management Development Process

The management incentive system should include monetary and non-monetary incentives. As far as monetary incentives are concerned arbitrary executive bonus schemes and bonuses which are linked to the overall company's dividends are becoming less effective in providing motivation. In addition to the salary which is linked to their level, managers (or better still management teams) should be offered bonuses which depend on the manager's contribution to the achievement of individual goals and corporate operational and strategic goals. Managers at different levels and at different phases in their careers should be offered different incentives. So management incentive systems should provide the opportunity to offer a variety of incentives. The variations should cover increases in salary as well as different kinds of prerequisites.

Although equity ownership is not usually included systematically in German companies as part of a management incentive scheme, i.e. stock options for managers usually made available at a specific time, are a useful and important way of motivating management. Furthermore, stock options may encourage entrepreneurial behaviour. In divisions or subsidiaries concerned with services, such as software or consulting, stock options are useful to retain senior managers in the company, and to dissuade them from establishing their own businesses. On the other hand, it is difficult to introduce stock options at a division level in large companies because key strategic issues are often decided at the corporate level.

Non-financial incentives are also becoming increasingly important. Changes in personal values, the demand for more job satisfaction and work which provides opportunity for self-development – not just a higher material standard of living– have caused companies to pay more attention to non-financial incentives like enlarged job responsibilities, changes in responsibilities, autonomy and independence, recognition and status in the company and in society.

To cope with these changes and to achieve their strategic tasks, companies need to have clear and well defined visions, missions, and management policies which reflect management's strategic intentions. Successful corporate development in a turbulent and complex environment requires management to reconcile conflicting pressures for:

- innovation, and tradition;
- self-fulfilment and participation; and
- decentralization and integration.

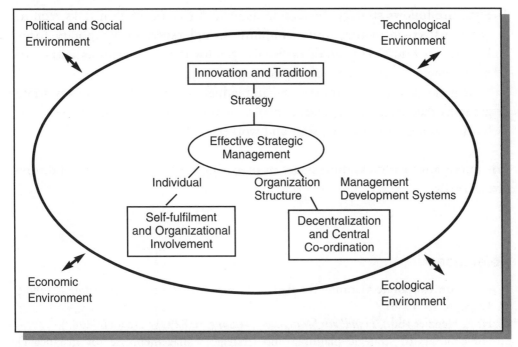

Figure 12. The Requirements for Effective Strategic Management in the 1990s

These tensions may be resolved through goal-oriented and well co-ordinated:

- strategies;
- organization structures, management systems; and
- highly motivated staff and workers

Conclusions and Recommendations for Action

We need a vision-oriented, goal-oriented and well co-ordinated strategic management approach within an integrative framework. For the 1990s we advocate the inclusion of the following five points in all strategic management considerations:

1. Senior management needs capabilities that allow for a pro-active influence on corporate philosophy and culture.
2. Corporate goals and objectives should explicitly include those requirements which are essential for a supportive business climate e.g. the development and commercialization of innovative environmentally-friendly technologies.
3. Business, functional, and regional strategies have to be combined more closely to achieve strategic fit.[14]

4. Structure follows strategy. Increasing demand for co-ordination tasks requires additional co-ordinating units, committees, and especially temporary forms like project teams. This holds especially true for the organizational structures management-concept and holding-concept.

5. Systematic succession planning and individual career planning are key strategic tasks requiring management involvement at all organizational levels, and leading to highly motivated staff and workers.

It is important to address these issues in preparing for the demanding conditions of the 1990s.

References

1. B. Taylor, Corporate planning for the 1990s, the new frontiers, *Long Range Planning.* 19 (6), p. 13 (1986).

2. H. A. Henzier (Ed.), *Handbuch Strategische Fuehiung,* p. 829, Wiesbaden (1989).

3. For concepts of strategic planning and strategic management see for instance D. Hahn, B. Taylor (Ed.), *Strategische Unternehmungsplanung.* 4th edn, Heidelberg (1986); H. H. Hinterhuber, *Strategische Unternehmungsfuehrung.* 3rd edn, Berlin (1984); W. Krueger, *Die Erklaerung von Unternehmungserfolg: theoretischerAnsatz und empirische Ergebnisse.* DB W, 48, p. 27 (1988); A. C. Hax and N. S. Majluf. *Strategic Management - An Integrative Perspective.* Englewood Cliffs (1984); K. R. Andrews, *The Concept of Corporate Strategy,* 3rd edn, Homewood (1987); T, L Wheelen and J. D. Hunger, *Strategic Management*, 2nd edn, Reading (1987); L L. Byars, *Strategic Management*, 2nd edn, Cambridge (1987).

4. E. Reuter, Die kuenftige Rolle des Managements in der Gesellschaft, in H. A. Henzier (Ed.). *Handbuch Strategische Fuehrung.* p. 47, Wiesbaden (1989).

5. D. Hahn, Strategische Unternehmungsfuehrung–Stand und Entwicklungstendenzen unter besonderer Beruecksichtigung US-amerikanischer Konzepte, in E. Seidel and D. Wagner (Eds), *Organisation. Evolutionaere Interdependenzen von Kultur und Struktur der Unternehmung.* p. 55, Wiesbaden (1989).

6. H. A. Henzier. Vision und Fuehrung, in H. A. Henzier (Ed.), *Handbuch Strategische Fuehrung.* p. 17. Wiesbaden (1989).

7. G. Hoehler, *Offener Horizont. Junge Strategien veraendem die Welt.* p. 13, Duesseldorf (1989).

8. D. Hahn, Stand und Entwicklungstendenzen der strategischen Planung, in D. Hahn and B Taylor (Eds) *Strategische Unternehmungsplanung,* 4th edn, p. 3, Heidelberg (1986); D. Hahn, Zweck und Standort des Portfolio-Konzeptes in der strategischen Unternehmungsplanung. in D. Hahn and B. Taylor (Eds). *Strategische Unternehmungsplanung.* 4th edn. p. 128, Heidelberg (1900); W. Pfeiffer and R. Dögl, Das Technologie

Portfolio-Konzept zur Beherrschung der Schnittstelle Technik und Untemehmens-strategie, in D. Hahn and B. Taylor (Eds), *Strategische Unternehmungsplanung*. 4th edn, p. 149, Heidelberg (1986).

9. F.J. Contractor and P. Lorange (eds), *Co-operative Strategies in International Business*, Lexington (1988): P. Lorange and J. Roos, *Increasing the Pace of Implementing Global Strategies through Strategic Alliances*. Working Paper No. 89-109 of the Wurster Center for International management Studies at the Wharton School, University of Pennsylvania (1989).

10. G. Spur, CIM – Die informationstechnische Herausforderung an die Produktions-technik, *Produktionstechnisches Kolloquium*, ZWF/CIM, No. 11/1986, p. 5, Berlin (1986); G.Seliger.CIM – was ist das? – Grundkonzept, *DIN-Mitteilungen*. 67 (6), p. 325 (1988); H.-J. Warnecke, Fabrikautomatisierung zwischen technischen Zielvorstellungen und wirtschaftlich sozialer Realitaet, *Produktionstechnisches Kolloquium*. ZWF/CIM, No. 11 /1986, p. 37, Berlin (1986); H. Wildemann, Strategische Investitionsplanung fuer neue Technologien in der Produktion, in H. Albach and H. Wildemann (Eds), *Strategische Investitionsplanung fuer neue Technologien*. ZfB-Ergaenzungsheft No. 1 /1986, p. 1, Wiesbaden (1986).

11. H. Albach, K. Bock and T. Warncke, *Kritische Wachsturnsschwellen in der Unter-nehmensentwicklung.* Stuttgart (1985).

12. B. Taylor *et al.* Strategy and leadership in growth companies, *Long Range Planning.* 23 (3), p. 66 (1990).

13. See Arbeitskreis 'Integrierte Unternehrnungsplanung' der Schmalenbach-Gesellschaft, Integrierte Fuehrungskraefteplanung, in A. G. Coenenberg (Ed.), *Betriebliche Aus- und Weiterbildung von Fuehrungskraeften*, ZftbF-Sonderheft 24, p. 121, Duesseldorf (1989).

14. N. Venkatraman and J.C. Camillus, Exploring the concept of 'fit' in strategic man-agement. *Academy of Management Review.* p. 513 (1984); W. Krueger, Patterns of suc-cess in German businesses. *Long Range Planning.* 22 (2), p. 106 (1989); C. Scholz, *Strategisches Management.* Berlin (1987).

Pressures from Stakeholders Hit Japanese Companies

By *Mark E Steadman, Thomas W. Zimmerer* and *Ronald F. Green*
Long Range Planning, Vol 28, No. 6, pp 29-37, 1995, with permission from Elsevier Science.

Dr Mark E. Steadman is Assistant Professor of Accountancy at the College of Business East Tennessee State University, USA.

Dr Thomas W. Zimmerer is Professor of Management and holds the Allen & Ruth Harris Chair of Excellence in Business at the College of Business, East Tennessee State University, USA.

Dr Ronald F. Green, Associate Professor of Management, College of Business, East Tennessee State University, USA.

In recent years few US and European executives have been faced with the task of managing in a highly complex, dynamic business environment. There is a growing awareness of the need to consider the interests of a variety of stakeholder groups when making business decisions. This awareness has quickly become a requirement for executives across the globe, even among those in Japanese firms who have historically been less encumbered due to different societal, cultural, and business expectations. This article addresses these differences and discusses the global evolution of stakeholder group influence with an emphasis on US, European, and Japanese executives.

Strategic management is a dynamic and pragmatic process of developing goals, objectives and strategies designed to create a defendable position that allows a firm to combat the competitive forces of the marketplace. This militaristic definition views competitors as the primary adversary upon which strategic plans must focus. Firms continually alter their tactical actions to create a competitive advantage by out-positioning the competition. The traditional measures of success have been higher earnings and the growth necessary to satisfy stockholders. This profit maximization strategy has been the foundation for management decision making and the focus of strategy since the advent of the modern corporation.

As society and the external environment of business have become more complex, executives have been forced to broaden their focus to include a wider array of stakeholders. This pluralistic view holds that society has a legitimate stake in the operations of corporations. Constituents in this societal view include stockholders, bondholders, employees, suppliers, customers, the financial community, gov-

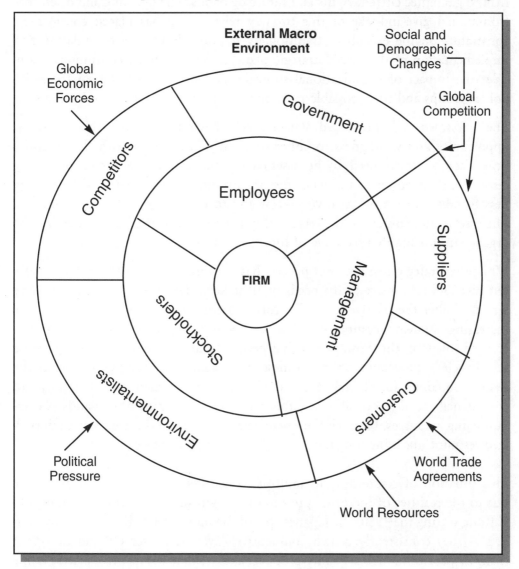

Figure 1. Stakeholder Groups and External Pressures

ernment, and various special interest groups such as environmentalists (see Figure 1). These groups can be defined as the stakeholders of the firm.[1] Stakeholder groups are, to some degree, dependent upon the firm for the realization of their personal or institutional goals.[2]

Executives have the responsibility for developing long-term, stable relationships with the firm's stakeholders in order to maintain the current competitive position while enhancing future profitability and growth. Stakeholder groups look to the firm to guarantee current rights and future demands. The dynamic and often confrontational give-and-take of this two-way relationship has placed considerable constraints on the executives traditionally responsible for the formulation and implementation of the firm's strategic plans. Executives must continuously consider the impact of organizational strategies and policies on each of the stakeholder groups and their possible reactions to the firm's decisions and actions.

The assessment of anticipated stakeholder behaviours captures their capacity, opportunity and willingness to either threaten or co-operate with the organization. Factors which need to be assessed are the stakeholders' control of key resources, their power to influence the organization's performance, their willingness to take positive or negative actions and to co-operate and form coalitions. The history and context of the relationship between a specific stakeholder and the organization is highly predictive of future behaviours.[3]

While the strategic management process has continually evolved to make it more sensitive and responsive to the needs of all stakeholders, these same changes have served to alter the relatively simple profit maximization paradigm and to create increasing strategic complexity. The competitive equation that traditionally focused solely on the 'bottom line' has been substantially modified by a growing set of societal expectations that business will operate in a way that optimizes the desired outcomes for all stakeholders. Some view these changes as a step toward enlightened social responsibility. Other see the new constituent demands as overburdening resources, blurring the organizational focus and acting as an internalized restraint upon the long-term success of global businesses.

This situation of responding to multiple constituents is especially troublesome due to the realities of increased pressures from global competition. On the global front, during the 1980s the Japanese posed the most serious threat in many markets as they consistently gained competitive advantages over US and European firms by providing higher quality products at extremely competitive prices. While Japanese executives have many potential sources of competitive advantage, one prominent factor during this period was the relative lack of constraints placed on these executives by various stakeholder groups. However, recent developments around the globe indicate changing attitudes that may require re-evaluation of the competitive equation for firms competing globally. US firms which were once competitors now find that strategic alliances are an effective means of matching the advantages achieved by Japanese and European competitors. For example, Corning has a long and very positive track record in establishing highly focused strategic alliances with a dozen or more Asian and European firms.[4]

The purpose of this article is to describe the past and current influence of stakeholders on the comparative management styles of executives around the globe. While particular emphasis will be placed on the contrasts between US and Japanese firms, changes in the European market will also be addressed. Recent developments in stakeholder rights and influence and their subsequent effects on the strategic behaviour of executives and managers will be examined. Conclusions and recommendations for executives who deal with these changing influences will be presented.

Traditional Organizational Cultures

The existence of various stakeholder groups clearly influences the strategic decisions of corporate managers. As a result, the firm's management strategies cannot be based solely upon the profit capability of the various alternatives. In recent years, corporations have been confronted with an increasing number of external and internal constituencies, or stakeholders, whose demands have affected the strategic and operational behaviour of the firm. Management is now expected to 'increase total stakeholder value'. The most difficult questions still revolve around operationalizing the concept of stakeholder value in a global market with a highly volatile competitive environment. Table 1 summarizes the traditional stakeholder influences on the firm.

This shift in managerial focus has been manifested in the corporate culture in the United States and, to a lesser extent, in Europe. These firms are continually striving to become 'good corporate citizens' and to appease various stakeholder groups. When a particular stakeholder group feels that the company has failed to comply with their expectations, the firm is faced with adverse stakeholder reactions in the form of product boycotts, hostile proxy battles, or other disruptive acts. Firms are expected to be environmentally proactive, loyal to their work force,

Stakeholder	United States	Japan	Europe
Customers	independent	*keiretsu*	independent
Employees	employment at will	life-long employment	long-term emploment encouraged by government law
Suppliers	independent	*keiretsu*	less independent but not formally linked
Stockholders	volatile ownership pattern based short-term	stable pattern and emphasis on long-term performance	varies
Government	lack of defined industrial policy and antitrust laws	promotes business through national policy	varies
Competitors	adversarial behaviour and mostly national or regional in scope	global with controlled competition among Japanese firms	larger multicountry competitors some with support of government
Environment-alists	major external influence	little influence	well established 'Green' movement and political parties

Table 1. The Traditional Influence of Stakeholders

a contributor to humanitarian efforts, and economically and socially sensitive to employee needs, all the while increasing stockholder wealth. To compound the situation, today's executives must optimize each outcome in terms of stakeholder interests while striving to compete in an increasingly competitive global economy. This situation is not unlike that facing European executives who have been forced to manage their organizations in an environment of strong labour unions, an extensive ecological movement, and changing political and social environments.

Alternatively, the interests of stakeholder groups are less ingrained into the corporate culture of Japan. The nature of corporate ownership and numerous cultural differences make the concept of stakeholder interests somewhat less relevant to Japanese executives. Japanese firms have traditionally operated in corporate groups, or *keiretsus.* These groups consist of firms from eight to ten industries and are centred around a banking institution.[5] Members of a group usually have an equity interest in other member firms, but the operation of the group is based upon firm interdependence rather than legal encumbrances. The existence of formal business 'partners' reduces the risk of the aggressive strategies employed by Japanese firms in global competition. There are numerous recent examples of a *keiretsus* bailing out a member firm that has encountered financial difficulties.[6]

In addition to the existence of *keiretsus*, other societal factors in the Japanese culture have limited the amount of stakeholder influence on corporate strategic management. The majority of stockholders in Japanese firms have been stable investors who have demonstrated a long-term financial focus. This fact, coupled with the cross-ownership features of the corporate groups, limits the amount of shares which are openly traded on the Japanese stock exchange to 25-35%. In comparison, 70% of shares in US firms are regularly traded.[7] Also, dividend payouts in Japan represent 30% of corporate profit compared to a 54% rate in the United States.[8] This unique Japanese financial environment alleviates some of the external stakeholder pressure for producing short-term financial results that is found by firms in the US and Europe which must face the reality of highly demanding equity markets.

Japanese executives traditionally have not been faced with stakeholders with aggressive agendas. Employment in Japan is often a life-long commitment by both employee and firm. Organized labour is virtually non-existent. Suppliers tend to be members of the same *keiretsu*. Environmental concerns have not been a high priority. Corporate charitable contributions in Japan are less than one-quarter the rate for US firms.[9] A combination of these factors result in fewer constraints in the decision-making process of the Japanese executive.

Given the contrast between the corporate cultures of the US and Europe with that of Japan, specifically the influence of stakeholder groups, the emergence of Japan as a power in the global economy can be better understood. However, recent developments around the globe have begun to alter the environment in which executives must operate. The next section will present these developments and discuss their impact upon the strategic management process.

Strategic Developments in US Stakeholder Influence

Recent developments in the global corporate environment can be associated with the increasing influence of stakeholder groups on the strategies and decisions of corporate management. Executives must operate in an increasingly competitive

Stakeholder	United States	Japan	Europe
Customers	independent	more independent	single market led to more linkage
Employees	more involvement	less life-long employment	recession driven 'downsizing'
Suppliers	formal relationships	none	more compertitive relationship
Stockholders	proactive in management and long-term performance	change toward an increasingly shorter term investment horizon	increased concern for 'corporate citizenship'
Government	emerging industrial policy	none	varies with each country
Competitors	strategic alliances, less anti-trust restrictions	new emphasis in 'open markets' and strategic alliances	strategic alliances
Environment-alists	major influence	growing influence	strong 'Green' movement

Table 2. The Changing Influences of Stakeholders

global environment while attempting to meet the increasing demands of stakeholders whose measures of success are not necessarily congruent. This situation has resulted in significant changes in the strategic management philosophies of nearly all firms. Table 2 illustrates the changing influence of stakeholder groups on the firm's management.

The effect of this new environment can be best observed in US firms by the growing number of corporate 'partnerships' between firms and various stakeholder groups. An example of a 'partnership' between a firm and its stakeholders involves the environmental aspects of corporate operations. The 'Big Three' US auto makers recently announced a plan to pool research concerning measures to meet or exceed clean air standards imposed by the Federal government.[10] Relaxed US Justice Department restraints against sharing technology allowed for this development. As another example, General Motors has solicited the Environmental Defense Fund (EDF) as an independent consultant concerning emission controls.[11] The environmental group will not be paid by GM, and the goal of the alliance is to develop policy proposals that will reduce emissions without increased governmental regulations. Also, EDF aided McDonald's, the US fast food giant, in dramatically reducing the restaurant chain's solid waste.

US firms are also forming alliances (usually as joint ventures) with competitors. The common impetus for such partnerships is the realization that no one firm can accumulate the resources and talent to develop projects that are often very complicated and global in nature. For example, IBM has formed separate joint ventures with Apple Computer, Toshiba, Mitsubishi, Siemens, Borland, Lotus, and Novell.[12] Motorola has entered into an agreement with Phillips Electronics to co-design consumer electronic chips.[13] Examples of this new adversarial alliance, 'co-opetition', can also be found in the auto industry.

Corporations around the globe are changing their actions in order to meet the needs of suppliers and customers. Electronic data interchange (EDI) systems allow firms to develop enduring relationships with both groups. In today's business world, more customers and suppliers are part of global markets, and EDI permits firms to maintain constant contact with both groups. The result is that firms are becoming increasingly aware of customer differences and are continually attempting to reconfigure products and services to adapt to and meet the needs of clients. These 'partnerships' create an operational system which allows firms to strategically compete on a global basis.

Another important partnership group involves the firm's employees. In recent years, many companies have instituted employee stock ownership plans (ESOPs) and have formed more self-directed work groups that result in structured decision-sharing programmes. An example of this latter development is the Eaton Corporation which shares extensive financial data with employees in an attempt to tie employee performance with overall corporate results.[14]

While employee involvement is often difficult to ensure, numerous potential benefits can lead to long term improvements in corporate performance.[15] This appears to be one area in which Japanese firms may have a clear historical advantage in developing employee stakeholder groups. While firms from the United States and Europe have traditionally been seen as being involved in adversarial relationships with employees, firms from Japan have benefited from the strong sense of family inherent within their culture. Employees in Japan are often portrayed as highly motivated with a commitment to a unified implementation of the organization's strategies and tactics. The level of commitment can be measured by the number of hours employees are willing to work and the personal sacrifices often made in their private lives. As US firms have become more aware of the productive power of employees, they have begun to develop and implement human resource strategies to maximize employee involvement.

While this relationship is still developing in the US, Japanese firms face growing problems with employee groups. Recent problems with the Japanese economy have led to employee layoffs and the global trend toward downsizing has led to additional reductions in the Japanese work force. The strong sense of family once found within the Japanese work culture may possibly be eroding. As the Japanese become pressured to respond to external stakeholder groups, internal pressures may also be felt from employee groups.

Changes in Japan: Increased Awareness of Stakeholder Needs

Not only is the strategic management process of US firms being affected by the presence of various stakeholder groups, but Japanese executives are also being called upon to become more sensitive to stakeholder interests. As detailed earlier, Japanese firms have traditionally not been influenced to any major degree by the interests of employees, environmentalists, suppliers unions, and other stakeholder groups. However, recent developments in the corporate culture of Japan reveal an increasing degree of awareness of these groups and the firm's responsibility to meet the needs of various stakeholders.

In the February 1992 issue of Bungei Shanju, Akio Morito, the chairman of Sony, discussed the lack of stakeholder concern in Japanese firms. Mr. Morita admitted that Japanese firms may have sacrificed their concern for employees, shareholders, suppliers, and their communities in their singular focus on the creation and implementation of global competitive strategies. Morita also concluded that such practices may have reached their limits and argued that Japanese firms should begin to pay attention to various stakeholder groups.[16]

Specifically, Mr. Morita stated that Japanese firms must begin to provide their employees with more holidays to ensure a better quality of life, increase the dividend payout rate, treat suppliers as partners, contribute to their community, and consider the environmental aspects of corporate management. This 'new management philosophy' would result in firms which are more responsive to the needs of stakeholders. Morita concluded that in order to adhere to this paradigm, Japanese firms may have to raise prices and abandon the current 'market-share at any price' strategy.

Another top Japanese executive who has begun to recognize the validity of the rights expressed by stakeholder theory is Minoru 'Ben' Makihara, the newly named president and CEO of Mitsubishi Corporation. Makihara believes that 'the expectations of employees, shareholders and the outside world are changing' and that 'new directions have to be sought'.[17] In Makihara's opinion, Japanese firms must make jobs more satisfying, pay more attention to the environment, and give shareholders a larger dividend.

Other Japanese top executives are also beginning to change their views on the relationship of their firms with stakeholder groups. Ryuzaburo Kaku, chairman of Canon, states that his firm's corporate mission is to 'make a positive difference in the world' by becoming a responsible corporate citizen. Nippon Steel is sponsoring social and cultural activities as part of its 'corporate citizen' programme. Hitachi is placing a strong emphasis on the development of environmentally sound products and production techniques. Omron Corporation has established a 'corporate citizenship' department and has affirmed its commitment to work for a better society. Konica Corporation is promoting public awareness of environmental issues.[18] With so many of Japan's leading executives espousing these views, the concepts of stakeholder interests should gain increased acceptance in the future Japanese corporate culture. The acceptance of stakeholder needs will in turn lead to changes in the focus of the strategic planning process and the way in which these firms are managed.

Another factor which will lead to increased acceptance of stakeholder theory in Japanese firms is the changing investor attitudes in the Japanese financial community. No longer are investors as willing to wait for long term payouts on their investments. Richard Koo, a senior economist at the Nomura Research Institute, predicts that Japanese firms will have to increase prices or withdraw from unprofitable product lines in order to meet investors' new attitudes.[19] Koo states that firms wishing to raise capital in the Japanese financial market will have to begin to meet investors' short-term return objectives. Compared to the traditional long-term focus of Japanese investors, this development could lead to a dramatic change in the corporate strategies of Japanese executives.

Global Changes and the Interaction Between Stakeholder Groups

Quite often organizations undertake monumental change due to pressures from external stakeholder groups. Ciba-Geigy, Switzerland's largest chemical and pharmaceutical firm, is a global organization that recognized changing societal values toward the chemical industry. After an environmental accident in 1986 that, in the words of Ciba-Geigy's president Heini Lippuner, revealed a 'pent-up resentment at the chemical industry', the diversified corporate giant altered its entire business portfolio and related divisional relationships.[20] By restructuring to become less bureaucratic, Ciba-Geigy implemented a new organizational culture calling for a more enlightened relationship to the ecological environment. Central to this change was the adoption of the public values of 'self-fulfillment, fairness, cultural identity, and also environmental regard'.[21] The Ciba-Geigy commitment to the future integrates strategic performance with the professional and personal growth of its employees. Corporate growth and individual growth are viewed in the new culture as linked. Individual initiative, risk-taking, and the autonomy to act become the generators of change.

One interesting outcome of this reaction to external stakeholders is the effect on internal stakeholders. Quite often, a firm's response to one group interacts with the conflicting desires of other groups. In the case of Ciba-Geigy, a central component of changing the organizational culture was staff reductions and reducing the average age of management.[22] While the normal Swiss retirement age is 65, everyone over the age of 60 was offered early retirement. While 'new blood' is often necessary in order to enact organizational change and the reductions were also designed to reduce operating costs, mandatory retirement can have a dramatic effect on employee morale if not handled properly.

The Ciba-Geigy illustration also supports the contention that changing stakeholder pressures are not simply within the domain of firms competing in the United States. The 'green movement' has been quite prominent in Western Europe and other regions around the globe. Firms who can convince the buying public of their environmental sensitivity may have a tremendous advantage over competition, globally as well as domestically. Yet there is no doubt that business organizations in different regions of the world face varying degrees of pressure from stakeholder groups. This may be the result of different levels of governmental influence or may come from cultural differences within the country itself. While the cultural difference associated with countries such as Japan are readily identifiable, the equally prominent differences of other countries may be less recognized by most. For example, Western Europe is made up of numerous countries that are quite dissimilar in terms of culture, yet most observers would have a difficult time assessing how these differences may affect a firm's strategic orientation. It should be noted, however, that much of the increasing pressure for change comes from sources other than the defined stakeholder groups. The need for change may be partially attributed to the economic reality of global recession and the resultant emphasis on improved operating efficiencies.

While many organizations enact change due to external stakeholder groups, many changes are simply the result of bowing to economic reality. While Ciba-Geigy's workforce reduction may have been primarily to enact change resulting from societal pressure, the firm also gained economically from reduced overhead. Likewise, firms who make their products or processes more environmentally sound often reap significant economic benefits in addition to the positive public relations outcomes. Firms who recycle are prime examples. Recycling can result in an enhanced corporate image, a closer tie with consumers and employees, and a stronger position when dealing with governmental legislation and environmental liabilities. These benefits all seem to result from the firm's acknowledgment of the needs of various stakeholder groups. Yet benefits also include reduced material disposal costs during manufacture, improved material economies in dealing with end-of-life product waste and reduced dependence on those in the value chain who are responsible for disposal.[23]

This discussion does not imply that those changes with significant economic benefit are not without benefit to various stakeholder constituencies. Obviously stockholders, the primary internal stakeholder group, reap the gains from these activities. Other societal groups also benefit from ecologically oriented strategies, even if an economic benefit to the firm exists. The implication should be that, when examining organizations to determine the level of influence from different stakeholder groups, the confounding factor is the economic benefit that the firm may be seeking. Firms under relatively little pressure from external stakeholders may design strategies entirely oriented around economic gain, but may give the appearance that these actions are, in fact, in response to increased stakeholder group influence.

In addition to economic pressures, there are a number of other forces contributing to many of the changing perspectives discussed. Figure 2 summarizes how numerous external pressures have resulted in new perspectives on the value-added chain which globally link suppliers, manufacturers and consumers. Changing

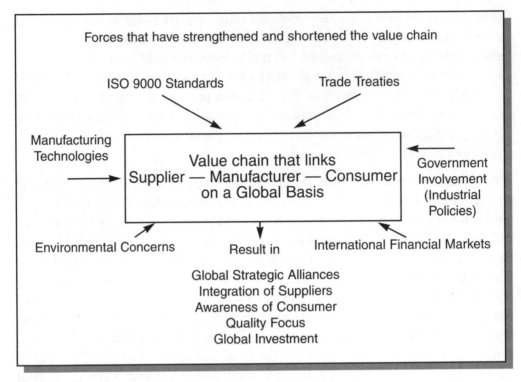

Figure 2. Forces for Change

pressures to shorten and strengthen the value-added chain can be viewed as another force requiring restructuring of the global strategic planning process.

Summary and Conclusions

Firms in the United States, Europe, and Japan are facing increasing pressure from stakeholder groups, many of which have never been part of the corporate strategy process in the past. The dramatically changing nature of global competition resulting from evolving corporate cultures must be acknowledged. The future of the global business environment will be met with new forms of competition, integration, and co-operation. Models that interconnect an array of stakeholders have begun to become more commonplace. These models attempt to map strategically the relationships among players involved in the broadly defined environmental arena. Previous adversaries must work co-operatively in a systems fashion to optimize outcomes for each stakeholder group.[24]

Gary Hamel of the London Business School speculates that future corporate competition will not be concerned so much with market position, cost or quality but rather industry structure.[25]

Hamel states that developing basically new businesses will be the main obstacle for firms in the future. In order to meet this new requirement, four ingredients will be needed: intellectual leadership, core competencies, fertile corporate imagination, and expeditionary marketing.

Strategic alliances will also be increasingly important as they have become a means of achieving breakthroughs in the marketplace through effective partitioning. These alliances must become co-operative efforts that blend the inputs of both external and internal stakeholders. The broader the base of the stakeholder involvement, the higher the level of commitment to and enthusiasm for the strategic alliance.[26] An example of such alliances is the IBM, Siemens, and Toshiba partnership that integrates the efforts of firms from three continents to develop semiconductor technologies. The goal is a 21st Century chip with capacity to link together as many as 600 million transistors. Such a chip will create a microcomputer with the capacity of today's super computer.[27]

Firms which strive to survive in the new corporate world order will have to adopt new corporate strategies. A main factor in this process will be the consideration of stakeholder interests. Only by satisfying the needs of all valued constituencies can a firm compete in a global marketplace. US and European firms have been faced with this concept for some time, and Japanese firms are now accepting this view. As Japanese firms begin to integrate the interests of various stakeholders into their corporate strategies, the current competitive advantage of Japan should dissipate to some degree. Given this development, the 'level playing field' for global competition may finally be achieved.

Does this mean that the global executive should expect Japanese firms to become immediately less competitive? Should they expect Japanese corporations to become more bureaucratic as they attempt to respond strategically to a variety of stakeholder groups? Should they examine how firms in other regions of the world are affected? While this scenario may reflect what happened to US firms in the 1980s, it is doubtful that it will happen to Japanese firms in the 1990s. Having witnessed their global counterparts struggle with the often conflicting needs of various stakeholder groups, Japanese executives will be better prepared for the growth of this influence in their strategic management process. Thus, rather than causing the decision making process to come to a screeching halt, Japanese executives are more likely to become even more parsimonious in their search for higher efficiency through higher quality.

References

1. R.E. Freeman, *Strategic Management: A Stakeholder Approach*, Pitman Publishing, Boston, MA (1984).
2. Eric Rhenman, *Strategic Management*, John Wiley and Sons, New York (1986).
3. Grant T, Savage, Timothy W. Nix, Carlton J. Whitehead and John D. Blair, Strategies for assessing and managing organizational stakeholders, *Academy of Management Executive* 5 (2), 61-75 (1991).
4. David Lei, Offensive and defensive use of alliances, *Long Range Planning* 26 (4), 32-41 (1993).
5. P.R, Brown and C.P. Stickney, Instructional case: Tanaguchi Corporation, *Issues in Accounting Education* 7 (1), 57-79 (1992).
6. For bankrupt companies, happiness is a warm *Keiretsu, Business Week*, October 26, 48-49 (1992).
7. Howard D. Lowe, Shortcomings of Japanese consolidated financial statements, *Accounting Horizons,* September, 1-9 (1990).
8. A.T. Demaree. What now for the US and Japan, *Fortune*, February 10, 80-95 (1992).
9. Ibid.
10. *Wall Street Journal,* June 2, B6 (1992).
11. Paul Raeburn, GM recruits experts to reduce emissions, *Johnson City Press,* July 9, 17 (1992).
12. Global management in the 1990s, *Fortune*, July 27, 44-47 (1992).
13. J.B. Levine, A helping hand for Europe's high-tech heavies, *Business Week*, July 13, 43-44 (1992).
14. Thomas F. O'Boyle, A manufacturer grows efficient by soliciting ideas from employees, *Wall Street Journal.* June 5, A1,A4 (1992).
15. R.S. Ahlbrandt, C.R. Leana and A.J. Murrell, Employee involvement programmes improve corporate performance, *Long Range Planning* 25 (5), 91-98 (1992).
16. *Time,* March 23, 46 (1992).
17. R. Neff and W.J. Holstein, The Harvard man in Mitsubishi's corner, *Business Week,* March 23,50 (1992).
18. Global management in the 1990s, *Fortune,* July 27, 44-47 (1992).
19. *Time,* March 23, 46 (1992).
20. C. Kennedy, Changing the company culture at Ciba-Geigy, *Long Range Planning* 26 (1), 18-27 (1993).
21. Ibid., p. 18.
22. Ibid., p. 23.
23. R. Roy and R.C. Whelan, Successful recycling through value-chain collaboration, *Long Range Planning* 25 (4), 62-71 (1992).
24. Ibid.
25. B.H. Peters and J. Peter, The new corporate order, *Business Week*, April 27, 113-116 (1992).
26. P. Lorange, J. Roos and P.S. Bronn, Building successful strategic alliances, *Long Range*

Planning 25 (6), 10-17 (1992).

27. Talk about your dream team, *Business Week,* July 27, 59-60 (1992).

SECTION TWO

THE BUSINESS ENVIRONMENT

Macroenvironmental Analysis for Strategic Management

By *Peter M. Ginter* and *W. Jack Duncan*
Long Range Planning, Vo. 23, No. 6, pp 91-100, 1990, with permission from Elsevier Science

W.Jack Duncan is Professor and University scholar in Management and **Peter M. Ginter** is Professor of Management, both at the University of Alabama at Birmingham.

Macroenvironmental analysis is an integral part of systematic strategic planning. Even though the literature on macroenvironmental analysis is fragmented, there are useful guidelines for making sense out of this complex and important aspect of strategic planning. This article highlights five important questions managers should ask about macroenvironmental analysis, develops a model for the process, and summarizes what research and experience tell us about each question.

For many people of today's organizations, success or failure, profit or loss, growth or decline depend on technological, or political/regulatory changes – the external macroenvironment. For instance, Ford Motor Company's market success with the Tarus and Sable automobiles illustrates Ford's early recognition and response to society's emerging preference for superior product design (function plus fashion). In contrast, the failure of Caterpillar Tractor Company in the early 1980s to anticipate and respond to world-wide economic shifts, resulted in a dramatic decline for the company.

Trends in the technological environment have also had profound effect on firms, boosting some to industry leaders and driving others into bankruptcy. For example, advances in the networking capabilities of the newer PCs have seriously questioned the advantages of the minicomputer and leadership position of Digital

Equipment Corporation in the midrange computer market. Similarly, macro political/regulatory trends toward less government involvement in business have affected, dramatically, many industries. Specifically, deregulation has completely changed the keys to success in the trucking industry. Deregulation has contributed to overcapacity within the industry and new methods of competition, which were formally prohibited, have become prevalent. As Chairman George E. Powell, Jr. of Yellow Freight System reflected. 'deregulation makes the big firms stronger, forces the smaller firms into niches, and allows the medium sized firms to get squeezed.[1] Clearly, changes in macroenvironments will significantly affect an organization's success and perhaps its survival.

Macroenvironmental Analysis

For purposes of analysis, macroenvironmental forces typically are classified as social, economic, technological, and political/regulatory. Analysis of these areas involves the study of current and potential change and the assessment of the impact of changes on the organization.[2] Certainly, trends within these areas, like the aging of the population, the shift from manufacturing to service industries, and the increasing use of robotics will have profound effects on organizations regardless of the industry.

Sport shoes provide a good example of the importance of environmental forces. Adidas, Converse, and Keds all missed or underestimated the size and strength of the upper price running shoe market and the extensive emphasis on health it signaled. A lack of response to such signals provided just the opportunity Nike needed to successfully enter the market. It is important that managers acknowledge macroenvironmental factors and study their potential impact.

---

1. Inability to organize for effective environmental scanning;
2. Difficulty in matching individual beliefs and detectable trends;
3. Inability to obtain pertinent and timely information;
4. Delays between the occurrence of external events and management's ability to interpret them;
5. General inability to respond quickly enough to take advantage of the trends detected; and
6. Motivation of the management team to discuss the issues.

Box 1. Major frustrations in macroenvironmental analysis

Macroenvironmental Analysis Process

While macroenvironmental analysis is a crucial part of systematic strategic planning, there may be many frustrations in its management (see Box 1) and few guidelines to help managers understand and use the process. In fact, as William Dill has pointed out, one of the primary problems facing the effective use of macroenvironmental analysis is the fact that we do not even understand completely the concept of environment. Dill argues:[3]

'At one level, environment is not a very mysterious concept. It means the surroundings of an organization; the climate in which the organization functions. The concept becomes challenging when we try to move from simple description of the environment to analysis of its properties.'

Generally, the process of macroenvironmental analysis consists of four interrelated activities – scanning, monitoring, forecasting, and assessing. More specifically, macroenvironmental analysis involves:

- Scanning macroenvironments for warning signs and possible environmental changes that will effect the business;
- Monitoring environments for specific trends and patterns;
- Forecasting future directions of environmental changes; and
- Assessing current and future trends in terms of the effects such changes would have on the firm.

Scanning. RJR detected warning signals as the implications of the Surgeon General's report on the harmful affects of smoking and the growing fitness movement became evident. Clearly, there were important changes in social values that would adversely affect the tobacco industry in general and RJR in particular.

Monitoring. Keeping in contact with public attitudes further convinced RJR's management, because of growing concerns over the secondary affects of inhaling tobacco smoke exhaled by others, that the Company should not bet its future exclusively on tobacco products.

Forecasting. RJR could see no reasons why the trend away from smoking and toward fitness would not continue and therefore anticipated a long term decline in the use of tobacco products. This trend suggested the need for diversification.

Assessing. RJR's assessment of the situation led to them to believe the best course of action was to reduce the firm's reliance on tobacco products and to expand into the familiar, and promising, area of consumer goods.

Box 2. Macroenvironmental analysis at R.J. Reynolds

How these activities were important for R.J. Reynolds in responding to macroenvironmental change is illustrated in Box 2.

Engaging in Macroenvironmental Analysis

Before beginning macroenvironmental analysis, the following five questions should be considered. Answers to these questions will provide insight into the level of commitment that will be required by the organization. The sequence in which the question should be asked is illustrated in Figure 1.

Q1. Does my organization need macroenvironmental analysis?

Q2. If the answer is yes to Q1, which areas of the macroenvironment should I analyse?

Q3. How much information do I need and where do I get it?

Q4. What techniques can I use to analyse important trends and events?

Q5. What procedures and organization structures are most appropriate for analysing the macroenvironment?

Fortunately, these questions have been addressed sufficiently to offer some practical guidelines to managers. The remainder of this discussion will be devoted to examining what we know about these questions and illustrating how each assists managers in doing a better job of analysing the macroenvironment. The relevance

---

Scanning. RJR detected warning signals as the implications of the Surgeon General's report on the harmful affects of smoking and the growing fitness movement became evident. Clearly, there were important changes in social values that would adversely affect the tobacco industry in general and RJR in particular.

Monitoring. Keeping in contact with public attitudes further convinced RJR's management, because of growing concerns over the secondary affects of inhaling tobacco smoke exhaled by others, that the Company should not bet its future exclusively on tobacco products.

Forecasting. RJR could see no reasons why the trend away from smoking and toward fitness would not continue and therefore anticipated a long term decline in the use of tobacco products. This trend suggested the need for diversification.

Assessing. RJR's assessment of the situation led to them to believe the best course of action was to reduce the firm's reliance on tobacco products and to expand into the familiar, and promising, area of consumer goods.

Box 2. Macroenvironmental analysis at R.J. Reynolds

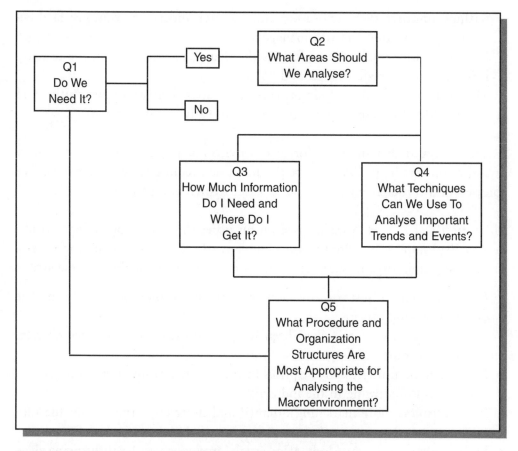

Figure 1. Five Questions About Macroenvironmental Analysis.

of these questions in a large, well known, multinational firm, Royal Dutch/Shell which will be discussed as the questions are examined.[4]

Q1. Does my Organization Need Macroenvironmental Analysis?
Macroenvironmental analysis, like other aspects of managerial action, must be economical if it is to be successful. That is, the benefits must exceed the costs. Therefore, in answering the first question, managers need to look at the potential benefits of systematic macroenvironmental analysis. A few of the more important are:

- Macroenvironmental analysis increases managerial awareness of environmental changes;
- A higher environmental awareness enhances strategic planning by enriching industry and market analysis; increasing our understanding of multinational

settings; improving diversification and resource allocation decisions; facilitating energy planning and risk management.

- Macroenvironmental analysis focuses the manager's attention on the primary influences of strategic change; and
- Macroenvironmental analysis provides time to anticipate opportunities and carefully develop responses to change (i.e. an early warning system).

It can be argued that the need for macroenvironmental analysis increases when organizations are large, have diverse product lines, require large investments, face complex and turbulent markets, and experience high competitive threats.[5]

More specifically, A. H. Mesch, based on his experiences in an operating division of Sun Exploration and Production Company, developed seven specific criteria for deciding if an organization needs macroenvironmental analysis. These are:[6]

- Does the external business environment influence capital allocations and the decision making process?
- Have previous long-range plans been scrapped because of unexpected changes in the environment?
- Have there been unpleasant surprises in the external business environment?
- Is competition growing in the industry?
- Is the business more marketing oriented and more concerned about the ultimate customer?
- Do more and different kinds of external forces seem to be influencing decisions, and does there seem to be more interplay among them?
- Is management unhappy with past forecasting and planning efforts?

A 'yes' to any of these questions suggests the need to consider adding or expounding the macroenvironmental analysis efforts in your organizations. The more 'yes' answers, the more urgent the need.

In the late 1960s and early 1970s, Royal Dutch/Shell answered a strong yes to these seven questions, particularly number four. A scenario planning technique emphasing macroenvironmental shifts was developed that allowed Royal Dutch/Shell to be more prepared for the 1973 crisis and to sell off its excess oil supplies before the world-wide glut developed in 1981. The technique began by carefully sorting out the differences between environmental factors that were 'predetermined' events and those that were 'uncertainties'. Predetermined events are those that have already occurred or will almost certainly occur. Heavy rains in one part of a country during a particular time of year will almost certainly set off events that will happen 'downstream' at predictable intervals.

Until the 'downstream' distinction was made, management of Royal Dutch/Shell had not been satisfied with it macroenvironmental analysis and forecasting techniques. They had achieved only 'first generation scenarios'. While first generation scenarios were useful in gaining understanding of the environment and were the necessary first step in planning macroenvironmental 'downstreaming' this led to an appreciation of the predetermined factors and their interrelationships with the uncertainties and provided the foundation for more sophisticated plans.[7]

Q2. Which Areas of the Environment Should I Analyse?
After establishing the need for macroenvironmental analysis, the next question is 'which areas of the macroenvironment should we scan, monitor, forecast and assess?' the theoretical and empirical literature suggest that there is a need to engage in scanning, monitoring, forecasting, and assessing in at least the macro social, economic, technological, and political/regulatory environments. It is no longer sufficient to monitor only those events and trends in your own industry.

For example, by the turn of the century it is estimated that 30 per cent of a new car's cost will be accounted for by aerospace-style computer electronics. Such technological improvements include computer gear shift, heads-up display, collision avoidance and navigation systems, and adaptive lights. Automobile industry management must scan, monitor, forecast, and assess these changes (changes in the technological environment) if their products are to be competitive in the year 2000.

Similarly, consumer goods firms planning expansions into multinational settings must be sensitive to a range of world-wide demographic trends. Projections show that by the year 2000 of the 25 largest cities in the world only six will be in economically developed nations. The implications for the amount and types of goods and services that will be demanded by the world's population are significant.[8] Clearly, consumer goods firms like Beatrice Foods must monitor and assess worldwide population trends.

Firms should have analysis activities in at least the four macroenvironmental areas identified above. However, since these external environments are vast and diverse, managers must carefully select the most promising trends and events to analyse. In fact 'It has become necessary to restrain executives from roaming the external environment with enthusiastic indiscipline.'[9]

Royal Dutch/Shell was careful not to display excessive indiscipline in their development of planning scenarios. Attention was focused on variables like oil demand by market class (economic), refining capacity construction world-wide (political and economic), likelihood of government intervention into different markets (political), alternative sources of fuels (technological), and so on.

However, through their analysis of the macroenvironment, planners at Shell came to realize that their task was not to produce a documented view of the business environment 5 to 10 years in the future. It was decided instead, through their scanning, forecasting, assessing, and monitoring, to develop a 'corporate microcosm' that was a view of the real world (Shell called this the 'macrocosm' that was accurate and one that would build management confidence in the planning staff. In fact, the director of planning at Royal Dutch/Shell stated that until the manager's mental picture of the world was altered through environmental analysis, the scenarios were like 'water on a stone'. [10] Only through an analysis of the social, economic, technological, and political/regulatory environments can a complete macrocosm be constructed.

Q3. How Much Information Do I Need and Where Do I get It?

Managers are justifiably concerned about the amounts and sources of information for macroenvironmental analysis. Sometimes only a little information is needed to make strategic decisions and at other times it is necessary to gather large amounts of data. There are at least conditions under which large amounts of information are required.[11]

1. The need for information increases as the scope or magnitude of the decision under consideration increases. Magnitude is measured in terms of the decision's potential impact on long-term return on investment and other goals and sub-goals of the total organization or any of its component parts.
2. The need for information increases as the urgency or timelines of the decision increases.
3. The need for information increases when the decision involves a problem as opposed to an activity that is going well. If the decision relates to something with which we have less experience, our need for information increases.
4. The need for information increases as the relationship of the decision to some major long range plan increases.

When these conditions are present it is important that we have an ongoing macroenvironmental analysis effort and established sources of information.

Examples of major issues requiring extensive macroenvironmental information are presented in Box 3.

Companies use a number of information sources inside and outside the organizations. Some of the more important can be classified as illustrated in Figure 2. Inside sources should always be exploited while outside sources should be used to a greater or lesser extent, depending on the nature of the decision under consideration.

For most companies, personal sources greatly exceed impersonal sources in terms of importance. Inside the company, subordinates and other managers are the greatest source of information. In fact, most companies have far more internal information than they expect. Vast amounts of relevant decision making data frequently exist in research personnel, planners, economists, and executive specialists in geographical areas of the firm's operations or relevant functions. People inside the firm provide rich and valuable industrial, technological, and political infor-

---

Scope of Decision. Honda's decision to locate major manufacturing facilities in the United States is an example of a decision with the potential for tremendous impact on the Company's future. With global markets shrinking, the success of Honda will depend on the success of its American production operations. Decisions of this nature require great amounts of macroenvironmental information in areas like international politics/regulation, consumer tastes, and economic conditions.

Urgency of Decision. When Proctor and Gamble was faced with the evidence associating the incident of toxic shock syndrome and the use of tampons, the Company immediately required vast amounts of macroenvironmental information in order to consider the economic, ethical, and legal implications of the removal of Rely tampons from the market.

Solving a Problem. Coca-Cola acquired its position of industry leadership with a product that had become an American, and perhaps world-wide institution. Coke's decision to change its formula in 1985 was not in response to familiar technical factors relating to the formula but to an eroding market share resulting from the 'Pepsi Challenge' — a problem. Information required about the changing nature of consumer tastes (desire for sweeter foods and beverages) was instrumental in addressing the issue.

Part of Long Range Planning. Progressive banks in the United States are sensitive to demographic trends. A necessity for long-run survival in the commercial banking industry is to seek new and profitable markets. This long necessity has prompted many banks to develop programmes attractive to large groups of older people who account for an increasin percentage of the American population.

Box 3. Decision requiring extensive macroenvironmental information

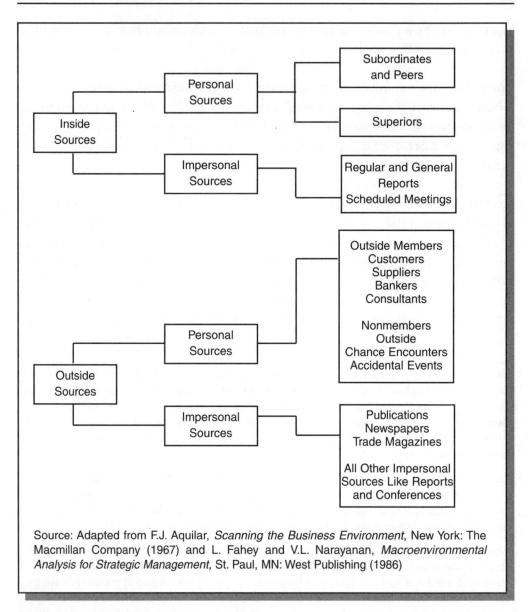

Source: Adapted from F.J. Aquilar, *Scanning the Business Environment*, New York: The Macmillan Company (1967) and L. Fahey and V.L. Narayanan, *Macroenvironmental Analysis for Strategic Management*, St. Paul, MN: West Publishing (1986)

Figure 2. Classification of Information Sources

mation that may not be available elsewhere. Often the macroenvironmental analysis staff will find it useful to personally interview informed personnel within the company.

Outside sources are usually quite numerous and include customers, suppliers, bankers, and consultants.[12] Also included in this category are business associates and chance encounters with people outside the manager's organization who possess valuable strategic information. External impersonal sources are trade publications, conferences, and activities of trade associations.[13] Outside agencies that supply forecasts and technical information about the environment can be useful as can private consultants. Outside forecasts typically consider a broader range of issues and variables and often fill gaps left in the less objective analyses of in-house specialists. Consultants can frequently provide in-depth studies on topics selected by the analysis staff and provide more objective assessments of the information uncovered in the process of analysis.

Royal Dutch/Shell, in evolving to its sophisticated scenarios, used almost every source of information one can imagine. In 1965 the Company introduced its Unified Planning Machinery (UPM) designed to look ahead 6 years. This was replaced by experimental studies exploring the business environment in the year 2000. Later 'Horizon Year Planning' for 15 years into the future was introduced before the scenario approach was initiated. Throughout this period, extensive use was made of secondary data bases, computer facilities, and personal expertise in Shell's many operating companies and business sectors. Government projections and statistical studies were frequently part of the inputs used in the experimental studies.

Q4. What Techniques Can I Use to Analyse Important Trends and Events?
This is the most neglected of the five questions addressed. It is the least examined because it is not quantitative and is the most subjective. As William Dill noted: 'the complexity of what we find and the grossness of most of the data that we collect are not consistent with the standards of precision and parsimony that social scientists have come to respect.[14]

There are few procedures for incorporating 'fuzzy' issues into the planning process. The ones that are available are usually characterized as judgemental, speculative, or conjectural. In recent years a variety of techniques have been suggested for dealing more effectively with this confusing aspect of macroenvironmental analysis. Three methods most frequently mentioned as being effective are the delphi technique or the systematic solicitation of expert opinion, the diffusion process, and scenario development. These techniques can be used to study emerging trends in the macro social, economic, political, and technological environments.

Traditional delphi techniques have undergone a great deal of change in the context of macroenvironmental analysis. The revised methodology involves; (1) identifying recognized experts in the area of interest; (2) seeking their co-operation and participation; (3) providing these experts with an initial position paper on the status of the issue; and (4) personal interviews with each expert. Sometimes more than a single interview is necessary but nothing that compares to the traditional multiple iterations of feedback rounds.

In addition, some authors have suggested studying the 'diffusion' of ideas that may eventually influence the environment.[15] Based on the product adoption process, the Battelle approach traces the adoption of emerging values throughout society. This process traces ideas from their initial inception through various stages of adoption. Continuous observation and plotting of values and new ideas through this process allows key influences to be identified, monitored, and evaluated in terms of their affect on relevant environmental areas.

Few techniques of environmental analysis have been as extensively reported as the Royal Dutch/Shell scenario models. These scenarios served two main purposes that are important to any serious planner. First, the process had a protective goal whereby the Company was able to anticipate and understand the risks involved in doing its business. Second, the process had an entrepreneurial goal. Its aim was not just to protect but to discover new strategic options of which Shell was previously unaware. Scenarios, at least as they are used at Royal Dutch/Shell, are fundamental aids to changing the mental models and altering the corporate microcosm in ways that allow managers to generate options for the future while assuming acceptable levels of risk.[16]

For any method adopted for macroenvironmental analysis, Terry proposed the use of a simple philosophy. The macroenvironmental analysis process becomes operational through the following principles:[17]

1. Macroenvironmental scanning should consider possible influences on the company. Only when the major issues are considered should the refining process, weighting, and priority setting process be initiated.
2. Recognize that the purpose of the scanning process is not to accurately predict the future but to identify those issues that are most likely to impact on the company and be prepared to cope with them when they arise. Fayol, for example, in his classic book captured the essence of this idea in his discussion of planning which, according to him, was merely part of a larger concept of prevoyance. The latter involved not only planning and forecasting but systematically preparing for the future.[18]

3. The results of macroenvironmental analysis should be used proactively rather that then company assuming a reactive stance toward the environment.
4. It is not sufficient for managers to understand the plan that results from the macroenvironmental analysis; it is crucial that they understand the thinking that has led to the development of strategic and tactical key issues. It is advantageous for as many managers as possible to take place in macroenvironmental analysis.
5. An important aspect of macroenvironmental analysis is that it focus managers' attention on what lies outside the organization and allows them to create an organization that can adapt to and learn from that environment.

Q5. What Procedures and Organization Structures are Most Appropriate for Analysing the Macroenvironment?
Having answered all the preceding questions, the manager's attention should now turn to developing procedures for the process and an organization structure to accomplish it. Unfortunately, most macroenvironmental analysis activity in the past was informal, unsophisticated, and largely an individual effort to person-specific interests. As a consequence, there are few useful frameworks for developing models and procedures.

Procedures

The literature reports three general types of macroenvironmental analysis procedural models. These are regular, irregular and continuous.[19] The regular model is comprehensive and systematic. Its focus is retrospective in that it employs simple extrapolations of the recent past into the near future. The irregular model is a type of *ad hoc* macroenvironmental analysis generally activated by some unexpected environmental event. The continuous model emphasizes the monitoring of various environmental subsystems rather than specific events. The scenario approach we have used previously, while being activated by unexpected events, is continuous in character and intent.

Structuring the Process

Most companies use one of several variations to position their macroenvironmental analysis units. Some of the more common variations are corporate/strategic planning departments; product/market areas, divisions, or strategic business units; marketing research departments; legal departments; public relations or public affairs departments; think tanks; and concept groups. The corporate/strategic planning department, the product/market group, and strategic business unit are the most frequently used. However, companies in the most advanced stages of strategic planning prefer to place their macroenvironmental analysis units in separate departments.[20]

One study of United States and foreign firms found that most macroenvironmental analysis units are located organizationally within formal planning departments.[21] When found elsewhere, macroenvironmental analysis units are housed in public affairs and governmental relations departments. In a study of 10 'leading edge' corporations there was considerable variety in the designs of macroenvironmental analysis units – 'a variety of position within organizational hierarchies serve as the primary locus of environmental intelligence gathering and interpretation'. Where structures existed, the variations could be classified according to the role the unit was designed to play in the organization. These roles logically fell under three headings – public policy role, strategic planning integrated role, and function oriented role.[22]

Firms exhibiting a public policy role placed primary attention on early detection of emerging issues that were suspected to be harbingers of large scale shifts in societal attitudes, laws, social norms and roles. Most units organized in this manner have direct access to top-level executives in the corporation while linkage with the strategic planning process is tenuous at best and sometimes virtually non-existent.

Companies using the strategic planning integrated structure in macroenvironmental analysis focus on both general and industry levels of the environment and subsequently play an integrative role in the strategic planning process. In contrast to the public policy role, companies with a function-oriented role for scanning centered activities on only those aspects of the environment that impinge directly on the activities of the function within the organization as a whole. As a result these units may be housed in functional departments. The advantages and disadvantages of these administrative structures are presented in Table 1.

A continuous or proactive approach is most appropriate for firms committed to strategic planning and concerned about the influence of the macroenvironment. Companies in advanced stages of strategic planning will benefit most by separating the macroenvironmental analysis operations from the unit primarily responsible for strategic planning. Companies with fewer environmental influences may benefit by incorporating macroenvironmental analysis within the strategic planning of other functional departments. Even with a separate macroenvironmental analysis unit, it may be useful to have certain line managers continually monitoring specific aspects of the external environment and periodically providing

Structure	Advantages	Disadvantages
Public Policy	Direct access to power structure. New perspective for top executive group. Stimulates long-term strategic thinking. Access to the 'corporate vision'.	Establishing legitimacy. No direct planning linkage. Survival depends on 'sponsoring' manager. Must compete with strategic planners for top management attention.
Integrated Planning	Direct access to strategic planning process. Can integrate corporate and business level environmental issues. Opportunity to directly influence corporate strategy.	Pressure to become short range in analysis. Need to conform to planning procedures and formats. Tension between line and staff viewpoints.
Function oriented	Environment is more easily defined. Direct input to key strategy decisions. No competition with planning for management attention. Close line-staff interaction.	Restricted environmental focus. Limited prospect for unconventional thinking. Short-term orientation. Requires clear and stable concept of strategy.

Source: R.T. Lenz and J.L. Engledow, Environmental analysis units and strategic-decision making. *Strategic Management Journal*, **7**, 69-89 (1086).

Table 1. Advantages and Disadvantages of Different Macroenvironmental Analysis Administrative Structures.

environmental information to the macroenvironmental analysis unit. At a minimum, periodic interviews with key line managers and executives should be conducted.

Conclusions

Macroenvironmental analysis is widely acknowledged to be an important part of the strategic planning process; yet there are few guidelines for conducting macroenvironmental analysis activities. While the critical questions concerning macroenvironmental analysis are clear, precise answers are not always available.

Managers initiating the macroenvironmental analysis process must proceed using trial and error.

Structuring macroenvironmental analysis is helpful both conceptually and functionally. Consideration of the social, economic, technological, and political/regulatory environments is crucial for most firms. However, management experience and judgement must be used in determining the extent to which environments are to be scanned, monitored, forecasted, and assessed.

There are variety of useful sources of environmental information. Many of the sources are inside the organization. Key managers often have important information and insight concerning the environment. Therefore, internal interviews are an essential part of the scanning effort. Also, the macroenvironmental analysis staff can identify emerging trends through analysis of data in periodicals and government publications. With the direction provided by internal sources and the macroenvironmental analysis staff's activities, indepth studies by outside experts may be commissioned. These analyses can be evaluated and integrated into the overall macroenvironmental analysis.

The organization of the macroenvironmental analysis effort will depend on the size of the firm and its stage in, and commitment to, strategic planning. Most companies should have an ongoing macroenvironmental analysis effort that acquaints top management with the general opportunities and threats in the external environment. These issues must ultimately be integrated into the strategic plan for the business. Companies in advanced stages of strategic planning will likely get the best results through a separate macroenvironmental analysis unit that reports directly to top management. Less advanced organizations in terms of strategic planning will do well to place the macroenvironmental analysis function under strategic planning.

Regardless of its position in the organization structure, the assessment of environmental information should: (1) be systematic; (2) consider diverse opinions; and (3) divorce the findings from the personal beliefs of the managers. Judgemental techniques such as brainstorming, scenarios, and impact analysis can identify emerging issues but management must still speculate about their impact. Macroenvironmental analysis, like general management, requires a good deal of judgement and experience.[23]

As a final summary, Box 4 illustrates how all five of the questions addressed in this paper were approached by a large telecommunications firm.

Regular, formal macroenvironmental analysis currently is practiced in a large telecommunications firm. In instituting macroenvironmental analysis, management had to address each of the important questions in the process. The following are the answers one firm obtained.

The Need for Macroenvironmental Analysis?
The field of telecommunications currently is undergoing dramatic change. Perhaps no other field has merged so many once distinct technologies and has wider potential applications. Management at a large telecommunications firm realized this trend would probably continue and, in an effort to anticipate the direction of change and achieve a position from which the firm could respond, an understanding of the external environment was considered essential.

Management found that: (1) the external environment greatly affected capital allocations; (2) long-range plans had been dramatically affected by changes in the external environment; (3) world-wide telecommunications competition was increasing; (4) because of regulatory changes, the company had become more marketing oriented; (5) more and different forces were influencing decisions; and (6) past forecasting techniques were no longer adequate. Therefore, a strategic analysis unit was established to scan, monitor, forecast, and assess the external environment.

Areas of Macroenvironment
The strategic analysis unit identified eight initial macro areas for analysis: (1) Lessons of the past for the Future, (2) Future Market Needs Assessment,(3) Telecommunications Technology, (4) Competitive Issues, (5) General Demographic, (6) Finance and Economics, (7) Public Policy Issues, and (8) General technology.

Initial studies in the areas were conducted by in-house experts and outside university professors specializing in the area. The primary objective of these studies was to conduct a broad analysis across each area in order to identify opportunities and threats over the next 10 years.

From the initial studies, it was determined that the strategic analysis unit would conduct on-going scanning, monitoring, forecasting, and assessment in the following macroenvironmental areas; demographics, life-styles, social values, economic, technological, political, and regulatory environments. The following common terminology was developed to aid in analysis of each area.

Issues — environmental changes with important implications for an organization.

Trends — systematic variation of indicators over time.

Patterns — meaningful clusters of trends.

Projection/Forecasts — future states or trends or patterns.

Prediction — projections of forecasts accepted for strategic purposes.

Change — change in indicators, trends, or patterns in one or more areas.

Forces — the causes underlying changes or factors that cause such change.

Box 4. Macroenvironmental Analysis for Telecommunications *(continued on next page)*

(Box 4 continued)

Sources of Information
The strategic analysis unit realized that the scanning and monitoring processes were essentially information gathering activities. Therefore, an in-house library was established where subscriptions to relevant periodicals and related publications were stored for reference. In addition, the firm subscribed to the publications of several research groups such as Stanford Research Institute (primarily for life style and demographic information). As further sources of information, in-house units, such as market and economic research, and outside authorities were identified and periodically consulted for updates in their area.

Analysis Techniques
The study of each macroenvironment was assigned to an individual in the strategic analysis unit who obtained additional support from in-house or outside sources (most used a modified delphi approach). Their primary charge was: (1) the development of a report that discussed the major issues and the associated implications for the company over the next 10 years; and (2) the identification of the most significant issues that needed additional study.

The responsible strategic staff member identified the major issues, trends and patterns and forecasted possible impacts on the company. Simple trend extrapolation and delphi consultation were utilized. The fundamental forces underlying these issues and trends were also identified and assessed. Identified sources, issues, trends, and implications for the firm were summarized and forwarded to the strategic planning group as an input to the strategic planning cycle (which focused on a 3-5 year horizon).

Organization Structure
The strategic analysis unit operated as a separate concept group, autonomous from and independent of the strategic planning department. This autonomy allowed the group to pursue issues unconstrained by the planning unit's bias or short term perspective. The strategic analysis unit performed in a public role identifying emerging issues that were expected to affect the firm and providing a long-term perspective to the planning function.

References

1. *New York Times*, 22 December, Section 3, 17 (1985)
2. Liam Fahey and V.K. Narayan, *Macroenvironmental Analysis for Strategic Management*, West Publishing, St Paul, MN, p. 3 (1986)
3. William R. Dill, The Impact of Environment on Organizational Development, *Concepts and Issues in Administrative Behavior*, in S Millick and E. H. Van Ness (eds.), Prentice Hall, Englewood Cliffs, NJ, pp 95-96 (1962)
4. Pierre Wack, Scenarios: Uncharted waters, *Harvard Business Review*, pp 73-89 September/October (1985), and Pierre Wack, Scenarios: Shooting the rapids, *Harvard Business Review*, pp. 139-150, November/December (1985).
5. G.S. Yip, Who needs strategic planning? *Journal of Business Strategy*, 6, 30-42 (1985).
6. A.H. Mesch, Developing an Effective Environmental Assessment Function, *Managerial Planning*, 32, 17-22 (1984).
7. Wack, *Uncharted Waters*, pp 74-78.
8. Robert W. Fox, Population Images, *The Futurist*, 22, 29-32, March/April (1988).
9. J.J. O'Connell and J.W. Zimmermann. Scanning the international environment, *California Management Review*, 22, 15-23 (1979).
10. Wack, *op cit.*, p. 84.
11. F.J. Aquilar, *Scanning the Business Environment*, Macmillan Company, New York, p. 25 (1967).
12. L.C. Rhyne, Strategic Information: The key to successful planning, *Long-Range Planning*, 32, 4-10 (1984).
13. S.C. Jain, Environmental Scanning in U.S. Corporations, *Long Range Planning*, 17, 117-128 (1984).
14. Dill, *op cit.*, p. 96.
15. W.A. Reinhardt, An early Warning System for Strategic Planning, *Long Range Planning*, 17, 25-34 (1984).
16. Wack, *op cit.*, pp. 145-150.
17. P.T. Terry, Mechanisms for Environmental Scanning, *Long Range Planning*, 10, 1-9 (1977).
18. Henri Fayol, *General and Industrial Management*, C. Storrs, trans., Pitman Publishing Company, London (1949).
19. L. Fahey and W.R. King, 'Environmental Scanning for Corporate Planning, *Business Horizons*, 20, 61-71 (1977).
20. Jain, *op cit.*, 117-128.
21. H.E. Klein and R.E. Linneman, Environmental Assessment: An International Study in Corporate Practice, *Journal of Business Strategy*, 5, 66-75 (1984).
22. R.T. Lenz and J.L. Engledow, Environmental analysis units and strategic decision making: A field study of selected 'leading edge' corporations, *Strategic Management Journal*, 7, 69-89 (1986).
23. L, Fahey and V.L. Narayan , *Macroenvironmental Analysis for Strategic Management, op cit.*

How Competitive Forces Shape Strategy

By *Michael E. Porter*

Mr. Porter is a specialist in industrial economics and business strategy. An associate professor of business administration at the Harvard Business School, he has created a. course there entitled "Industry and Competitive Analysis." He sits on the boards of three companies and consults on strategy matters, and he has written many articles for economics journals and published two books. One of them, *Interbrand Choice, Strategy and Bilateral Market Power* (Harvard University Press, 1976) is an outgrowth of his doctoral thesis, for which he won the coveted Wells prize awarded by the Harvard economics department. He has recently completed two book manuscripts, one on competitive analysis in industry and the other (written with Michael Spence and Richard Caves) on competition in the open economy.

Awareness of these forces can help a company stake out a position in its industry that is less vulnerable to attack

The nature and degree of competition in an industry hinge on five forces: the threat of new entrants, the bargaining power of customers, the bargaining power of suppliers, the threat of substitute products or services (where applicable), and the jockeying among current contestants. To establish a strategic agenda for dealing with these contending currents and to grow despite them, a company must understand how they work in its industry and how they affect the company in its particular situation. The author details how these forces operate and suggests ways of adjusting to them, and, where possible, of taking advantage of them.

The essence of strategy formulation is coping with competition. Yet it is easy to view competition too narrowly and too pessimistically. While one sometimes hears executives complaining to the contrary, intense competition in an industry is neither coincidence nor bad luck.

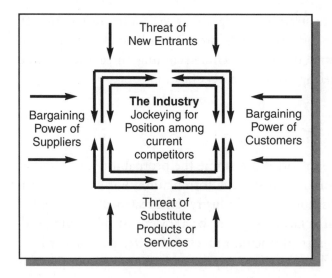

Threat of
New Entrants

The Industry
Jockeying for
Position among
current
competitors

Bargaining
Power of
Suppliers

Bargaining
Power of
Customers

Threat of
Substitute
Products or
Services

Exhibit 1. Forces Governing Competition in an Industry

Moreover, in the fight for market share, competition is not manifested only in the other players. Rather, competition in an industry is rooted in its underlying economics, and competitive forces exist that go well beyond the established combatants in a particular industry. Customers, suppliers, potential entrants, and substitute products are all competitors that may be more or less prominent or active depending on the industry.

The state of competition in an industry depends on five basic forces, which are diagrammed in Exhibit 1. The collective strength of these forces determines the ultimate profit potential of an industry. It ranges from *intense* in industries like tyres, metal cans, and steel, where no company earns spectacular returns on investment, to *mild* in industries like oil field services and equipment, soft drinks, and toiletries, where there is room for quite high returns.

In the economists' "perfectly competitive" industry, jockeying for position is unbridled and entry to the industry very easy. This kind of industry structure, of course, offers the worst prospect for long-run profitability. The weaker the forces collectively, however, the greater the opportunity for superior performance.

Whatever their collective strength, the corporate strategist's goal is to find a position in the industry where his or her company can best defend itself against these forces or can influence them in its favor. The collective strength of the forces may be painfully apparent to all the antagonists; but to cope with them, the strategist must delve below the surface and analyze the sources of each. For example, what makes the industry vulnerable to entry? What determines the bargaining power of suppliers?

Knowledge of these underlying sources of competitive pressure provides the groundwork for a strategic agenda of action. They highlight the critical strengths and weaknesses of the company, animate the positioning of the company in its industry, clarify the areas where strategic changes may yield the greatest payoff, and highlight the places where industry trends promise to hold the greatest significance as either opportunities or threats. Understanding these sources also proves to be of help in considering areas for diversification.

Contending forces

The strongest competitive force or forces determine the profitability of an industry and so are of greatest importance in strategy formulation. For example, even a company with a strong position in an industry unthreatened by potential entrants will earn low returns if it faces a superior or a lower-cost substitute product – as the leading manufacturers of vacuum tubes and coffee percolators have learned to their sorrow. In such a situation, coping with the substitute product becomes the number one strategic priority.

Different forces take on prominence, of course, in shaping competition in each industry. In the ocean-going tanker industry the key force is probably the buyers (the major oil companies), while in tyres it is powerful OEM buyers coupled with tough competitors. In the steel industry the key forces are foreign competitors and substitute materials.

Every industry has an underlying structure, or a set of fundamental economic and technical characteristics, that gives rise to these competitive forces. The strategist, wanting to position his company to cope best with its industry environment or to influence that environment in the company's favor, must learn what makes the environment tick.

This view of competition pertains equally to industries dealing in services and to those selling products. To avoid monotony in this article, I refer to both products and services as "products." The same general principles apply to all types of business.

A few characteristics are critical to the strength of each competitive force. I shall discuss them in this section.

Threat of entry

New entrants to an industry bring new capacity, the desire to gain market share, and often substantial resources. Companies diversifying through acquisition into the industry from other markets often leverage their resources to cause a shake-up, as Philip Morris did with Miller beer.

The seriousness of the threat of entry depends on the barriers present and on the reaction from existing competitors that the entrant can expect. If barriers to entry are high and a newcomer can expect sharp retaliation from the entrenched competitors, obviously he will not pose a serious threat of entering.

There are six major sources of barriers to entry:

1. *Economies of scale* – These economies deter entry by forcing the aspirant either to come in on a large scale or to accept a cost disadvantage. Scale economies in production, research, marketing, and service are probably the key barriers to entry in the mainframe computer industry, as Xerox and GE sadly discovered. Economies of scale can also act as hurdles in distribution, utilization of the sales force, financing, and nearly any other part of a business.

2. *Product differentiation* – Brand identification creates a barrier by forcing entrants to spend heavily to overcome customer loyalty. Advertising, customer service, being first in the industry, and product differences are among the factors fostering brand identification. It is perhaps the most important entry barrier in soft drinks, over-the-counter drugs, cosmetics, investment banking, and public accounting. To create high fences around their businesses, brewers couple brand identification with economies of scale in production, distribution, and marketing.

3. *Capital requirements* – The need to invest large financial resources in order to compete creates a barrier to entry, particularly if the capital is required for unrecoverable expenditures in up-front advertising or R&D. Capital is necessary not only for fixed facilities but also for customer credit, inventories, and absorbing start-up losses. While major corporations have the financial resources to invade almost any industry, the huge capital requirements in certain fields, such as computer manufacturing and mineral extraction, limit the pool of likely entrants.

4. *Cost disadvantages independent of size* – Entrenched companies may have cost advantages not available to potential rivals, no matter what their size and attainable economies of scale. These advantages can stem from the effects of the learning curve (and of its first cousin, the experience curve), proprietary technology, access to the best raw materials sources, assets purchased at pre-inflation prices, government subsidies, or favorable locations. Sometimes cost advantages are legally enforceable, as they are through patents. (For an analysis of the much-discussed experience curve as a barrier to entry, see the insert overleaf.)

The experience curve as an entry barrier

In recent years, the experience curve has become widely discussed as a key element of industry structure. According to this concept, unit costs in many manufacturing industries (some dogmatic adherents say in all manufacturing industries) as well as in some service industries decline with "experience," or a particular company's cumulative volume of production. (The experience curve, which encompasses many factors, is a broader concept than the better known learning curve, which refers to the efficiency achieved over a period of time by workers through much repetition.) The causes of the decline in unit costs are a combination of elements, including economies of scale, the learning curve for labor, and capital-labor substitution. The cost decline creates a barrier to entry because new competitors with no "experience" face higher costs than established ones, particularly the producer with the largest market share, and have difficulty catching up with the entrenched competitors.

Adherents of the experience curve concept stress the importance of achieving market leadership to maximize this barrier to entry, and they recommend aggressive action to achieve it, such as price cutting in anticipation of falling costs in order to build volume. For the combatant that cannot achieve a healthy market share, the prescription is usually, "Get out."

Is the experience curve an entry barrier on which strategies should be built? The answer is: not in every industry. In fact, in some industries, building a strategy on the experience curve can be potentially disastrous. That costs decline with experience in some industries is not news to corporate executives. The significance of the experience curve for strategy depends on what factors are causing the decline.

If costs are falling because a growing company can reap economies of scale through more efficient, automated facilities and vertical integration, then the cumulative volume of production is unimportant to its relative cost position. Here the lowest-cost producer is the one with the largest, most efficient facilities.

A new entrant may well be more efficient than the more experienced competitors; if it has built the newest plant, it will face no disadvantage in having to catch up. The strategic prescription, "You must have the largest, most efficient plant," is a lot different from, "You must produce the greatest cumulative output of the item to get your costs down."

Whether a drop in costs with cumulative (not absolute) volume erects an entry barrier also depends on the sources of the decline. If costs go down because of technical advances known generally in the industry or because of the development of improved equipment that can be copied or purchased from equipment suppliers, the experience curve is no entry barrier at al — in fact, new, less experienced competitors may actually enjoy a cost advantage over the leaders. Free of the legacy of heavy past investments, the newcomer or less experienced competitor can purchase or copy the newest and lowest-cost equipment and technology.

If, however, experience can be kept proprietary, the leaders will maintain a cost advantage. But new entrants may require less experience to reduce their costs than the leaders needed. All this suggests that the experience curve can be a shaky entry barrier on which to build a strategy.

While space does not permit a complete treatment here, I want to mention a few other crucial elements in determining the appropriateness of a strategy built on the entry barrier provided by the experience curve:

- The height of the barrier depends on how important costs are to competition compared with other areas like marketing, selling, and innovation.
- The barrier can be nullified by product or process innovations leading to a substantially new technology and thereby creating an entirely new experience curve.* New entrants can leapfrog the industry leaders and alight on the new experience curve, to which those leaders may be poorly positioned to jump.
- If more than one strong company is building its strategy on the experience curve, the consequences can be nearly fatal. By the time only one rival is left pursuing such a strategy, industry growth may have stopped and the prospects of reaping the spoils of victory long since evaporated.

* For an example drawn from the history of the automobile industry, see William J. Abernathy and Kenneth Wayne, "The Limits of the Learning Curve," HBR September-October 1974. p. 109.

5. *Access to distribution channels* – The new boy on the block must, of course, secure distribution of his product or service. A new food product, for example, must displace others from the supermarket shelf via price breaks, promotions, intense selling efforts, or some other means. The more limited the wholesale or retail channels are and the more that existing competitors have these tied up, obviously the tougher that entry into the industry will be. Sometimes this barrier is so high that, to surmount it, a new contestant must create its own distribution channels, as Timex did in the watch industry in the 1950s.

6. *Government policy* – The government can limit or even foreclose entry to industries with such controls as license requirements and limits on access to raw materials. Regulated industries like trucking, liquor retailing, and freight forwarding are noticeable examples; more subtle government restrictions operate in fields like ski-area development and coal mining. The government also can play a major indirect role by affecting entry barriers through controls such as air and water, pollution standards and safety regulations.

The potential rival's expectations about the reaction of existing competitors also will influence its decision on whether to enter. The company is likely to have second thoughts if incumbents have previously lashed out at new entrants or if:

- The incumbents possess substantial resources to fight back, including excess cash and unused borrowing power, productive capacity, or clout with distribution channels and customers.
- The incumbents seem likely to cut prices because of a desire to keep market shares or because of industrywide excess capacity.
- Industry growth is slow, affecting its ability to absorb the new arrival and probably causing the financial performance of all the parties involved to decline.

Changing conditions

From a strategic standpoint there are two important additional points to note about the threat of entry.

First, it changes, of course, as these conditions change. The expiration of Polaroid's basic patents on instant photography, for instance, greatly reduced its absolute cost entry barrier built by proprietary technology. It is not surprising that Kodak plunged into the market. Product differentiation in printing has all but disappeared. Conversely, in the auto industry economies of scale increased enormously with post-World War II automation and vertical integration – virtually stopping successful new entry.

Second, strategic decisions involving a large segment of an industry can have a major impact on the conditions determining the threat of entry. For example, the actions of many U.S. wine producers in the 1960s to step up product introductions, raise advertising levels, and expand distribution nationally surely strengthened the entry roadblocks by raising economies of scale and making access to distribution channels more difficult. Similarly, decisions by members of the recreational vehicle industry to vertically integrate in order to lower costs have greatly increased the economies of scale and raised the capital cost barriers.

Powerful suppliers and buyers

Suppliers can exert bargaining power on participants in an industry by raising prices or reducing the quality of purchased goods and services. Powerful suppliers can thereby squeeze profitability out of an industry unable to recover cost increases in its own prices. By raising their prices, soft drink concentrate producers have contributed to the erosion of profitability of bottling companies because the bottlers, facing intense competition from powdered mixes, fruit drinks, and other beverages, have limited freedom to raise their prices accordingly. Customers likewise can force down prices, demand higher quality or more service, and play competitors off against each other – all at the expense of industry profits.

The power of each important supplier or buyer group depends on a number of characteristics of its market situation and on the relative importance of its sales or purchases to the industry compared with its overall business.

A *supplier* group is powerful if:

- It is dominated by a few companies and is more concentrated than the industry it sells to.

- Its product is unique or at least differentiated, or if it has built up switching costs. Switching costs are fixed costs buyers face in changing suppliers. These arise because, among other things, a buyer's product specifications tie it to particular suppliers, it has invested heavily in specialized ancillary equipment or in learning how to operate a supplier's equipment (as in computer software), or its production lines are connected to the supplier's manufacturing facilities (as in some manufacturers of beverage containers).
- It is not obliged to contend with other products for sale to the industry. For instance, the competition between the steel companies and the aluminum companies to sell to the can industry checks the power of each supplier.
- It poses a credible threat of integrating forward into the industry's business. This provides a check against the industry's ability to improve the terms on which it purchases.
- The industry is not an important customer of the supplier group. If the industry is an important customer, suppliers' fortunes will be closely tied to the industry, and they will want to protect the industry through reasonable pricing and assistance in activities like R and D and lobbying.

A *buyer* group is powerful if:

- It is concentrated or purchases in large volumes. Large-volumes buyers are particularly potent forces if heavy fixed costs characterize the industry – as they do in metal containers, corn refining, and bulk chemicals, for example – which raise the stakes to keep capacity filled.
- The products it purchases from the industry are standard or undifferentiated. The buyers, sure that they can always find alternative suppliers, may play one company against another, as they do in aluminum extrusion.
- The products it purchases from the industry form a component of its product and represent a significant fraction of its cost. The buyers are likely to shop for a favorable price and purchase selectively. Where the product sold by the industry in question is a small fraction of buyers' costs, buyers are usually much less price sensitive.
- It earns low profits, which create great incentive to lower its purchasing costs. Highly profitable buyers, however, are generally less price sensitive (that is, of course, if the item does not represent a large fraction of their costs).
- The industry's product is unimportant to the quality of the buyers' products or services. Where the quality of the buyers' products is very much affected by the industry's product, buyers are generally less price sensitive. Industries in which this situation occurs include oil field equipment, where a malfunction

can lead to large losses, and enclosures for electronic medical and test instruments, where the quality of the enclosure can influence the user's impression about the quality of the equipment inside.

- The industry's product does not save the buyer money. Where the industry's product or service can pay for itself many times over, the buyer is rarely price sensitive, rather, he is interested in quality. This is true in services like investment banking and public accounting, where errors in judgment can be costly and embarrassing, and in businesses like the logging of oil wells, where an accurate survey can save thousands of dollars in drilling costs.
- The buyers pose a credible threat of integrating backward to make the industry's product. The Big Three auto producers and major buyers of cars have often used the threat of self-manufacture as a bargaining lever. But sometimes an industry engenders a threat to buyers that its members may integrate forward.

Most of these sources of buyer power can be attributed to consumers as a group as well as to industrial and commercial buyers; only a modification of the frame of reference is necessary. Consumers tend to be more price sensitive if they are purchasing products that are undifferentiated, expensive relative to their incomes, and of a sort where quality is not particularly important.

The buying power of retailers is determined by the same rules, with one important addition. Retailers can gain significant bargaining power over manufacturers when they can influence consumers' purchasing decisions, as they do in audio components, jewellery, appliances, sporting goods, and other goods.

Strategic action

A company's choice of suppliers to buy from or buyer groups to sell to should be viewed as a crucial strategic decision. A company can improve its strategic posture by finding suppliers or buyers who possess the least power to influence it adversely.

Most common is the situation of a company being able to choose whom it will sell to – in other words, buyer selection. Rarely do all the buyer groups a company sells to enjoy equal power. Even if a company sells to a single industry, segments usually exist within that industry that exercise less power (and that are therefore less price sensitive) than others. For example, the replacement market for most products is less price sensitive than the overall market.

As a rule, a company can sell to powerful buyers and still come away with above-average profitability only if it is a low-cost producer in its industry or if its product enjoys some unusual, if not unique, features. In supplying large customers with electric motors, Emerson Electric earns high returns because its low cost position permits the company to meet or undercut competitors' prices.

If the company lacks a low cost position or a unique product, selling to everyone is self-defeating because the more sales it achieves, the more vulnerable it becomes. The company may have to muster the courage to turn away business and sell only to less potent customers.

Buyer selection has been a key to the success of National Can and Crown Cork & Seal. They focus on the segments of the can industry where they can create product differentiation, minimize the threat of backward integration, and otherwise mitigate the awesome power of their customers. Of course, some industries do not enjoy the luxury of selecting "good" buyers.

As the factors creating supplier and buyer power change with time or as a result of a company's strategic decisions, naturally the power of these groups rises or declines. In the ready-to-wear clothing industry, as the buyers (department stores and clothing stores) have become more concentrated and control has passed to large chains, the industry has come under increasing pressure and suffered falling margins. The industry has been unable to differentiate its product or engender switching costs that lock in its buyers enough to neutralize these trends.

Substitute products

By placing a ceiling on prices it can charge, substitute products or services limit the potential of an industry. Unless it can upgrade the quality of the product or differentiate it somehow (as via marketing), the industry will suffer in earnings and possibly in growth.

Manifestly, the more attractive the price-performance trade-off offered by substitute products, the firmer the lid placed on the industry's profit potential. Sugar producers confronted with the large-scale commercialization of high-fructose corn syrup, a sugar substitute, are learning this lesson today.

Substitutes not only limit profits in normal times; they also reduce the bonanza an industry can reap in boom times. In 1978 the producers of fiberglass insulation enjoyed unprecedented demand as a result of high energy costs and severe winter weather. But the industry's ability to raise prices was tempered by the plethora of insulation substitutes, including cellulose, rock wool, and styrofoam. These substitutes are bound to become an even stronger force once the current round of plant additions by fiberglass insulation producers has boosted capacity enough to meet demand (and then some).

Substitute products that deserve the most attention strategically are those that (a) are subject to trends improving their price-performance trade-off with the industry's product, or (b) are produced by industries earning high profits. Substitutes often come rapidly into play if some development increases competition in their industries and causes price reduction or performance improvement.

Jockeying for position

Rivalry among existing competitors takes the familiar form of jockeying for position – using tactics like price competition, product introduction, and advertising slugfests. Intense rivalry is related to the presence of a number of factors:

- Competitors are numerous or are roughly equal in size and power. In many U.S. industries in recent years foreign contenders, of course, have become part of the competitive picture.
- Industry growth is slow, precipitating fights for market share that involve expansion-minded members.
- The product or service lacks differentiation or switching costs, which lock in buyers and protect one combatant from raids on its customers by another.
- Fixed costs are high or the product is perishable, creating strong temptation to cut prices. Many basic materials businesses, like paper and aluminum, suffer from this problem when demand slackens.
- Capacity is normally augmented in large increments. Such additions, as in the chlorine and vinyl chloride businesses, disrupt the industry's supply demand balance and often lead to periods of over-capacity and price cutting.
- Exit barriers are high. Exit barriers, like very specialized assets or management's loyalty to a particular business, keep companies competing even though they may be earning low or even negative returns on investment. Excess capacity remains functioning, and the profitability of the healthy competitors suffers as the sick ones hang on.[1] If the entire industry suffers from overcapacity, it may

---

1. For a more complete discussion of exit barriers and their implications for strategy, see my article, "Please Note Location of Nearest Exit," *California Management Review*, Winter 1976, p. 21.

seek government help – particularly if foreign competition is present.
- The rivals are diverse in strategies, origins, and "personalities". They have different ideas about how to compete and continually run head-on into each other in the process.

As an industry matures, its growth rate changes, resulting in declining profits and (often) a shakeout. In the booming recreational vehicle industry of the early 1970s, nearly every producer did well; but slow growth since then has eliminated the high returns, except for the strongest members, not to mention many of the weaker companies. The same profit story has been played out in industry after industry – snowmobiles, aerosol packaging, and sports equipment are just a few examples. An acquisition can introduce a very different personality to an industry, as has been the case with Black & Decker's takeover of McCullough, the producer of chain saws. Technological innovation can boost the level of fixed costs in the production process, as it did in the shift from batch to continuous-line photo finishing in the 1960s.

While a company must live with many of these factors – because they are built into industry economics – it may have some latitude for improving matters through strategic shifts. For example, it may try to raise buyers' switching costs or increase product differentiation. A focus on selling efforts in the fastest-growing segments of the industry or on market areas with the lowest fixed costs can reduce the impact of industry rivalry. If it is feasible, a company can try to avoid confrontation with competitors having high exit barriers and can thus sidestep involvement in bitter price cutting.

Formulation of strategy

Once the corporate strategist has assessed the forces affecting competition in his industry and their underlying causes, he can identify his company's strengths and weaknesses. The crucial strengths and weaknesses from a strategic standpoint are the company's posture vis-à-vis the underlying causes of each force. Where does it stand against substitutes? Against the sources of entry barriers?

Then the strategist can devise a plan of action that may include (1) positioning the company so that its capabilities provide the best defense against the competitive force; and/or (2) influencing the balance of the forces through strategic moves, thereby improving the company's position; and/or (3) anticipating shifts in the factors underlying the forces and responding to them, with the hope of exploiting change by choosing a strategy appropriate for the new competitive balance before opponents recognize it. I shall consider each strategic approach in turn.

Positioning the company

The first approach takes the structure of the industry as given and matches the company's strengths and weaknesses to it. Strategy can be viewed as building defenses against the competitive forces or as finding positions in the industry where the forces are weakest.

Knowledge of the company's capabilities and of the causes of the competitive forces will highlight the areas where the company should confront competition and where avoid it. If the company is a low-cost producer, it may choose to confront powerful buyers while it takes care to sell them only products not vulnerable to competition from substitutes.

The success of Dr Pepper in the soft drink industry illustrates the coupling of realistic knowledge of corporate strengths with sound industry analysis to yield a superior strategy. Coca-Cola and Pepsi-Cola dominate Dr Pepper's industry, where many small concentrate producers compete for a piece of the action. Dr Pepper chose a strategy of avoiding the largest-selling drink segment, maintaining a narrow flavor line, foregoing the development of a captive bottler network, and marketing heavily. The company positioned itself so as to be least vulnerable to its competitive forces while it exploited its small size.

In the $11.5 billion soft drink industry, barriers to entry in the form of brand identification, large-scale marketing, and access to a bottler network are enormous. Rather than accept the formidable costs and scale economies in having its own bottler network – that is, following the lead of the Big Two and of Seven-Up – Dr Pepper took advantage of the different flavor of its drink to "piggyback" on Coke and Pepsi bottlers who wanted a full line to sell to customers. Dr Pepper coped with the power of these buyers through extraordinary service and other efforts to distinguish its treatment of them from that of Coke and Pepsi.

Many small companies in the soft drink business offer cola drinks that thrust them into head-to-head competition against the majors. Dr Pepper, however, maximized product differentiation by maintaining a narrow line of beverages built around an unusual flavor.

Finally, Dr Pepper met Coke and Pepsi with an advertising onslaught emphasizing the alleged uniqueness of its single flavor. This campaign built strong brand identification and great customer loyalty. Helping its efforts was the fact that Dr Pepper's formula involved lower raw materials cost, which gave the company an absolute cost advantage over its major competitors.

There are no economies of scale in soft drink concentrate production, so Dr Pepper could prosper despite its small share of the business (6%). Thus Dr Pepper confronted competition in marketing but avoided it in product line and in distribution. This artful positioning combined with good implementation has led to an enviable record in earnings and in the stock market.

Influencing the balance

When dealing with the forces that drive industry competition, a company can devise a strategy that takes the offensive. This posture is designed to do more than merely cope with the forces themselves; it is meant to alter their causes.

Innovations in marketing can raise brand identification or otherwise differentiate the product. Capital investments in large-scale facilities or vertical integration affect entry barriers. The balance of forces is partly a result of external factors and partly in the company's control.

Exploiting industry change

Industry evolution is important strategically because evolution, of course, brings with it changes in the sources of competition I have identified. In the familiar product life-cycle pattern, for example, growth rates change, product differentiation is said to decline as the business becomes more mature, and the companies tend to integrate vertically.

These trends are not so important in themselves; what is critical is whether they affect the sources of competition. Consider vertical integration. In the maturing minicomputer industry, extensive vertical integration, both in manufacturing and in software development, is taking place. This very significant trend is greatly raising economies of scale as well as the amount of capital necessary to compete in the industry. This in, turn is raising barriers to entry and may drive some smaller competitors out of the industry once growth levels off.

Obviously, the trends carrying the highest priority from a strategic standpoint are those that affect the most important sources of competition in the industry and

115

those that elevate new causes to the forefront. In contract aerosol packaging, for example, the trend toward less product differentiation is now dominant. It has increased buyers' power, lowered the barriers to entry, and intensified competition.

The framework for analyzing competition that I have described can also be used to predict the eventual profitability of an industry. In long-range planning the task is to examine each competitive force, forecast the magnitude of each underlying cause, and then construct a composite picture of the likely profit potential of the industry.

The outcome of such an exercise may differ a great deal from the existing industry structure. Today, for example, the solar heating business is populated by dozens and perhaps hundreds of companies, none with a major market position. Entry is easy, and competitors are battling to establish solar heating as a superior substitute for conventional methods.

The potential of this industry will depend largely on the shape of future barriers to entry, the improvement of the industry's position relative to substitutes, the ultimate intensity of competition, and the power captured by buyers and suppliers. These characteristics will in turn be influenced by such factors as the establishment of brand identities, significant economies of scale or experience curves in equipment manufacture wrought by technological change, the ultimate capital costs to compete, and the extent of overhead in production facilities.

The framework for analyzing industry competition has direct benefits in setting diversification strategy. It provides a road map for answering the extremely difficult question inherent in diversification decisions: "What is the potential of this business?" Combining the framework with judgement in its application, a company may be able to spot an industry with a good future before this good future is reflected in the prices of acquisition candidates.

Multifaceted rivalry

Corporate managers have directed a great deal of attention to defining their businesses as a crucial step in strategy formulation. Theodore Levitt, in his classic 1960 article in HBR, argued strongly for avoiding the myopia of narrow, product-oriented industry definition.[2] Numerous other authorities have also stressed the need to look beyond product to function in defining a business, beyond national boundaries to potential international competition, and beyond the ranks of one's competitors today to those that may become competitors tomorrow. As a result of these urgings, the proper definition of a company's industry or industries has become an endlessly debated subject.

One motive behind this debate is the desire to exploit new markets. Another, perhaps more important motive is the fear of overlooking latent sources of competition that someday may threaten the industry. Many managers concentrate so single-mindedly on their direct antagonists in the fight for market share that they fail to realize that they are also competing with their customers and their suppliers for bargaining power. Meanwhile, they also neglect to keep a wary eye out for new entrants to the contest or fail to recognize the subtle threat of substitute products.

The key to growth – even survival – is to stake out a position that is less vulnerable to attack from head-to-head opponents, whether established or new, and less vulnerable to erosion from the direction of buyers, suppliers, and substitute goods. Establishing such a position can take many forms – solidifying relationships with favorable customers, differentiating the product either substantively or psychologically through marketing, integrating forward or backward or establishing technological leadership.

---

2. Theodore Levitt, "Marketing Myopia," reprinted as an HBR Classic, September-October 1975, p. 26.

Assessing and Enhancing Strategic Capability: A Value-Driven Approach

By *Mike Partridge* and *Lew Perren*
From: *Management Accounting* June 1994

Mike Partridge and Lew Perren of the University of Brighton continue the theme that they introduced in the November issue – that firms should maintain an external strategic perspective. They move on this month to examine the strategic capability of the firm through the use of Porter's value chain analysis.[1] They introduce the fundamentals of the value chain, examine some emergent issues and explore its practical application. Readers unfamiliar with the five forces model, the competitive arena, generic strategies or the Porter approach to strategy development are directed to their earlier articles in the series.[2]

Strengths and weaknesses analysis is a useful way of appraising a firm's resources and competencies relative to industry norms and also to the opportunities and threats perceived in the competitive environment. Historically, the SWOT approach to strategic analysis has, when used thoughtfully, offered useful signals for strategic change. What it has lacked is an explicit focus on strategic capability, differentiation and strategic advantage. This the value chain seeks to remedy.

Activities and the value chain

Porter suggests that firms can be viewed as a flow of activities performed to provide products or services to customers.[1] These activities can be organised into a value chain that portrays how the firm creates value (see Figure 1, which describes the fundamentals of the value chain). Firms competing in the same industry sector are likely to have similarly configured value chains. However, it is the differences in the configuration of competing firms that are interesting as these provide the potential for competitive advantage.

Firms should adjust the activities in their value chain to create a 'value package' that certain customers will perceive as providing the 'best' value compared with the competition. The value chain should be arranged either to achieve overall low-

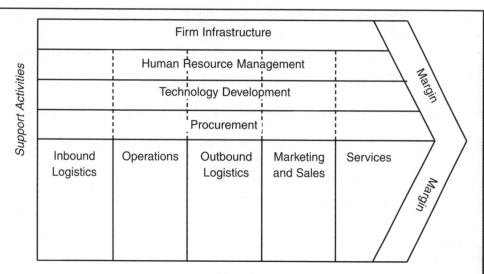

Primary Activities

Figure 1 classifies value activities into two main types, support and primary. The support activities contribute the infrastructure required for primary actvities to function. The primary activities are those directly concerned with the provision of the product or service and its distribution to the customer.

The support activities are segmented into four areas:

Procurement:	acquired inputs needed by the firm's value chain.
Technology development:	develops improvements in products or processes.
Human resource management:	recruits, trains, develops and rewards people in the firm.
Firm infrastructure	plans, finances and controls the firm's entire value chain.

The primary activities are segmented into five areas:

Inbound logistics:	receives, stores and transfers inputs to the operational stage.
Operations:	processes inputs into final product form.
Outbound logistics:	collects, stores and delivers product to customer.
Marketing and sales:	persuades customer to purchase product.
Service:	maintains the value of the product.

Figure 1. The Value Chain Diagram

est cost or to identify and provide specific product or service attributes that allow the firm to meet specific customer needs better than competing firms.

If there are alternative ways of configuring the value chain and so altering the attributes of the value package, so also can the costs of building the value chain alter. The strategic objective is to maximise the difference between value (price or volume) and cost.

Porter suggests that value chain activities should be isolated and separated if:

1. they represent a significant or growing proportion of operating costs;
2. the cost behaviour of the activities is different;
3. they are performed by competitors in a different way;
4. they have a high potential of being able to create differentiation.

Linkages

Linkages between activities can be vital in creating competitive advantage. Linkages exist within the firm, both horizontally and vertically, and outside the firm with suppliers and customers.

Porter suggests that many of the recent philosophies in manufacturing are an acknowledgment of the importance of linkages. The possible advantages of employing Japanese manufacturing techniques result from careful consideration of the linkages between activities. For example: *Just-in-time (JIT)* aspires to create a seamless flow across activity boundaries, thus reducing work-in-progress and giving instant feedback of quality problems to the previous activity. *Total quality management (TQM)* devolves quality issues to all operatives and empowers them to act. This allows quality issues to be dealt with at the linkage between activities rather than by waiting for a quality check at the end of the line.

Conventional reporting systems along functional lines operate against the development and exploitation of linkages by stressing individual responsibility for discrete organisational sub-units. The traditionally veiled hostility that can operate between supplier and customer along the chain can mitigate against the development of mutually rewarding partnerships.

Value systems

To perceive the value chain as existing solely within the boundaries of the firm would be less than realistic.

Most firms operate within a part of a vertically integrated chain of manufacture and supply and so may be insulated from their ultimate marketplace. Yet it is there that the customer's value perception is most important. A buyer's perception of a new car depends on the value added by the manufacturer, the component suppliers, the agent or distributor and the final customer. Porter calls this the value system (see Figure 2).

It is this area of value chain design that is currently seeing some of the most exciting developments. Strategic alliances are moving the buyer-seller relationship from one that is 'arm's length and adversarial'[3] towards one that is beneficial to both parties. Bowman and Faulkner,[4] with Webster,[3] argue that firms should avoid trying 'to do everything'. Identification of core or key competencies[5] should help a firm to identify which products and services it should produce or perform in-house and which it should outsource.

Marks & Spencer is a firm whose core competencies include retail and inventory management and who deliberately outsource their products via tightly managed supplier/buyer alliances. Other retailers that have sought greater degrees of verti-

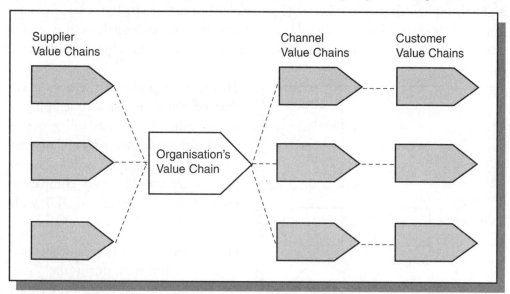

Figure 2. The Value System

cal integration, from design and manufacture through to retail, have been less successful.

There has been an increasing trend towards integrating customers into the value system.[6] Early examples include self-service retailing and catering. More recently, firms such as MFI and IKEA have successfully involved the customer in creating value through self-assembly of furniture. Currently, technology is offering new ways of involving the customer in the value system; for example, 24-hour banking and petrol retailing.

Another trend has been towards sharing activities within the value system to achieve economies of scale while retaining product or service offerings that are tailored to specific customer needs. This has been prevalent in the car industry where mergers and strategic alliances have led firms to share manufacturing capability but still achieve distinctive branding through the activities of assembly, marketing and distribution.

Using the value chain

The value chain can be used to audit the firm's current activities as well as developing improvements for the future (see Figure 3).

It offers a systematic way of analysing the firm's value creating activities and of highlighting the degree to which the particular bundle of attributes satisfies customer needs (A in Figure 3). In addition to customer-focused analysis, it is useful next to compare the firm's value chain with those of its principal competitors[7] (B).

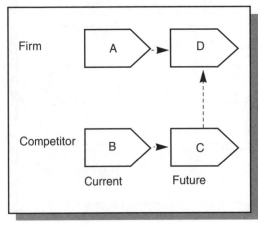

This leads logically to the next stage, that of designing and developing a future value chain that will generate competitive advantage (D) relative to competitors' *potential* value chains (C). Firms should avoid comparing their future value chains (D) with competitors' present value chains (B).

Firms need to test the value perceptions of customers down the value system and not just rely on their own perceptions of value. This needs to be

Figure 3. Designing the Value Chain

repeated regularly and benchmarked against competitor offerings as they alter their value packages and customer expectations increase. Accuracy and reliability were major value ingredients in the watch industry prior to the development of the quartz crystal watch in the late 1960s.

These characteristics moved from being 'order winning' to 'qualifying' attributes and new forms of differentiation had to be developed.

The objective is to build a value package which customers perceive to be better than those offered by competitors. It is vital when designing such a package that the firm relates the costs of activities to the customer's perception of the value created by them.

References

1. Porter, M.E.: *Competitive Advantage: Creating and Sustaining Superior Performance.* Free Press, 1985.
2. The articles in the series are: Partridge, M.J. and Perren, L.J.: 'Achieving competitive advantage', Vol 71, No 10, November 1993; 'Defining the competitive arena: a flexible and innovation-driven approach', Vol 72, No 4, April 1994; 'Developing strategic direction: can generic strategies help?', Vol 72, No 5, May 1994.
3. Webster, F.E.: 'The changing role of marketing in the corporation'. *Journal of Marketing,* Vol 56, October 1992.
4. Faulkner, D. and Bowman, C.: 'Generic strategies and congruent organisational structures: some suggestions', *European Management Journal,* Vol 10, No 4, December 1992.
5. Prahalad, C.K. and Hamel, G.: "The core competence of the corporation'. *Harvard Business Review,* May-June 1990.
6. Norman, R. and Ramirez, R,: 'From value chain to value constellation: designing interactive strategy', *Harvard Business Review,* July-August 1993.
7. Day, G.S. and Wensley, R,: 'Assessing advantage: a framework for diagnosing competitive superiority', *Journal of Marketing,* Vol 52, April 1988.

SECTION THREE

THE VISION AND MISSION

Brief Case: Mission, Vision and Strategic Intent

By *Andrew Campbell* and *Sally Yeung*

Long Range Planning, Vol. 24, No. 4, pp. 145 to 147, 1991, with permission from Elsevier Science

Andrew Campbell is a Fellow and **Sally Yeung** an Associate of the Ashridge Strategic Management Centre.

Brief Case is a portfolio of commentary, opinion, research and experience. The editors welcome contributions, comments and ideas from readers. These should be sent to Andrew Campbell and Michael Goold at Ashridge Strategic Management Centre, 17 Portland Place, London W1 N 3AF.

The Ashridge Strategic Management Centre has recently concluded a research project into mission and mission statements (see pp. 10-20). In talking about mission with audiences of managers and academics, we have been asked to explain the difference between the concepts of mission and vision. In addition, since the publication of an article by Gary Hamel and C. K. Prahalad called 'Strategic Intent',[1] we have been asked to explain the difference between mission and strategic intent. We would also like to explain in this column our view of the position of mission in the strategic planning process.

Mission

Our research exposed the need to formulate a definition of the word mission. Some organizations take the view that mission is primarily a strategic tool, an intellectual discipline which defines their commercial rationale and target market. In this context, it is perceived as the first step in strategic management. It exists to answer two fundamental questions: "What is our business, and what should it be?" Other organizations see mission as the cultural 'glue' which enables them to function as a collective unity. This cultural glue consists of strong norms and values that heavily influence the way in which people behave, how they work together and how they pursue the goals of the organization.

Our view is that mission is about culture *and* about strategy. In fact a mission exists when strategy and culture are mutually supportive. An organization has a mission when its culture fits with its strategy.

Mission is an organization's character, identity and reason for existence. It can be divided into four inter-relating parts: purpose, strategy, behaviour standards and values. Purpose addresses why an organization is in being: for whose benefit is all this effort being put in? Strategy considers the nature of the business, the desired positioning vs other companies and the source of competitive advantage. Behaviour standards are the norms and rules of 'the way we do things around here'. Values are the beliefs and moral principles that lie behind the behaviour standards, beliefs that have normally been formulated within the organization by a founding dynasty or a dominant management team.

Mission provides a rationale for action. It links behaviour standards with purpose in two ways: the strategy link explains that certain behaviour will help make the organization successful; the values link explains that certain behaviour is morally upright, the right way to behave.

Vision

Warren Bennis and Burt Nanus identify vision as a central concept in their theory of leadership.[2] To choose a direction, a leader must first have developed a mental image of a possible and desirable future state of the organization. This image, which we call a vision, may be as vague as a dream or as precise as a goal or mission statement', they say. 'The critical point is that a vision articulates a view of a realistic, credible, attractive future for the organization, a condition that is better in some important ways than what now exists.' So far as the word vision has a meaning in business language, this quote captures its distinguishing features as well as its vagueness.

A vision and a mission *can* be one and the same. A possible and desirable future state of the organization can include all of the elements of mission – purpose, strategy, behaviour standards and values.

But vision and mission are not fully overlapping concepts. Vision refers to a future state, 'a condition that is better ... than what now exists', whereas mission more normally refers to the present. Marks and Spencer's mission, 'to raise the standards of the working man', was being achieved throughout the 1950s and 1960s and is still being accomplished today. It is a timeless explanation of the organization's identity and ambition. When a vision is achieved, a new vision needs to be developed; but a mission can remain the same and members of the organization can still draw strength from their common and timeless cause.

A vision is, therefore, more associated with a goal whereas a mission is more associated with a way of behaving. We believe that mission is the more powerful concept and we take issue with Bennis and Nanus for using the word vision without separating the two concepts. Vision is valuable because goals are valuable, but it is the clarity of mission rather than vision that we believe is the strength of a great leader.

In times of change, a new mission will be difficult to distinguish from a vision because the new mission will be a mental image of a desirable future state. Hence, our difference of opinion is not, in practice, a serious one. Nevertheless we have two concerns with vision as a concept. First, a vision begins to lose its power when it is achieved. It is no longer a driving force for action and the organization can begin to lose direction. This can happen to companies that strive for market leadership: once achieved, the ambition that drove the company drains away, leaving it directionless. Second, if a vision is so ambitious that it is unlikely to be achieved in the next 5 or 10 years, it loses its power to motivate and stimulate. It becomes too ambitious and unrealistic.

Mission is a much more timeless concept. It is concerned with the way the organization is managed today (behaviour standards) and its purpose. Both of these are enduring ideas and can supply an unbounded source of fulfilment and energy.

Strategic Intent

Strategic intent is another concept that overlaps with vision and mission. Hamel and Prahalad comment: 'On the one hand strategic intent envisions a desired leadership position and establishes the criterion the organization will use to chart its progress. Komatsu set out to "encircle Caterpillar". Canon sought to "beat Xerox", Honda strove to become a second Ford, an automotive pioneer. All are expressions of strategic intent. At the same time, strategic intent is more than just unfettered ambition. (Many companies possess an ambitious strategic intent yet fall short of their goals.) The concept also encompasses an active management process that includes: focusing the organization's attention on the essence of winning; motivating people by communicating the value of the target; leaving room for individual and team contributions; sustaining enthusiasm by providing new operational definitions as circumstances change; and using intent consistently to guide resource allocations.'

Strategic intent is a concept that draws from both vision and mission. It includes a desired future state, a goal defined in competitive terms that is more a part of vision than of purpose. It also encompasses a definition of strategy that is fundamentally the same as the use of strategy within mission. Strategic intent is, therefore, closest in concept to the traditional definition of mission: 'what business are we in and what strategic position do we seek?'

However, we see strategic intent as suffering from the same problem as vision, in that once the intent has been achieved the organization is liable to lose direction. The problem with goals is that they have to be reset as they are achieved. Purpose has the advantage of being everlasting.

We also see strategic intent as being a left brain concept. Hamel and Prahalad argue that intent should motivate people 'by communicating the value of the target'. We have not found many managers who are motivated by a target, unless it is a short term objective or milestone.[3] Managers we have spoken to are motivated more by the organization's current values than by some distant ambition. Strategic intent is, in our view, a less powerful concept than mission because it fails to include values and behaviour standards, the keys to long-standing employee commitment and enthusiasm.

Mission Planning

Our research has shown us that mission can be analysed and discussed in as rigorous a way as strategy. In other words, managers can do mission planning in the same way that they do strategic planning. In fact, strategic planning is a subset of mission planning. Mission planning is more sophisticated than strategic planning; it helps managers formulate strategies that will fit their organization.

One of the reasons that so many strategies fail to get further than the pages of a beautifully bound planning document is that they are strategies not missions: they fail to build on the values and behaviour standards that already exist in the organization and they do not inspire the emotions of the managers and employees who are expected to put them into practice.

Mission planning goes beyond strategic planning in three ways:

- it involves an analysis of employee values and organization behaviour to assess the changes needed;
- it focuses on identifying behaviour standards that are central to the implementation of strategy and symbolic of the new value system;
- it encourages discussion of the organization's commitment to its stakeholders and to some higher level purpose.

Mission planning forces managers to think through the behavioural implications of their plans; it prompts them to articulate an inspirational reason for any new plans; and it prevents them from sidestepping the issue of whether existing managers and employees are capable of responding to the challenge. Mission planning is where strategy, organization and human resource issues come together. It asks managers to take a holistic view of their organization and its environment before developing a plan of action.

We believe that leaders of multi-business companies should be promoting mission planning at the business unit level in the same way that most companies currently promote strategic planning. The first step is to extend mission thinking into the periodic strategic planning process:

- Ask managers in charge of business units to include issues of purpose, values and behaviour standards along with their presentation at the strategy review.
- Ask them whether or not their organization is culturally aligned with their strategy.
- Ask them what their three most important behaviour standards are.

Initially these questions will get little attention, superficial discussion and insufficient analysis. But the process will have started. Managers at the centre will be able to identify issues of concern and ask for further clarification or follow up with the business unit informally. The mission questions at the next strategy review can be more targeted, moving the thinking forward again.

In a highly developed process it may become necessary to separate the mission discussion from the strategy discussion in the same way that most companies have found it beneficial to separate the strategy discussion from the budget discussion.

Many managers at headquarters have argued to us that although they can see the relevance and importance of mission thinking at the business unit level, they can see no value in it at the headquarters level of a diversified company. A corporate level mission would be considered as an imposition, discouraging diverse businesses from developing their own diverse missions.

We do not disagree with this view, yet we still consider that it is possible to have a headquarters mission and a set of diverse business unit missions. Mission can be treated in the same way as strategy. Because it is possible, in fact necessary, to have a corporate strategy and a different strategy for each business unit, it is possible to have a corporate mission and a different mission for each business unit. With good strategic planning the strategies at different levels and between sister companies do not clash and can reinforce each other. In the same way, good mission planning ensures compatibility between the different missions.

References

1. Gary Hamel and C. K. Prahalad, Strategic intent, *Harvard Business Review*. May-June (1989).
2. Warren Bennis and Burt Nanus, *Leaders: The Strategies for Taking Charge.* Harper & Row, New York (1985).
3. See Michael Goold with John J. Quinn, *Strategic control.* Economist/Hutchinson (1990).

Note:
This article is drawn from *A Sense of Mission* by Andrew Campbell, Marion Devine and David Young (Economist/Hutchinson. 1990).

Demystifying Vision

By *Mark Lipton*

Executive Excellence March 1997. Used with permission of Executive Excellence Publishing. For subscription information, call 1-800-304-9782.

> **Mark Lipton** is chair of the department of human resources management and director of The Leadership Center, Milano Graduate School of Management and Urban Policy, New School for Social Research.

A well conceived vision statement serves like a set of architectural drawings to give structure to ideas

Clarifying a vision and communicating it to everyone can have powerful results. Unfortunately, the need for a vision does not necessarily lead to one, and an ill-conceived or poorly managed process can lead to a vision that is worse than none at all. One survey of leaders asked for the key traits that CEOs should have. The trait most frequently mentioned was that they convey a "strong sense of vision," followed by "strategy formulation to achieve the vision." My studies arrive at a clear conclusion: managers who develop and communicate a vision skillfully can make a profound impact. Performance measures such as profit, return on shareholder equity, employee turnover, and rate of new product development improve when visions are used as strategic tools to manage cultures.

A vision serves as a road map for companies as they move through accelerated change. Lack of vision is why transformation efforts frequently fail. The use of vision as a management tool is the most significant determinant for easing the transition from a bureaucratic to a flexible organization.

Culture change can be agonizingly slow, but when vision becomes the vehicle to drive change, the speed picks up. Many faltering organizations and their leaders share an inability to adjust to a world radically changed by collapsed time frames.

They do not try to see into the future, and because they lack vision, they are unprepared for it.

An initial vision is crucial if strategic planning is to work at all. Focusing on a "plan" rather than a vision may be too constraining, reduce individual incentive, and lead to paralysis. But, a plan conceived as a vision, even if it is communicated in imagery or metaphors, may prove a much greater incentive to action.

A vision motivates individuals and facilitates the recruitment of talent. A shared vision can energize people by connecting them to the purpose of the organization. People need to feel that they are making a useful contribution to a worthwhile venture; the vision enables them to see how their effort contributes to the larger picture.

When managers' values are clear, employee pride, motivation, and performance increase. Managers who have difficulty communicating their values find it much easier to convey them in the framework of a vision. In fact, younger employees often pressure managers to develop visions.

Visions provide focus and direction. Without a vision, people are exposed to short-term opportunities that they may feel endlessly compelled to seize. Without focus, the organization may never develop a strong distinctive competence. When visions help individuals focus their attention on what is most important, people eliminate a myriad of unproductive activities.

A shared vision can also provide a context for decision making. As organizations become leaner and flatter, decision making becomes inherently more decentralized. A clear vision, in effect, gives people a compass. If it is properly developed and implemented, vision can affect the perspectives or premises that people use to make decisions in the absence of rules, direct supervision, or threats. When senior executives effectively communicate the vision, we see a significantly higher level of job satisfaction, commitment, loyalty, esprit de corps, and clarity about the organization's values, pride, productivity, and encouragement

What is a Vision?

A vision must focus on the future and serve as a concrete foundation, an enduring promise. Unlike goals and objectives, a vision does not fluctuate from year to year. A successful vision paints a vivid picture and, though future based, is in the present tense, as if it were being realized now. It illustrates what the organization will do in the face of ambiguity and surprise. A vision must give people the feeling that their lives and work are intertwined and moving toward legitimate goals.

Many organizations that manage with a vision articulate it through a vision statement. The statement can be as short as four sentences or as long as five pages; written in conversational prose or crisply outlined as bullet points; and vague and abstract on some topics, while clear and precise on others. There is no template for the style of a vision statement.

A vision statement fulfills two useful functions. First, it provides a way for managers to integrate an amorphous collection of goals, dreams, challenges, and ideas. The process of creating a vision statement ultimately yields the vocabulary for the vision.

A second function is to serve as a constitution, a public document from which there can be no equivocation. People's response to a vision increases when it is perceived as an enduring commitment, made in writing.

No two visions should be alike. My template allows for variations in style:

Vision = Mission + Strategy + Culture.

The visions of highly effective organizations communicate three messages or principal themes: the mission or purpose, the strategy for achieving the mission, and elements of the culture that seem necessary to achieve the mission and support the strategy.

- *Mission.* Mission addresses the question of why an organization exists and why it is in business. Many vision statements define a mission that identifies the stakeholders and defines what they expect. A mission must appeal to the broadest stakeholder constituency possible and rise above the interests of any single stakeholder group. It must engage people and require little or no explanation.
- *Strategy.* To achieve a mission, there must be a strategy to give the logic for what the company hopes to achieve. If its purpose is to be the best at providing a particular service, the strategy must explain the principles that will make this possible. Strategy defines the business in which a company competes and the distinctive competence or competitive advantage that it has or plans to develop. It is related to strategic positioning – the place an organization assumes in relationship to its competitors.

- *Culture.* Culture is typically missing from the standard mission statement, which is why the statement alone is ineffectual. The value of the vision as a management tool is undermined if the vision is nothing more than a statement of purpose and strategy. These lack the power to enhance performance unless they can be converted into action, policy, and job-related behavioral guidelines. When people understand the desired culture – the values that support the purpose and strategy – they know what is expected of them.

Match the Walk with the Talk

An idealistic vision can raise employees' hopes, but those hopes will be dashed when they see that management's behavior is inconsistent with the vision. For many leaders, vision is a sloganeering campaign of new buzzwords and empty platitudes. Without substantive ideas and concrete programs to ensure that behavior is consistent with the vision, the platitudes quickly become a joke. Culture is changed and managed only when a leader's behavior matches the message. Some managers are surprised at the repercussions of not practicing what they preach. When their behavior runs contrary to guidelines prescribed by the vision, others perceive it, quite viscerally, as betrayal. The impact of not walking the talk can devastate a manager's credibility.

After the vision is complete and communicated, each individual must ask whether he or she can commit to it. If the vision is a vehicle for communicating strategy and managing the culture, it requires difficult decisions and actions by everyone. In more than a few incidents, the vision was announced, many managers pledged their commitment, and others walked away, resolved to seek jobs where a different organizational culture might be a better fit.

Although the vision must have broad appeal, it is not a one-size-fits-all proposition. The difficult decisions throughout the vision process are not limited only to the development of a vision statement. People must eventually determine whether the vision fits with their personal goals and values and decide whether they can grow with it.

Mission Statements Make Cents

By *Charles A. Rarick* and *John Vitton*
From the *Journal of Business Strategy, 1995. © Faulkner & Gray Inc., reprinted by permission.*

Charles A. Rarick is associate professor and director of management, Transylvania University, Lexington, Kentucky. **John Vitton** is an associate professor of management, University of North Dakota, Grand Forks.

Few things have been better documented over the past decade than the decline of formal – read big and heavily-staffed – strategic planning departments. Recently, however, there seems to be a planning renaissance of sorts with smaller, streamlined departments cropping up in U.S. companies (see 'The New Lean Planning Machine' Business Strategy, July/August 1994). Now there are some new data that are guaranteed to warm the down-sized, down-trodden hearts of corporate planners everywhere – especially those looking to keep those seedling departments alive. The results of some recent research (by the authors of this piece) suggest that a key aspect of strategic planning – getting senior executives to agree on, and put into writing, a definition of the purpose and scope of the company – can actually translate into profits.

A year-end 1994 study of the companies listed in the Business week 1000, analyzing randomly selected firms across industrial groups, shows that having a mission statement (or creed, purpose, statement of corporate philosophy/values) significantly increases shareholder equity. In fact, the average return for firms with mission statements is 16,1%. The return for firms without mission statements (or the equivalent) is 9,7%.

Of course, what a mission statement should say is still open to debate. To some of the companies surveyed it is merely a venue to stress organizational values. To others, it is straightforward outline of who-we-are, what-we-do, and where-we're-headed. To another group, it is a few words on vision.

Surprisingly few mission statements in this group mention one of the latest buzz-words, "diversity." Meridian, an exception, states "... increasing diversity of our workforce in terms of race, gender, and cultural backgrounds adds richness to our lives". Not surprising however, is that many mission statements of corporations in heavy industry include references to safety. Phillips Petroleum has given itself the mission: "Be the industry leader in safety."

Common elements

While simply having a mission statement is good, the study asserts, having one with content is even better. Corporate planners looking to compose – or rewrite – a high-performing mission statement might want to consider which mission statement components are identified in this study. The percentages in parentheses indicate how many of all the mission statement-using companies contain that particular element.

Concern for Public Image (73%)

This refers to the social responsibility of the organization. Perhaps this is because the mission statement is the most public component of the organization's strategic plan. The Reader's Digest statement is typical of this concern for public interest.

> "Becoming involved as good corporate citizens wherever we work and live around the world. Treating customers and suppliers with integrity, fairness, and respect. Avoiding even the appearance of conflict of interest. respecting and preserving our environment. Providing leadership in industry, trade, and regulatory associations."

Concerns for Quality (73%)

Commitment to quality ran neck and neck with public image. Typical of such phrases is that voiced by the Deere & Company statement:

> "The foundation of the John Deere vision has always been quality."

Commitment to Survival, Growth, Profitability (70%)

Typical of the type of reference is the Adolph Coors Company statement of company values:

"We are committed to the long-term financial success of our stockholders through consistent dividends and appreciation in the value of the capital they have put at risk. Reinvestment in facilities, research and development, marketing, and new business opportunities which provide long-term earnings growth take precedence over short-term financial optimization."

Identity of customers and Markets (60%)

Although some mission statements name specifics, most do not. The following phrasing from Microsoft's mission statement is fairly representative:

"... to push technology forward, making products that help businesses operate more efficiently as organizations and help people perform more effectively as individuals."

Identity of Products and Services (60%)

The Sunstrand corporate mission statement is typical:

"To satisfy the needs of selected worldwide aerospace and industrial markets by developing and manufacturing high quality, proprietary, technology-based components and subsystems and by achieving customer satisfaction."

Statement of Company Philosophy (43%)

Almost half of the organizational mission statements include the basic beliefs or values of the firm. Perhaps the most striking and simple is the Harley-Davidson mission statement which contains a separate sheet referred to as "Harley-Davidson Values."

"Tell the Truth; Be Fair; Keep Your Promises; Respect the Individual; Encourage Intellectual Curiosity."

Differentiation from Competition (33%)

These sorts of statements are the least common of the features. Those that do cover the topic use phrases similar to an excerpt from the Merck mission statement:

"To be the world's most innovative company in our chosen fields, measured both by the flow of new products into the global marketplace and by the significance of those products for the health and well-being of society."

Cashing In ▪

In addition to simply having a mission statement, the results of the study suggest that it's better to say more than less.

The report analyses mission statements using a content-analysis research format – noting how many of the above features are mentioned. Mission-statement content was then correlated with the firm's financial performance using return on common shareholder equity for the latest fiscal year.

When the "high content" mission statements are compared with the "low content" mission statements, the average return for firms with "high content" statements is 26,2% and the average return for firms with "low content" statements is 13,7%

Although it is impossible to make a definitive causal assumption, it would appear that firms engaged in the type of formal strategic planning process that produces a mission statement are more likely to achieve good financial and bottom-line performance.

Creating A Mission Statement

A mission statement contains the strategic intent and business direction for an organization. Therefore, the first step in writing or revising any mission statement document is getting the full support of top management.

The second step is to produce a rough outline of the proposed mission statement. The next step is to get feedback on this draft. Feedback should come both from management and lower level employees. Seeking meaningful employee input is important. While management sets strategy, employees must understand what this strategy is if they are to implement it. Involving employees in the process of shaping the identity and direction of the organization provides the employees with a sense of ownership.

The next step is to revise the statement. This includes not only tinkering with the language — avoid buzzwords and convey complex thoughts in understandable terms — but considering layout and format. Getting management approval and support is the final step.

The process of writing or revising a mission statement does not simply offer a chance to send another communication to employees and stakeholders. It offers the chance for management and employees to re-define and re-create their organizations. Writing a mission statement ultimately challenges organizations to measure their performance.

Excerpted from Mission Statements: A Guide to the Corporate and Nonprofit Sectors, *by John W. Graham and Wendy C. Havlick. Published 1994, Garland Publishing New York.*

Leadership and Vision

By *Neil H. Snyder* and *Michelle Graves*, Guest Editors
From *Business Horizons*: January-February 1994. Copyright 1994 by Indiana University and Kelley School of Business.

Neil H. Snyder is the Ralph A. Beeton Professor of Free Enterprise at the McIntire School of Commerce. University of Virginia. Charlottesville. **Michelle Graves** is a staff associate with Price Waterhouse in Washington, D.C. The material in this article is adapted from *Vision, Values, and Courage: Leadership for Quality Management,* by Neil H. Snyder, James J. Dowd, Jr., and Dianne Morse Houghton (New York: The Free Press. 1994).

In the Book of Proverbs it is said, "Where there is no vision, the people perish." This is as true in business as it is in life. Organizations whose leaders have no vision are doomed to work under the burden of mere tradition. They cannot prosper and grow because they are reduced to keeping things the way they have always been; they are guided by the saying, "If it ain't broke, don't fix it."

True leaders see things differently. They are guided by another belief more in keeping with the competitive world in which we live. They believe, "If it ain't broke, you're not looking hard enough." Realizing that there is always room for improvement, they believe that no one has ever done anything so well that it cannot be done better.

For leaders, a vision is not a dream; it is a reality that has yet to come into existence. Vision is palpable to leaders; their confidence in and dedication to vision are so strong they can devote long hours over many years to luring it into being. In this way, a vision acts as a force within, compelling a leader to action. It gives a leader purpose, and the power of the vision and the leader's devotion to it work to inspire others – who, sensing purpose and commitment, respond. Warren Bennis, having spent many years working with leaders, has concluded:

> While leaders come in every size, shape and disposition - short, tall, neat, sloppy, young, old, male, and female - every leader I talked with shared at

least one characteristic: a concern with a guiding purpose, an overarching vision. They were more than goal-directed. (Bennis 1990)

Peter Kreeft, a professor of philosophy at Boston College, says that "to be a leader you have to lead people to a goal worth having – something that's really good and really there" (Stewart 1991). That essential "something" is the vision.

A Definition

What is vision? Because it operates on many levels, vision is difficult to define simply. When we say that a leader has vision, we refer to the ability to see the present as it is and formulate a future that grows out of and improves upon the present. A leader with vision is able to see into the future without being far-sighted and remain rooted in the present without being near-sighted. We also speak of having a vision for an organization, which looks at it from a slightly different perspective. A vision is an idea of the future; it is an image, a strongly felt wish.

Vision is a tremendously powerful force in any walk of life, but in business it is essential. A vision is a target toward which a leader aims her energy and resources. The constant presence of the vision keeps a leader moving despite various forces of resistance: fear of failure; emotional hardships, such as negative responses from superiors, peers, or employees; or 'real' hardships such as practical difficulties or problems in the industry.

Equally important, a vision, when shared by employees, can keep an entire company moving forward in the face of difficulties, enabling and inspiring leaders and employees alike. Moving toward the same goal, individuals work together rather than as disconnected people brought together because of having been hired coincidentally by the same organization. It can turn the stereotypical corporate hierarchy into a well-organized and harmonious matrix working together toward a common goal.

Vision refers to the force within a leader that spreads like wildfire when properly communicated to others. Vision refers to an image of the future that can be discussed and perfected by those who have invested in it. Vision is also the glue that binds individuals into a group with a common goal. This multiplicity of meanings does not weaken or obscure the concept; rather, it demonstrates how essential vision is to the success of a leader and to an organization.

Vision Adds Meaning to Corporate Life

When employees understand a leader's vision, they understand what the organization is trying to accomplish and what it stands for. Each employee can see what the future holds as a rational extension of the present. In addition, meaning is conveyed to each department, reaffirming that what individual departments contribute is crucial to organizational success. The vision must be logical, deductive, and plausible; at the same time it must be mind-stretching, creative, and able to capture the imaginations of individual contributors.

The role of a leader is not just to explain and clarify. Leaders "create meaning for people" by amassing large amounts of information, making sense of it, integrating it into a meaningful vision of the future, and communicating that vision so people want to participate in its realization. In this sense, visions have the power to lift employees out of the monotony of the daily work world and put them into a new world full of opportunity and challenge.

Visions excite people by appealing to their emotions. Jerry Wind, a professor at the University of Pennsylvania, refers to a vision as "something to rally around, a glue pulling the organization together" (Kiechel 1989). Because to some employees visions might seem almost impossible to meet, it is the leader's responsibility to bolster their courage with understanding. Experienced leaders do this so naturally that people do not even realize how courageous they are; their only concern is to do whatever is needed in pursuit of the vision. This is why leaders are so critical to the success of an organization. They have the ability to see through all the confusion in the workplace and focus on what matters. A vision helps leaders keep the frustrations of the workplace in perspective, enabling them to live with uncertainty in the short term because they can visualize accomplishment in the long term. They can then extend this ability throughout the organization.

Although vision guides a company in a particular direction, leaders do not typically produce specific "plans" for making a vision reality. They usually leave the more detailed planning to managers. However, "unless the leader has a sense of where the whole enterprise is going and must go, it is not possible to delegate ... the other functions" (Gardner 1990). It is as dangerous to leave others adrift by being too general as it is to cage them in by being too precise. "Typically, a vision is specific enough to provide real guidance to people, yet vague enough to encourage initiative and to remain relevant under a variety of conditions" (Kotter 1990).

Employee Buy-in and Commitment

To be effective, leaders cannot force their vision upon the organization. Imposing it will, in all likelihood, elicit rejection temporarily and, as a result, waste time and money. Additionally, this approach leads to frustration and anger, which can easily result in unnecessary failure. Under an autocratic leader, imposing a vision on the organization results in compliance rather than commitment, which is required for the long-term success of a vision. Ideally, a leader shares that vision with people in the organization. As employees come to comprehend the vision, they offer their commitment.

Having committed to a vision, organizational members begin to participate in shaping it, fashioning it to reflect their own personal visions – pictures or images they have in their hearts and minds about their futures and their contributions to the organization. At this point, the leader's vision becomes a shared one, after which people in the organization become even more committed. Shared vision creates a commonality of interests that enables people to see meaning and coherence in the diverse activities of the typical workday. Furthermore, a shared vision causes people to focus on the future and what it holds – not simply because they must, but because they want to.

The realization of a shared vision results in the "alignment of the individual energies" of all who take part. Realizing what an organization can achieve can generate a "unique rush of power", a level of energy high above what is considered normal that can be sustained for a relatively long period.

Possibly the most important variables contributing to a leader's success in implementing a vision is his level of commitment to it and the level of commitment it can inspire in employees. A leader who is wholly committed to a vision will find it much easier to motivate people and direct their energy toward making that vision reality.

Fear of Failure

Fear of failure prevents many otherwise capable people from pursuing their visions. Leaders must overcome their reluctance to risk falling on their face if they hope to succeed. Fear of failure is natural. True leaders, however, do not allow it to paralyze them and prevent them from pursuing their vision.

In 1982, at the height of the most severe recession in the U.S. since the Great Depression, Kemmons Wilson, the founder of Holiday Inns, spoke with a group of students in the McIntire School of Commerce at the University of Virginia to discuss the opportunities he saw for entrepreneurs in the future. Wilson's view of the future was bright. He told the students emphatically how fortunate they were to be living at a time when there was such an abundance of opportunity. When challenged by a student who declared that it was easy for him, an extremely successful businessman, to say such things because he had never experienced failure, Wilson responded, "I've failed more times than you've tried."

Wilson's point is that it does not matter how many times you try and fail. Everybody fails. What matters is your ability to try again. A leader simply must expect and deal with failure because it is such a fundamental part of the learning process. Everybody fails while learning to master something. It is an unavoidable and essential part of a process that leads to success.

Consider for a minute how much effort goes into learning golf. One never really masters the game; one is always learning to play regardless of skill level. Even professional golfers seek instruction from people who can help them improve their game. We bring this up because it is easy for most golfers to remember how atrocious they were when they started playing. A good golfer keeps playing and learns from the problems that hindered success. If your vision is to become a good golfer, you must deal with your failures along the way or your vision will never become a reality. That applies to leadership as well. Your vision will never become a reality if you are not able to deal with your failures.

Consider another example: major league baseball. In the major leagues, if a player hits .300 he is a very good hitter. If he hits around .320 or .330, he is among the best in the league. A player who has a .350 batting average is considered excellent. What this average actually means is that 65 percent of the time he either did not reach base, or he reached base as a result of an error. In major league baseball, a player who fails to get a hit 65 percent of the time is heading for the Hall of Fame. Interestingly, Babe Ruth is known as a great home run hitter. He was also a leader in strikeouts. Leaders must learn to deal with failure; they must master this experience. If they cannot cope with failure, they cannot lead.

Albert Einstein, who had great vision, was a leader in the scientific community. His theories changed the way we see the universe. But when once asked how many ideas he had in his lifetime, his answer was two. (Einstein considered ideas to be only those thoughts nobody had ever thought of before.)

A person can have an abundance of ideas, but success depends on what she does with these ideas, not on merely having them. Chances are that an idea believed to be original has already been conceived by somebody who has failed to do anything with it. It only takes one good idea to be a stunning success. Einstein is proof of this. The secret is to build on that idea. The fear of failure prevents many talented people from mentioning their ideas to others or from following through completely on them. What a shame! Because of the fear of failure, we deprive ourselves and others of so many benefits.

Nevertheless, many people believe that the key to success is to avoid failure. They stay with things they know, seldom trying anything new. These people fail because the surest way to fail in the long term is to continue doing what you did yesterday, to mindlessly follow proven tradition. Things are changing, and times are changing. If we do not change along with them, we will not succeed.

The willingness to confront and deal with failure is an important attribute of a leader. How many times should a leader try and fail before deciding it is time to quit. One? Two? Three? When Thomas Edison was working on the electric light bulb, he had to deal with much failure.

He tried thousands of filaments before he found the one that worked. He did not quit after the first, 500th, or 1 000th try. He believed in his vision, and he wanted to succeed more than anything else. He dealt with his own daily failures and kept his eye on the long-term success. Today we all benefit because Thomas Edison did not choose to give up.

Challenging the Status Quo

Leaders must make certain their people do not give up, that they continue to strive for success. It is natural for people to quit; organizational pressures keep many people from trying out new ideas. John D. Rockefeller III wrote in The Second American Revolution, "An organization is a system, with a logic of its own, and all the weight of tradition and inertia. The deck is stacked in favor of the tried and proven way of doing things and against taking risks and striking out in new directions." How true!

Walter Ulmer Jr., president of the Center for Creative Leadership, says, "The natural state of an organization is conservative, to maintain the status quo" (Main

1987). Many people in firms that have been around a long time believe their primary responsibility is to protect the status quo. Leaders must learn to deal with these obstacles in the path of success and to protect those who question the way things are done. Ram Charan, a management consultant, believes that "divine discontent with the status quo" (Main 1987) is an essential quality of a leader. We believe he is right. Abraham Zaleznik (1989), a Havard professor, says that people who have leadership talent have "a real fire in their belly ... a fire that has to do with having an effect on the world." You can tell when leaders have been in a firm because they leave their mark and, as a result, affect the destinies of many others.

Ridicule: A Technique Used to Make Leaders Quit

When employees in most organizations encounter a person with a vision that is significantly different from the status quo, it is common for them to resist the suggested changes and to put obstacles in the way of success. Their rationale is easily understood. Change means work and exertion for them. By preventing change, they save time and energy in the short term. But in the long run, their strategy is dangerous.

If the leader refuses to quit, employees turn to ridicule in hopes that the pressure will be sufficient to prevent the leader from moving forward. Leaders must learn to deal with this. They must understand that great leaders before them faced ridicule and prevailed over it. Marconi probably encountered a tremendous amount of ridicule as he sought support for the wireless radio. Imagine him trying to sell his idea to a group of would-be investors. Marconi had to convince a room full of bankers that his invention was capable of capturing "little waves" out of the air that could not be seen and converting them to sound that would come from a little box. A fair number of them must have thought he was crazy.

It is natural for some people to exhibit disbelief when unusual ideas are presented to them. It is also natural for them to ridicule the people who present those ideas.

When You Succeed, They Say You Are Lucky

Suppose a leader develops a vision to which she is committed, shares it with people, accepts failure, deals with ridicule, and after working tirelessly for many years actually turns that vision into a reality. It is now time to reap the rewards and hear praise for an amazing accomplishment, right? Wrong. In all likelihood, what she will hear is, "Oh, you were just lucky"- meaning, of course, "If it wasn't just plain dumb luck, I would have done it myself." In this situation, a leader should find comfort in the words of Emerson: "Shallow men believe in luck, wise and strong men in cause and effect."

Luck cannot explain accomplishment. Winning the state lottery may seem like a matter of luck, but you have to buy a lottery ticket to win. Ara Parseghian, football coach at Notre Dame several years ago, led his team lo beat the University of Alabama for the national championship two years in a row. Alabama was favored to win both times. Both years, Alabama took an early lead and held it until the end of the game. Both years, Notre Dame came back in the closing seconds of the game and won. When a reporter asked Parseghian after the second victory about "the luck of the Irish", he is reported to have said, "If by luck you mean the place where preparation meets opportunity, then we were lucky."

In this world, there is an abundance of opportunity for everyone. Parseghian knew that the Alabama football team was not infallible and that it would give his team opportunities to win. If his team prepared well and was ready for the game, it could take advantage of those opportunities. It took hard work and practice to be able to see and take advantage of the openings provided. Preparation met opportunity.

There is a story often told about professional golfer Gary Player's struggle to win the U.S. Open. On one hole he hit a terrible tee shot into the rough. To stay in contention, he needed to par the hole. His second shot sliced unmercifully, yet it rolled onto the green a few feet away from the pin. As he walked away from the slice, someone in the crowd yelled "Gary, you're lucky." He is reported to have turned to the man and said, "The more I practice, the luckier I get." Commitment, not luck, produced his success.

Communicating Vision

A leader must communicate his vision to others for it to become a shared vision. To accomplish this, leaders should act in a manner consistent with the vision in everything they do. They must set a personal example; they cannot afford to send mixed signals by saying one thing and doing another.

The first step in communicating a vision to a group is to stress its importance so that people will take an interest in it. If they believe the vision is important and worthwhile, many of them will want be involved with it, even if they do not understand all the details. As John W. Alexander, vice-president and general manager of 3D Distribution Systems, puts it, "Most people will co-operate and follow the leader with only a vague idea of what their participation, contribution, and reward might be" (1989) – if the leader's vision excites them.

In his book *A Force for Change*, John Kotter (1990) offers several suggestions for sharing a vision. Delivering a single, clear, and credible message is important in helping people understand the goals at hand. To communicate clearly and reinforce the vision, it is necessary to send frequent messages orally and in writing – messages that must be more than the typical day-to-day orders coming from "the boss."

Communication that motivates people to act tends to focus on the core values and beliefs that support the vision. Accurately communicating these values and beliefs simplifies implementation because it conveys simple images or words that make the vision easier to remember. In addition, repeating simple words and symbols communicates the message without clogging already overused communication channels. Written communication can be used in a similar manner to reinforce the vision by reporting progress for everyone to see, and progress toward achieving goals keeps peoples' spirits up and helps convince them they can do it.

Going From Communication to Commitment

After a vision has been explained simply and directly, people must decide whether they want to be a part of it. If they don't, they cannot be forced to produce quality results at competitive prices over the long term. They can be forced to do things in the short term, but they will abandon them as quickly as they figure out how to come out from under the strong arm of a leader who has not earned their commitment.

The day has almost passed when autocratic leaders can succeed over the long term. Strong-armed leaders typically do not last long; the cost of using this approach is too high in terms of the inferior quality output resulting from poor quality effort, lost employee loyalty and support, and money. Moreover, forcing people to do things they do not want to do requires a great deal of energy over the long term – more energy than most people can expend on a sustained basis.

Over the long term, most people are not motivated by being pushed. They are motivated by the desire to satisfy their own very basic human needs: those for achievement, belonging, recognition, self-esteem, control over their lives, and the sense of having lived up to their ideals. To be successful, leaders must connect with these human needs and let their people become excited about a vision. Further, they must involve people in deciding how to achieve the vision, or at least to achieve the part of it that is most relevant to them. Their involvement must be real, and the rewards and recognition they receive must be real as well.

To win continued support from a group, leaders must be willing to share their personal views, and to listen carefully to the group's ideas. Ultimately, leaders must be willing to assume a vulnerable position and ask a difficult question: "Will you follow me?" In reality, they are asking another question: "Is this vision worthy of your commitment?" Being vulnerable in this manner is difficult for many people who have grown up during a time when employees were expected to comply with the leader's orders and not ask too many questions.

Although a leader is responsible for introducing the vision to the group, people want and need to become personally involved with the vision. As we have said before, they cannot do this unless it reflects, to some extent, their own personal visions. It is critical for leaders to keep their minds open to suggestions and ideas that can improve the vision. Too often leaders present their visions to employees as cast in concrete, sending the subtle (or not so subtle) message that there is no room for compromise. As a result, the employees either reject the vision or simply go through the motions of supporting it. In either case, it is doubtful the vision will ever become reality.

Introducing the word "compromise" may surprise many people because they have been led to believe that once the leader is committed to the vision, she cannot afford to be flexible. Although it is true that the leader's commitment to the vision must be strong and unwavering, it is also true that she is incapable of predicting in advance precisely what the future holds. As the leader and the group move together toward making the vision a reality, they both learn more about their vision, and they have opportunities to improve upon it. Compromise as the vision unfolds should not be interpreted negatively. The leader's willingness to accept suggestions that result in some change in the vision will benefit the leader and improve both the quality of the vision and the intensity of the employees' commitment to it.

Stated another way, the development of a vision is an evolutionary process. As noted by Peter Senge, author of *The Fifth Discipline* (1990), "At any one point there will be a particular image of the future that is predominant, but that image will evolve." A vision should be constantly examined and modified to reflect important changes in the environment and ensure continued support and enthusiasm from everyone involved.

As people's commitment to the vision grows, it becomes more real to them; they will find it easier to dedicate the time and energy necessary to make the vision a reality. Those who have expertise in a particular field should be encouraged to use their knowledge to improve parts of the vision that are related to their specialty. According to Alexander (1989), employees supply "the details, missing steps, and concerns that confront the leader's visionary goals. When leaders solicit input, they discover the knowledge, interest, and evident parameters of support they can expect from others." A leader should expect that although parts of the vision may undergo alteration, its essence will remain intact.

If a leader cannot see the value in compromises and is too inflexible to accept them, the vision will never achieve its full potential. According to Senge (1990b), "when more people come to share a vision, the vision becomes more real in the sense of a mental reality that people can truly imagine achieving. They [the leaders] now have partners, co-creators; the vision no longer rests on their shoulders alone."

Empowering People to Do Their Jobs

Communicating the vision accurately and fully has the added advantage of creating the conditions under which employees can be empowered to do their jobs. The term "empowered" is used frequently today; unfortunately, many people using the term do not really understand what it means. Some who are familiar with management literature interpret empowerment to mean delegation of authority. The strict literalists will be quick to point out that a manager can delegate authority, but not responsibility. To them, empowerment is a formal (almost legalistic) passing down of a task from one level in the organization to another. Delegation is not empowerment, but empowerment does require good delegation.

Empowerment means giving employees jobs to do and the freedom they need to be creative while doing them. It means allowing employees to try new ideas, even ones that have never been considered or that have been previously rejected. It means allowing them to experiment and fail on occasion without fear of punishment.

Having said this, we must point out that leaders should avoid taking big risks without carefully considering the consequences. They must exercise judgment; as a general rule, they should establish an understanding with employees about the risks they are willing to take in the experimentation process. As we said earlier, experimentation is essential, so leaders must not be so restrictive that their employees fail to try new ideas. Empowerment means giving employees more than just the authority to do the job.

Leaders are not magicians, and they do not simply predict future events. They are strategic thinkers who are willing to take risks. Their actions, together with the actions of those who follow them, determine what the future will be. The point is, leaders do not create something out of nothing. They look at what they know to exist and search for relationships, the way things are meant to fit together. Once they find the connections, they share them with other people and work with them to bring about desired changes.

Leaders must maintain a balance between a clear understanding of the present and a clear focus on the future. Senge calls this balance "creative tension" and maintains that "an accurate picture of current reality is just as important as a compelling picture of a desired future."

References

John W. Alexander, "Sharing the Vision," *Business Horizons*, May-June 1989, pp. 56-59.

Warren Bennis, "Managing the Dream–Leadership in the 21st Century," *Training*, May 1990, pp. 43-46.

Warren Bennis, "The Pivotal Force," *Enterprise*, September 1985, p. 10.

John. W. Gardner, *On Leadership* (New York: The Free Press, 1990).

Walter Kiechel III, "A Hard Look at Executive Vision," *Fortune*, October 23, 1989, pp. 207-209.

John P. Kotter, *A Force For Change: How Leadership Differs From Management* (New York: The Free Press, 1990).

Jeremy Main, "Wanted: Leaders Who Can Make A Difference," *Fortune*, September 28, 1987, pp. 92-97.

John D. Rockefeller III, *The Second American Revolution* (New York: Harper & Row, 1973).

Peter M. Senge, *The Fifth Discipline* (New York: Doubleday/Currency, 1990a).

Peter M. Senge, "The Leader's New Work; Building Learning Organizations," *Sloan Management Review*, Fall 1990b, pp. 7-23.

Bryan Smith, "Vision: A Time to Take Stock," *Business Quarterly*. Autumn 1989, pp. 80-84.

Thomas A. Stewart, "Why Nobody Can Lead America," *Fortune*, January 14, 1991, pp. 44-45.

Noel Tichy and David Ulrich, "The Challenge of Revitalization," *New Management*, Winter 1985, pp. 53-59.

Abraham Zaleznik, *The Managerial Mystique* (New York: Harper & Row, 1989).

Abraham Zaleznik, "Why Managers Lack Vision," *Business Month*, August 1989, pp. 59-64.

Mission Statements Revisited

By *Romuald A. Stone*, Management Department, James Madison University
SAM Advanced Management Journal, Volume 1, No. 1, Winter 1996, pp. 31-37.

Dr. Stone, who teaches Strategic Management and other management subjects, has published numerous strategy case studies as well as articles in journals, including the Academy of Management Executive and Business Horizon.

"Corporate mission statements ... are the operational, ethical, and financial guiding lights of companies. They are not simply mottoes or slogans; they articulate the goals, dreams, behavior, culture, and strategies of companies" (Jones & Kahaner, 1996, p. ix)

By 1993, Quaker State Corporation had fallen on hard times. The company was losing 1,5 points of market share a year and experiencing declining sales and profits. Fearing a possible takeover, the Quaker State Board hired Herbert M. Baum, a marketer from Campbell Soup as CEO. Among his many initiatives was a management retreat where the firm redefined its core mission: "To funnel a wide range of lubricants through a massive network of mechanics, retailers and drive-through lube shops" (Murray, 1995). By 1995, Baum has successfully transformed the ailing Quaker state from an oil company selling motor oil to a branded consumer products company, a solid number two behind Pennzoil. Clearly, the new mission played a key role in shaping Quaker's turnaround.

Another company that had to undergo open heart surgery in order to respond to increased competition, a growing global marketplace, and increasing service demands by customers was United Parcel Service (UPS). By 1990, profit margins were slipping toward 4% from nearly 7% in 1988 (Hawkins, 1993). CEO Kent Nelson ordered UPS to develop a new strategy to respond to its rivals and changing marketplace. Spearheading the strategy change was the development of a new corporate mission statement. According to Clinton Yard, senior vice president of operations, "The mission statement gave a direction to go in" (Jones & Kahaner, 1995, p. 246). For example, UPS's mission now explicitly focuses on the customer, where in the past is was not as customer-driven as its competitors.

These examples and many others (e.g., GM Sears, IBM, Xerox, KMart) illustrate the need for all organizations to place more emphasis on reformulating their mission statements to respond to the current competitive landscape. Organizational leaders increasingly are faced with the challenge of how to reinvent and transform their organizations to adapt to the globalizations of markets, increased competition, deregulation, and wave of downsizing.

The starting point for effectively dealing with these issues is the organization's mission statements (sometimes called value statement, credo, or principles). Some years ago, Drucker (1974) observed, "That business purpose and business mission are so rarely given adequate thought is perhaps the most important single cause of business frustration and business failure" (p. 78). It is even more clear today that firms committed to developing and implementing clear and unambiguous strategic mission statements enjoy a competitive edge over rivals who do not.

The recent explosion of literature on this subject seems to fuel the notion that mission statements are just another management fad. Fad or not, mission statements serve a vital strategic role in organizations and should never be neglected. There are many books that offer collections of mission statements managers may review for samples (e.g., Abrahams, 1995; Graham & Havlick, 1994; Jones & Kahaner, 1995). The purpose of this article is to reexamine the relevance of mission statements in the 1990's and to review issues related to developing, writing, and implementing a mission guide to assist organizations in this process.

Why a Mission Statement is important

It is not uncommon for athletes to improve their performance in an upcoming event by creating a mental image of the perfect routine. using this proven method of enhancing performance, competitors create a mental image of a perfect home run, a perfect golf swing, a perfect ski run, or a flawless gymnastic routine. In the context of Olympic champions, Gouillart and Kelly (1995) comment on this process: "More than physical prowess, more than thinking about beating someone else, it's mental focus that makes the Olympian" (p.45).

If companies want to succeed in the 1990's they too need a mental focus, a vision, and sense of direction. Hamel and Prahalad (1994) note that "In business, as in art, what distinguishes leaders from laggards, and greatness from mediocrity, is the ability to uniquely imagine what could be" (p. 25). A mission statement specifying what the company does, how it does it, why it does it, and where it is going in the future can transform a leader's vision into substance. According to Drucker (1974).

> Defining the purpose and mission of the business is difficult, painful, and risky. But it alone enables a business to set objectives, to develop strategies, to concentrate its resources and to go to work. It alone enables a business to be managed for performance (p. 94).

Mission statements are not the sole property of for-profit enterprises, however. Perhaps one of the oldest statements is found in Philippians Chapter 2, verse 2, where Paul says "... make my joy complete by being of the same mind, maintaining the same love, united in spirit, intent on one purpose". Many consider the U.S. Constitution as an example of the world's most successful statement of purpose.

Mission Statements are crucial for nonprofit organizations, too. In their book, *Profiles of Excellence*, a study of achieving excellence in the nonprofit sector, Knauft, Berger, and Gray (1991) found that the key to success was having a clearly articulated mission statement along with goals to carry out the mission. In the nonprofit world, achieving the mission is analogous to making a profit in the private sector. According to Knauft *et al.*, "Nonprofit groups that give shrift to their missions will almost always find the going bumpy. Those that invest the time and effort necessary to formulate a sound mission statement build a platform from which to soar" (p 125).

What is a Mission Statement?

A mission statement is the starting point for an organization's entire planning process. Establishing the mission requires top management to sit down and seriously consider where the firm is now and where it should be in the future.

A mission statement provides a sense of direction, focus, and unity, and in Chester Barnard's words, " a spirit that overcomes the centrifugal forces of individual interest or motives" (Barnard, 1968, p 283). It contains both a strategic and a cultural perspective. Strategically, the mission statement is a tool that defines the company's business and target market. Culturally, the mission statement serves as the "glue" that binds the organization together through shared values and standards of behavior (Campbell and Nash, 1992). It can inspire employees and "stretch" the organization to achieve higher levels of performance. Bennis and Nanus (1985) focused on this important motivational tool:

> When the organization has a clear sense of purpose, direction and desired future state and when this image is widely shared, individuals are able to find their own roles both in the organization and in the larger society ... This empowers individuals and confers status upon them because they see themselves as part of a worthwhile enterprise. They gain a sense of importance, as they are transformed from robots blindly following instructions to human beings engaged in a creative and purposeful venture (p. 90).

Nicholls (1994) characterizes mission statements as a "strategic compass" that helps organizations find their way. "If the pace of change is rendering the business environment increasingly featureless, a compass is the essential tool. In the absence of landmarks, it [mission statement] shows the way ahead" (p. 22).

Campbell and Nash (1992) hold a perspective not widely shared by others. They see mission statements as creating more harm than good because "they imply a sense of direction, clarity of thinking, and unity that rarely exists" (p. 9). They suggest that many mission statements articulate values and behavior standards that are unrealistic and not a part of the organization's culture. Instead of motivating employees, they invite cynicism. As example of this kind of thinking, the authors cite some employees as saying, "If this is what the leaders think we should be believing and doing, then they are more stupid or out of touch than we thought" (p. 9). Instead of trying to write mission statements per se, Campbell and Nash argue that leaders should be trying to create a "sense of mission" among their employees that serves to cultivate a level of commitment and emotional attachment not attainable in a basic statement of purpose. Creating a sense of mission involves managing a blend of factors that include the organization's purpose, strategy, values, standards and behaviors such that employee values are congruent with the organization's philosophy and culture.

Mission Statement Elements

There is no simple formula that prescribes exactly what elements a mission statement should contain. In one collection of 622 mission statements, no two had the exact same format, formula, or pattern; they varied in length as well as tone

(Graham & Havlick, 1994). However, a review of the literature reveals that effective mission statements must be:

1. **Clearly articulated.** Mission statements should be simple and to the point (Jones & Kahaner, 1995), so that employees can clearly understand the values and principles that will guide them in their day-to-day and future activities. Avoiding jargon and buzzwords also will help keep the mission statement sufficiently universal for all employees to understand. Southwest Airlines' mission, for example, is succinct and easy to understand: "The mission of Southwest Airlines is dedication to the highest quality of Customer service delivered with a sense of warmth, friendliness, individual pride, and Company spirit."

2. **Relevant.** A mission statement should be appropriate to the organization in terms of its history, culture, and shared values (Quigley, 1993). It should also be consistent with the present situation and provide a realistic and informed assessment of what is attainable in the future (Nanus, 1992).

3. **Current.** A mission statement established years ago and unchanged may no longer be able to act as the driving force guiding the organization into the future. If the firm has been successful in achieving its strategic goals, the original vision and sense of direction may no longer be viable, resulting in a loss of focus and direction. Also, if the competitive environment changes significantly, the mission should be subject to revision. The Quaker state and UPS examples cited earlier highlight this important point. However, changes to the core statement are likely to be infrequent if the mission is cogently crafted.

4. **Written in a positive (inspiring) tone.** A mission statement should be written to encourage commitment and to energize all employees toward fulfilling the mission. A statement that does not do that is of limited value. The statement should be composed so that all stakeholders can identify with the organization and feel a sense of attachment. Creative and precise crafting will keep mission statements from being drab and uninspiring. Intel Corporation's mission does this well: "Our Mission: Do a great job for our customers, employees, and stockholders by being the pre-eminent building block supplier to the computing industry."

5. **Uniqueness to the organization.** An organization's mission statement should set is apart from other companies. It should establish the individuality, if not the uniqueness, of the company (Ackoff, 1987). Celestial Seasonings mission statement provides a good example: "Our mission is to grow and dominate the U.S. specialty tea market by exceeding consumer expectations with: The best tasting, 100% natural hot and iced teas, packaged with Celestial art and phi-

losophy, creating the most valued tea experience ...".

6. **Enduring.** Mission statements should serve to guide and inspire the organization for many years (Collins & Porras, 1994). In other words, a company
should be continually achieving its ultimate goal. Perhaps Walt Disney best
illustrated this enduring, never completed aspect of mission when he said
Disneyland would never be finished as long as there was imagination left in the
world. Other examples of enduring missions include Ritz-Carlton Hotel
Company's enduring commitment to guest satisfaction and AT&T's dedication
to being the world's best at bringing people together.

7. **Adapted to the target audience.** Some company mission statements are created for employees only, some for the general public and stockholders, and others are intended for all audiences. In any case, the target audience has a bearing on the length, tone and visibility of the statement (Abrahams, 1995). It is
essential to know who you're writing for before you decide what to say.

Mission statements that have these features can challenge and energize all employees in the organization and ensure that everyone is reading off the same page. A
well-crafted mission statement is a prerequisite to the strategy formulation process.
Without some form of direction, the resultant strategy is unlikely to be effective.
Table 1 reviews the seven essential features for mission statements.

Developing a Mission Statement

There is no standard length for a mission statement. Abrahams (1995) lists 88
companies whose mission statement is one sentences long: Cerner, an information
systems provider for the health care industry, states as its mission: "To automate
the process of health care"; Motorola's mission reads 'OUR FUNDAMENTAL
OBJECTIVE (Everyone's Overriding Responsibility) Total Customer
Satisfaction."

Other company missions are several sentences long, some even several paragraphs.
Beyond the actual statement of mission, most companies include vision statements, values, objectives, principles or philosophies, and strategies that support
and provide concrete guidance in fulfilling the mission (Abrahams 1995; Jones &
Kahaner, 1995). Abrahams addresses the question of the appropriate length of a
mission statement by reminding readers of the old story about President Lincoln.
when asked how long a man's legs should be, Lincoln is said to have replied,
"Long enough to reach the ground." The same philosophy should apply to design-

ing a mission statement. "All that's necessary is that the mission be long enough to reach the target audience" (p 47).

The ultimate form of the statement will largely be dependent on how organizations define themselves and the vision they wish to rally behind and project to their stakeholders. A key step in this process is to capture what the company truly believes its guiding philosophy should be, rather than emulating what some other company sees as its mission or philosophy. Exhibit 1 gives a suggested step-by-step guide to assist organizations in this process.

The following sections highlight the five phases of the mission development process set out in Exhibit 1.

Envision the Future.
The starting point for writing a mission statement is to articulate the vision and shared values the CEO or founders have for the organizations. Bennis and Nanus (1985) articulate this important step:

> To choose a direction, a leader must first have developed a mental image of a possible and desirable future state of the organization. This image, which we call a vision, may be as vague as a dream or as precise as a goal or mission statement. The critical point is that a vision articulates a view of a realistic, credible, attractive future for the organization, a condition that is better in some important ways than what now exists (p. 89).

In short, the vision creates the spark that brings the organization to life. It provides a future strategic direction, the foundation for its mission and related goals, and helps energize it to strive for success and a new level of performance.

Form a mission task force.
Although the CEO is ultimately responsible for developing an organization's mission statement, it is not realistic to expect him or her to do all the work. In this regard, forming a task force is often appropriate. Ideally, the task force should include representatives from every department, but in larger firms this may not be practical. This phase should be preceded by an announcement from the CEO formally creating the task force and outlining its purpose and objectives.

Develop a draft mission statement.
Before deciding what form the mission statement will take, the task force should conduct a situation analysis. A good situation analysis will identify where the

organization stands today, how it came to be where it is, what external forces will probably influence its future, and what it hopes to become (Tombazian, 1994). Once the analysis is complete, the task force should proceed to draft a mission statement that includes the essential features listed in Table 1. The draft should then be shared with all organization members for review and comment. This is an important step because it involves employees in shaping the identity and direction of the organization and ensures that they have an investment in its fulfillment. Following this process, the task force should present a final draft to the CEO for approval and prepare a budget to facilitate communicating and disseminating the final mission statement throughout the organization.

Communicate final mission statement.

Critical to the effectiveness of a mission statement is for all employees throughout the organization to be marching to the same drummer. Management should use every opportunity to communicate, confirm, and clarify the corporate mission (Bartlett & Ghoshal, 1991). This requires more than just publishing and distributing the mission or exhorting employees in various meetings; it requires a significant expenditure of personal time and effort by management to ensure the mission is shared by all.

Implement the mission statement.

Once the mission statement has been carefully developed and fits the history, culture, and values of the organization, the toughest challenge for management centers on how to generate the support and commitment necessary to use it as a blueprint for success. One commentator has compared the process to going to church. After hearing the homily, one still needs to know how to put the moral message into operation (Mathews, 1995).

Essential features of a Mission Statement
1. Clearly articulated
2. Relevant
3. Current
4. Written in positive (inspiring tone)
5. Unique to the organization
6. Enduring
7. Adapted to the target audience

Table 1. Essential Features of a Mission Statement

If the mission is correctly formulated, it will be aligned with the organization's strategies, tactics, operations, and administrative support systems. In addition to the crucial communication phase, managers at all levels need to translate the key elements of the mission into objectives and goals that guide the execution of the mission and are meaningful to all employees. The goals and objectives

Phase 1: Envision the Future
- ☛ CEO articulates his/her aspirations for the company (preferably with input from other in the company); develops a visual and verbal representation of what the future could be
- ☛ CEO defines the management practices and values that should guide behavior
- ☛ CEO validates the vision and values with the board of directors and senior officers

Phase 2: Form a Mission task Force
- ☛ CEO verbally announces to organization the purpose of the mission creation process and the level of involvement expected
- ☛ Establish a task force composed of representatives from every department

Phase 3: Develop a Draft Mission Statement
- ☛ Conduct a situation analysis to assess internal and external environment (e.g., core competencies, success factors, opportunities, obstacles, beliefs about future trends and events)
- ☛ Decide on what form and structure the mission statement will take (just a core mission statement or will it also include a vision and value statements, philosophies, principles, ethics, environmental policies and more)
- ☛ Write a draft that includes essential features listed in Table 1
- ☛ Post draft statements / beliefs and solicit input and feedback from employees and managers
- ☛ Synthesize rough statements / beliefs into an overall corporate mission and submit to CEO for approval
- ☛ Prepare a budget for mission dissemination and implementation

Phase 4: Communicate Mission Statement
- ☛ Determine in what format the mission statement will be communicated (e.g., annual report, brochure, poster, pamphlet, wallet-sized card, printed on company calendar / coffee mugs, T-shirts, displayed on front door, video, etc.)
- ☛ Mail company mission to each employee from the CEO's office and announce upcoming meetings
- ☛ Introduce mission to entire company in series of meetings
  - — Train managers as facilitators
  - — Schedule managers to introduce mission at departmental level
  - — Solicit employees for their ideas on how to turn the mission statement into a reality every day on the job

Phase 5: Operationalize Mission Statement
- ☛ Align the company's strategies, tactics, operations, and administrative support systems to be consistent with the mission
- ☛ Translate key elements of the mission into relevant performance objectives for employees at all levels
- ☛ Make mission statement review an integral part of the strategic planning process

Exhibit 1. Suggested Step-by-Step Guide to Developing a Mission Statement

should also be linked to the reward and performance evaluation system. At this stage the dangers of an overly ambitious mission will be abundantly clear. If, despite Herculean efforts, a company is unable to achieve its goals, the mission statement will be a failure. Management must also be totally committed to implementing the mission – to bringing the rhetoric to life. Otherwise, it serves no useful purpose and reinforces employee cynicism and apathy. Lastly, mission statement review should be an integral part of the strategic planning process.

Steelcase is an example of a company that revised its mission statement to reflect the realities of the office furniture industry. For much of the past two decades, Steelcase considered itself an "office environment" company providing office furniture for large companies. However, by 1992 Steelcase recognized that the office furniture market had changed dramatically. They found that customers wanted faster product-to-market times, quicker response to their needs, higher-quality goods, flexibility, ergonomic products, and all at a lower price. At the same time they recognized many organizations were moving toward "virtual" work, that is hiring employees to work at home either full- or part-time. In May 1994, Steelcase's board of directors approved a new mission statement: Helping people work more effectively." The new mission makes no mention of the company's product. According to Jerry Myers, former president and CEO, "The reason is that the product today may not be the product tomorrow" (Jones & Kahaner, 1995, p. 223). They also chose to use the word "people" instead of referring to customers and employees, people in this context encompassing both stakeholders.

Because companies now do battle in a competitive environment that is increasingly volatile and unpredictable, no mission statement can ever be considered a "once and for all" document. As Steelcase and other examples illustrate, companies should review the mission statements and formulate them with a broad vision in mind. At a minimum, the mission should be reviewed whenever the firm engages in a long-range planning process.

Conclusion

A well crafted mission statement is a key component of an effective strategic planning process. This is especially important as organizations undergo change and embark on new ways of doing business. Perhaps Drucker (1992) said it best:

> [The mission] focuses the organization on action. It defines the specific strategies needed to attain the crucial goals. It creates a disciplined organization. It

alone can prevent the most common degenerative disease of organizations, especially large ones; splintering their always limited resources on things that are 'interesting' or look 'profitable' rather than concentrating them on a very small number of productive efforts (p 205).

Like wine, words can describe a company's mission in some detail, but the real test comes when you taste it. A mission statement is worthless if it does not truly inspire and channel the energy of every employee in the same direction. Everyone has to believe the mission is reasonable and doable and not just empty rhetoric. Business leaders need to "walk the walk" by setting the example for all employees. They don't just talk mission statement, they become examples of the new philosophy; they live it every day. A mission statement is key to guiding the firm in these turbulent times and to creating a competitive advantage.

References

Abrahams, J. (1995). *The mission statement book: 301 Corporate mission statements from America's top companies.* Ten Speed Press.

Ackoff, R.L. (1987, July/August). Mission statements. *Planning Review*, 30-31.

Barnard, C. L. (1968). *The functions of the executive* (30th ed.). Cambridge, MA: Harvard University Press

Bartlett, C. A., & Ghoshal, S. (1991) *Managing across the borders.* Boston: Harvard Business School Press.

Bennis, W., & Nanus, B. (1985). *Leaders: The strategies for taking charge.* New York: Harper & Row.

Campbell, A., & Nash, L.L. (1992). *A sense of mission.* Reading, MA: Addison-Wesley Publishing Co.

Collins, J.C. & Porras, J.I. (1994). *Built to last: Successful habits of visionary companies.* Harper Collins Business.

Drucker, P.F. (1974). *Management: Tasks, responsibilities, practices.* New York: Harper & Row.

Drucker, P.F. (1992). *Managing for the future.* New York: Truman Talley Books.

Gouilart, F.J., & Kelly, J.N. (1995). *Transforming the organization.* New York: McGraw Hill Inc.

Graham, J.W. & Harvlick, W. C. (1994). *Mission statements: A guide to the corporate and non-profit sectors.* New York: Garland Publishing.

Hamel, G. & Prahalad, C. K. (1994). *Competing for the future.* Boston: Harvard Business School Press.

Hawkins, C. (1993, May 31). After a u-turn, UPS really delivers. *Business Week*, pp 92-93.

Jones, P., & Kahaner, L. (1995). *Say it and live it: The 50 corporate mission statements that hit the mark.* New York: Doubleday.

Knauft, E.B., Berger, R.A., & Gray, S.T. (1991). *Profile of excellence*, San Francisco: Jossey-Bass Publishers.

Mathews, J. (1995, January 8). Much ado about nothing? *The Washington Post*, pp. H1, H5

Murray, M. (1995, July 14). How the man from Campbell taught Quaker State to market oil like soup. *The Wall Street Journal*, p. B1.

Nanua, B. (1992). *Visionary Leadership*, San Francisco: Jossey-Bass Publishers.

Nichols, J. (1994). The strategic leadership star. A guiding light in delivering value to the customer, *Management Decision*, 32 (8), 21-26.

Quigley, J. V. (1993), *Vision: How leaders develop it, share it, and sustain it*. New York: McGraw Hill.

Tombazian, C.M. (1994). Mining for gold: Developing your strategic plan (part II). *Managers Magazine*, 69 (10, 16-21).

SECTION FOUR

FORMULATING LONG-TERM GOALS

Setting Business Objectives and Measuring Performance

By *Peter Doyle,* Professor of Marketing and Strategic Management, University of Warwick.
From *Journal of General Management*, Vol. 20 No. 2 Winter 1994, reprinted with permission.

Western companies tend to over-focus on profitability as a measure of performance.

The aim of this paper is to develop a rational model to assist managers in setting corporate goals. It raises fundamental questions on how business performance is assessed and leads to some recommendations on how to limit the 'short termism' which appears to handicap so many Western companies competing internationally.

Several factors stimulate a reassessment of corporate goal setting and conventional measures of business performance. One is the remarkably high failure rate of those Western businesses that only a little earlier were regarded as high performers or 'excellent companies'. Second is the widely held belief that Western companies are excessively short term orientated and that this has curtailed their investment in new markets and new technologies and so reduced their international competitiveness. Third are the obvious differences in objectives between Western and Japanese companies. American and British companies appear to be often narrowly focused around the achievement of return on investment targets. By contrast, Japanese companies appear to have multiple goals weighting approximately equally market share, profitability and innovation.

The following section reviews the most common measures of performance. It shows how each gives the perspective of a single stakeholder group and how the different performance objectives conflict with one another. Next, the normally constrained, non-aggressive nature of stakeholders expectations are discussed. It is suggested that unless management or external events trigger a heightening of tension, the interests of the various stakeholders are normally not difficult to reconcile. It is shown how the modern notion of 'excellence' – exceptional performance on a single objective, has however been a common factor triggering conflict between stakeholders (e.g. shareholders versus managers) with fatal consequences for many firms.

In the final sections, the concept of the 'tolerance zone' is introduced – a development path which makes it possible for management to reconcile the expectations of the different stakeholders. Recommendations are made on how to broaden this tolerance zone through developing an endorseable mission, consistent objectives, and supportable organizational structure and communication strategy.

Measuring Performance

There are many criteria for judging corporate performance but management and industry analysts tend to pick on one measure which they feel symbolises success or failure. Single measures have the practical advantage of permitting the unambiguous league tables so familiar in business journals. Others have justified their focus on theoretical grounds by arguing the primacy of some one measure or stakeholder group.

Such selections, however, normally give a biased and misleading picture of overall performance. In particular, they view performance from the perspective of a single stakeholder group. Further, most of the common performance targets have measurement and conceptual problems which make them hazardous predictors of future performance. Finally, each of these performance measures conflicts with others. Maximising on one measure implies minimising on others. Equivalently, optimising the interests of one stakeholder group means expropriating the resources perceived as belonging to others.

Profitability

As both an objective and a measure of performance, profitability is by far the most common in Western companies.[1, 2] Sometimes this is an absolute measure of profits, more often it is a ratio such as earnings per share, return on investment or return on shareholder funds. These indices are normally compared against other companies in similar lines of business and evaluated over a period of time, often

GOALS	US	JAPAN
Return on investment	2,43	1,24
Capital gain for shareholders	1,14	0,02
Increase in market share	0,73	1,43
New product ratio	0,21	1,06

Key: Managers were asked to range importance of goals: 3 = most important, 2 = second most important, 1 = third most important, 0 = all the rest. Score equals mean for all participating managers in each country.

Source: T. Kagono et al, Strategic vs Evolutionary Management, Englewood Cliffs, NJ: Prentice-Hall, 1985

Table 1. Ranking of Goals by American and Japanese Senior Managers

three to five years. Table 1, based on a sample of 500 American and Japanese managers, shows just how dominant as an objective it is in the West.[3] American management appear overwhelmingly geared to return on investment. By contrast, Japanese goals seem more balanced with profitability, market share and new product development equally placed.

Profitability is the basis for defining 'success' in virtually all the 'excellence' studies and is used in *Business Week, Management Today* (see Table 2) and similar journals as a basis for their widely quoted league tables of performance.

Profitability measures are also familiar as benchmarks in academic studies of organizational renewal, turnaround and corporate failure.[4,5,6] They are ubiquitous in organizations for measuring divisional and business unit performance and form the basis for the increasingly large bonus element in the compensation packages for senior executives.[7]

Despite their overwhelming popularity in both business and academic circles, these indices have been subject to a notable list of practical, methodological and conceptual criticisms. In practice, accounting profits are essentially an arbitrary choice by accountants and easily manipulated. Different methods of accounting for depreciation, stock valuation, research and development, foreign currency translations and especially different methods of accounting for acquisitions can change accounting losses into big reported profits and vice versa. For example, Polly Peck which was rated the most successful of British companies during the 1980s was subsequently shown to have lost money in many of these years. For instance, rather than show a loss of £15m in 1988, it chose to write off against reserves £170m so allowing it to state a profit of £155m. Such creative accounting explained the extraordinary, but temporary, excellence of many of these companies. Differences in legislation also create striking anomalies. For instance the same company, Smith Kline Beecham showed its profit as £130m in the UK but only £90m in the US!

Methodologically, financial analysts are familiar with a host of other crucial limitations of conventional profit measures. Earnings are easily boosted by financing growth through debt rather than equity. Earnings per share rise but the value of the shares drop due to the higher financial risk. For example, the multinational communications business WPP showed increasing earnings in the period up to 1991, while its share price eroded from £8 to £0,6. Profits also fail to take into account the additional capital required to generate them. Profit growth therefore can disguise a dwindling cash flow situation.

Finally, measures of accounting profit are fatally flawed as a conceptual measure of the value of the business. Earnings per share or ROI measure the past performance of the enterprise not its future cash generating performance. Profits can be quickly raised by trading off the future for the present. By cutting back on product development and brand support, earnings are boosted for a few years but at the expense of mortgaging the company's future. For instance the influential PIMS study of 7 000 businesses concluded that cutting back on investment was the swiftest way of boosting return on capital for most organizations.[8] Similarly, by firing workers and cutting education and training, current profitability can quickly be raised but at the cost of eroding the goodwill of the labour force and the community in which the business operates. Not surprisingly, studies have demonstrated the lack of correlation between growth in earnings and growth of shareholder value.[9] By focusing on short run profits, managers trade-off the interests of shareholders, employees, customers, the community and the firm's long run chances of survival.

In some ways, the prevalence of current earnings as a measure of performance is surprising. In public, the 'short term' outlook it creates in Western companies is frequently decried by executives. But the financial community has long recognized that short run profits are a very poor guide to shareholder value. For example, many studies have shown that while cutting back on R & D and other forms of investment boost short run profits, they generally have a negative effect on share prices. 'Short termism' appears to have more to do with how managers are motivated than with pressures from the City. Similarly, governments and employees also perceive that an obsession with short term profit improvement is inimical to their interests.

Market Share

Many studies have shown that growth in market share rather than profitability is the stronger objective in most Japanese companies.[10,1 1,12,13] This is illustrated in the Kagono study (Table 1) which contrasts the objectives of a matched sample of 90 US, British and Japanese companies.[14] There have been many explanations for the Japanese focus on market share. One of the most important appears to be the desire to maintain lifetime employment. To secure this, Japanese companies seek growth, the achievement of economies of scale and experience and to obtain strong control over markets and distribution channels.

Market share objectives receive less priority in Western companies because, at least in the short term, they conflict with the profitability goal. This is illustrated in Figure 1. Firms geared to market share characteristically start with ambitious objectives or 'strategic intent'.[15] Market segments are targeted and plans are made to achieve dominant shares. Central to these plans are market research and appraisal of the performance, price and service expectations of potential target customers. This process leads on to a programme of product development and marketing which aims to match the expectations of these target customers. In such companies the achievement of immediate profitability appears to be distinctly secondary to the achievement of the longer run market share objectives.

In contrast, most Western companies prioritize financial goals. Market share is of secondary importance. If earnings are under pressure it is normal to see share building investments cut back in an effort to boost profits. Today it is common to see Western companies facing fading market shares but boasting significantly higher profitability than their aggressive international competitors. This trade-off reflects the importance Western management give to financial objectives and the way their performance is popularly evaluated. It also reflects the priorities given to stakeholders – the Japanese see market share as the mechanism for protecting employees; the Western companies see earnings as a means of protecting the interests of shareholders.

Shareholder Value

Currently, the most intellectually respected business objective is shareholder value. This has considerable legal and conceptual merit. The company, it is argued, 'belongs to' its legal owners who are its shareholders. The task of management is to maximize the value these shareholders receive. Shareholder value is increased in three ways: dividends, appreciation in the value of the shares, and cash repayments. Operationally, this means managing the business to generate cash rather than accounting profit. The business should only invest if it can achieve a return greater than that shareholders could obtain for themselves investing this cash elsewhere. If a part of the business is worth more to another company than it is to its current management then it should be sold forthwith and the receipts handed

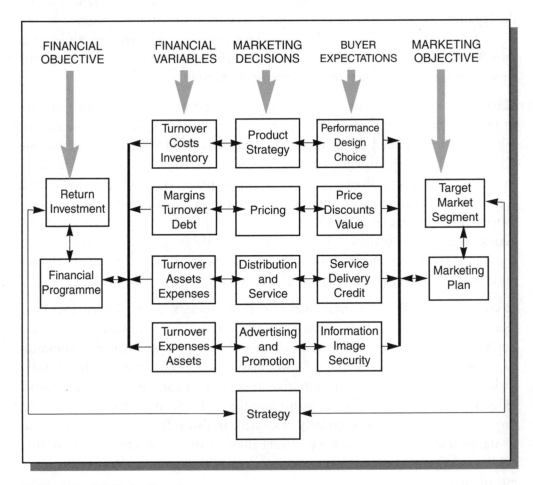

Figure 1. Market Share Objectives

back to shareholders. Management seeking to maximize shareholder value will normally pursue policies quite different from that geared to earnings or acquisitive growth. Several studies have shown policies to increase short term earnings tend to decrease shareholder value.[16] Similarly, the stock market is quickly sceptical of companies pursuing acquisitive growth strategies and the value of the acquirer's shares normally drops.

But, again, seeking to maximize shareholder value runs into several practical problems as well as severe conflicts of interests amongst other stakeholder groups. While it is a practical way to evaluate major acquisition or divestiture options, it is hardly a viable means of assisting the operational decisions of management, e.g. what price shall we charge next month? Shall a particular promotion be run? Even with major investment decisions there is a high degree of subjectivity in the shareholder value approach. Businesses rarely have planning horizons more than five years ahead, but only a small proportion of value can be attributed to estimated cash flows over this period. For example, Marsh, comparing the value of ICI shares and its current dividend, showed that only 8 per cent of ICI's current market capitalization is attributable to the current year's dividend; only 29 per cent can be explained by the present value of the dividends expected over the next five years; and over 50 per cent by the value of the dividend expected over the next ten years. The bulk of the value of the business is thus its residual value. Unfortunately there is no reliable way of estimating this key figure, and different techniques will give quite different estimates of shareholder value created.[17] These practical difficulties of using the shareholder value approach no doubt account for the pervasiveness of profitability targets. Managers see profits as a usable proxy for shareholder value.

Shareholder value goals also make it difficult for British and US companies to compete especially in manufacturing and high growth areas. The cost of capital used to discount investment decisions in the UK for example has been more than 70 per cent higher than in Germany and as much as three times that in Japan.[18] This means the British company needs to see a profit two or three times that which its competitors need to justify an investment decision. Put another way, a business in the UK. which looks for an investment to pay for itself over four years may be competing with a business in Japan content with a 12 year payback period. Not surprisingly, companies seeking to maximize shareholder value are predominately found in mature industries and the service sector where long term investment, research and development, and technical training can be minimized. The community cost is of course to bias the economy away from manufacturing and high growth sectors. To employees this means lower real income growth and less security. It also makes managers taking the long term view highly vulnerable to acquisition. Shareholder value in manufacturing can be released by selling the business to an acquirer with a lower cost of capital or one willing sharply to curtail long term investment.

Acquisitive Growth

Some companies have sought rapid growth – largely by acquisition – as their central objective. Saatchi and Saatchi propagated what it called 'the Law of Dominance' which said that 'being number one in the world is wonderful, two can be terrific, three is threatened and four is fatal'.[19] Size became the dominant goal of the Company and it pursued a hectic series of acquisitions in the 1980s to create the world's largest advertising agency. At the time, many business pundits hailed it as a visionary strategy and the Harvard Business School developed a case study on the Company.

Several explanations for the growth objective have been made. Baumol and later Williamson showed the link between managerial compensation and size.[20,21] Prestige and perks are also correlated to the growth of the business. Accounting conventions which allow the cost of acquisitions to be excluded from the income statement also inflate profits and earnings per share so disguising the true cost of acquisitions. By contrast, internal growth where investments are written off against revenues, has proved much less attractive than takeovers to these financial entrepreneurs.

Despite its appeal, when taken to excess, growth and the pursuit of size has proved even less robust as a strategy than profitability. Most of the companies that pursued it such as Saatchi, WPP, Next, Coloroll and Blue Arrow in the UK, and Texaco, PanAm, Campeau, Interco and the Savings and Loans Associations in the US proved very short-lived phenomena. A model to predict corporate failure recently tested by stockbrokers, County NatWest, found that very rapid turnover growth was the most important correlate of subsequent failure.[22,23] It is easy to see why. First, excessive rates of growth invariably involve higher levels of financial risk as a company takes on more debt. Second, given that the stock market values companies efficiently, then with bid premiums normally adding 50 per cent to the pre-bid share price, truly enormous improvements in the target companies' performance must be achieved by the acquirer. In fact, many of these companies appeared to make the most cursory examination of potential synergies.[24] Deals were often made on faith that rapid market growth and rising asset prices would make expensive purchases subsequently look good value.

When these forecasts proved too optimistic the real cost of the growth strategy became explicit. Shareholder value collapsed. For example the market valuation of Saatchi and Saatchi dropped from £7 to £0,2 over two years. Morale and motivation of employees declined in these groups as savage cutbacks became necessary to meet interest rate obligations and even creditors saw their loans written off.

Other Goals

The four goals above are not an exhaustive list of alternatives. Service companies in particular place satisfying employees as a key goal. The Chairman of Marriott Hotels identified three target groups to satisfy: customers, employees and shareholders and the most important of these he believed was the employee. He reasoned that if they like their jobs and feel a sense of pride and achievement they will serve the customer well. Satisfied customers who repeatedly used the business and spread good 'word of mouth' about it will be the basis of the profit for satisfying the shareholders. Hewlett-Packard is another company whose vision ('the H-P way') has historically been giving primacy to creating an excellent environment for its knowledge workers. At least two explanations are advanced for the superiority of this goal. First, unless employees are motivated and protected they will not give of their best and so customer satisfaction, profit, growth and shareholder value are not sustainable. Second, it has been argued that since shareholders are invariably institutional investors without long term commitment to the business or interested in being involved in its management, they are not the primary stakeholder group. As investors they are entitled to a reasonable return but not at the expense of other groups and in particular employees whose commitment is normally longer term and whose individual contributions are essential.

Again, however, focusing excessively on employees involves unacceptable trade-offs. Such companies as Hewlett-Packard, IBM and Marks & Spencer had, in the early 90s, to give up the vision of lifetime employment for their employees as competitive pressures forced them to cut costs to improve margins and de-layer administrative structures lo sharpen their focus on customers.

Interest groups have lobbied for other goals: the community interest – local and national; environmentalism, advancing the causes of minority groups, enhancing relationships with suppliers, or simply minimising risks.

Stakeholders: Objectives and Constraints

The above review suggests that no single goal is adequate for judging business performance. Partly this is because each measure suffers from operational and conceptual problems. More particularly it is because each gives a limited perspective, focusing on the rewards to one particular stakeholder group. Further, each of these goals partly conflict with one another. For example, maximising short run earnings will reduce the firm's long run competitiveness. Rapid growth leads to spiralling risks being absorbed by shareholders and creditors. The pursuit of shareholder value can erode the trust of employees and the local community as shareholder interests dominate.

When one or more stakeholder groups perceive that they are becoming disenfranchised then a disequilibrium situation is created which threatens the firm's survival. If shareholders believe they are obtaining unacceptable rewards then they can unseat the managers or sell the business. Creditors who conceive their assets placed at unreasonable risk can liquidate the business. Similarly, managers and employees can refuse to commit themselves to the organization's mission.

However, such disequilibrium situations are not normal. Stakeholders expectations are usually reasonable and easily met. They normally act as constraints on the behaviour of management rather than stretching objectives. There are two mechanisms moderating the expectations of stakeholders. One is that the perceived economic and *social costs of maximising behaviour* exceed the benefits stakeholders conceive that will be gained from disrupting the organization's current operational mode. Second, there are *dampening mechanisms* within the organization which facilitate its ability to adapt to stakeholder demands. Nevertheless, as we show, there are certain *triggering situations* which can change this optimistic scenario. In these situations stakeholders' expectations change from non-binding constraints to stressful objectives creating multiple sources of conflict and disequilibrium. The effect of these mechanisms on stakeholders are discussed next.

Shareholders

These are the most obvious stakeholders. They have invested in the enterprise with the expectation of rewards in terms of dividends, share appreciation and capital repayments. If dissatisfied, they can fire the executives and sell or close down the firm. While legally their power to maximize shareholder value is absolute, in practice it is normally severely constrained. Today's shareholders are predominantly institutional investors rather than active owners. These institutions have a large portfolio of shares and will invariably sell the shares of a disappointing performer rather than seek to oust its management. Often the terms of their charters prevent these institutions playing an active role in the companies whose shares they hold. The consequence is that companies rarely seek to maximize shareholder value and a substantial zone of tolerance is available. This is evidenced in both the relative low priority managers give to shareholder value (see Table 2) and the high bid premiums required to take over a company.

However, the power of shareholders can be activated if other stakeholder groups are not alert to their needs. If managers, employees or other groups are obtaining excessive rewards so that the dividends or equity values become completely unacceptable to shareholders then a disequilibrium situation is created. Then, investors do step in and change the top management. Or, more commonly, an outside group bids for the company taking advantage of its low valuation and seeks to create greater value for its own shareholders.

Managers

Salaries and bonuses, perquisites and power are among the major motivators of senior executives. The separation of corporate ownership and control has unquestionably increased the powers of managers. Evidence of this is in the salaries of chief executives and senior managers which have grown significantly faster than shareholder value over the last decade. It is also illustrated in the willingness of executives to invest in growth and diversification even though the return has been less than the true cost of capital. But again executives are normally sensitive to the risks of maximising their potential for personal gain. This zone of tolerance is evidenced in the premiums executives normally obtain when changing companies. Unduly high managerial rewards create jealousy and pressures among other members of the coalition on whom the business's stability depends. Most company boards also have compensation committees which dampen managerial expectations. Similarly, the pressures to grow and diversify are also constrained by the need to increase earnings per share, return on investment or maintain interest-cover conventions. When such constraints are breached then managers risk an eventual collision with other groups of stakeholders.

Customers

In a free enterprise system, customers are potentially the most powerful stakeholder group. If their expectations are not met they can switch to alternative brands and so erode the company's revenue base and ability to satisfy all other stakeholder groups. Again, however, customers appear to have substantial tolerance levels. Customers are normally reluctant to incur the risks and costs of changing their existing repertoire of suppliers. In well established markets it is very difficult for new entrants to succeed.[25] Only when customer service and product quality falls substantially below those of competitors will the company's market share fall precipitously. Nevertheless, British and American post-war industrial history is replete with examples of where the excess pursuit of other stakeholder interests, short term profit, workers' reluctance to change, or diversification, has led to an erosion of customer support and a loss of markets.

Employees

Workers outside the executive ranks seek a combination of employment security, compensation and job satisfaction. As stakeholders they are more dependent upon the firm for their livelihoods than shareholders and less able to control events than senior managers. Their power to achieve their goals depends upon their degree of organization, the tightness of the labour market for their special skills and the recognition of managers and shareholders of the importance of motivated employees. Again, workers are not maximisers. Consciousness of switching costs, uncertainty and interests outside their firm orientate them to accepting suboptimal returns from existing employers. However, a failure to meet their minimum expectations may create militancy; more certainly it will curtail the commitment of employees to provide high levels of quality and service to other stakeholders.

Creditors

Banks and other lenders have legal right to specified interest and capital repayments. Having limited upside potential in their assets, creditors want the firm to be risk averse. If the firm cannot meet its obligations to creditors then they can liquidate the firm's assets to meet their claims. Normally, however, creditors are reluctant to do this and will defer repayments if they believe the business can be turned round. Only if the assets are at increasing risk are creditors likely to liquidate the business.

Other stakeholders with claims on the enterprise can be extended to suppliers, governments, local community, minority groups and so on. The survival of the business depends upon the support or, at least, the non-active opposition of each of these. Again, for each of the groups, there is a broad tolerance zone, within which passivity can be expected. Figure 2 illustrates the relationships between stakeholders and their expectations.

In practice, the problem is more complex than Figure 2 suggests in that stake-holders are not homogeneous groups. Managers have functional and geographical loyalties so that conflicts among them can match conflicts between groups. Similarly, the interests of shareholder groups may diverge between say, family and 'outside' owners.

At the same time, the task of achieving reconciliation is generally easier than it might appear. As has been discussed above, stakeholders' demands are more about

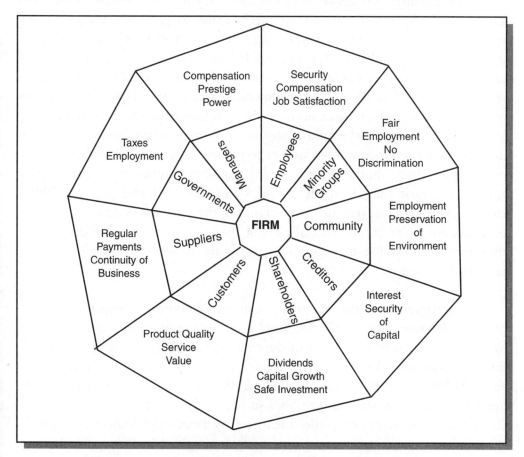

Figure 2. Stakeholders and Their Expectations

'satisficing' than maximising. Behavioural scientists have noted other mechanisms which dampen conflict.[26] One is that demands are normally *incremental* rather than unconstrained. Budgets within the firm and expectations of stakeholders outside it are related to past payments so that sudden shifts in demands are rare. Second, not all groups make demands simultaneously so that conflicts can be reduced by *selective attention*. Third, *managerial slack* in most organizations means that resources can be made available to a specific group by paring costs and reducing payments without breaking the tolerance limits of the other stakeholders. All these mean that senior executives have considerable discretion in running their organizations.

Triggering Mechanisms

However, the boards of firms are occasionally overturned and businesses are bankrupted or sold by stakeholders. Four mechanisms trigger such disequilibrium. First is simply poor *competitive performance* where the firm fails to generate sufficient resources from the market to meet the minimum payments required by stakeholders. Second is *environmental change*. Change can produce a mis-match of the firm's skills and assets with environmental requirements. For example, a sudden change in technology made obsolete the skill base of the Swiss watch companies who had dominated the industry for generations. Environmental change can also raise the importance and resource expectations of certain stakeholder groups. For example, labour shortages can raise the wage expectations of workers, capital shortages can raise the returns demanded by shareholders and creditors. Third, external *intervention* can activate the militancy of the stakeholder group. For example, a takeover offer can dramatically reveal the poor value shareholders are currently receiving, forcing management to promise substantial improvements to maintain its position.

These three triggers are either external or the non-intended consequences of management behaviour. The fourth, *'excellence'* is a direct result of management goals. Excellence here means the pursuit of outstanding results in one objective or measure of performance. Excellence has become a popular goal since the enormous success of Peters and Waterman's [27] study. Unfortunately, as has been noted subsequently, excellent companies exhibit a surprising lack of robustness. For example, of the 43 excellent companies identified by Peters and Waterman, only 14 were excellent five years later and only 6 eight years on. In fact, many of these companies had disappeared altogether.

Year	Company[1]	Market Value (£)	ROI[2]	Subsequent Performance
1979	MFI	57	50	Collapsed
1980	Lasmo	134	97	Still profitable
1981	Bejam	79	34	Acquired
1982	Racal	940	36	Still Profitable
1983	Polly Peck	128	79	Collapsed
1984	Atlantic Computers	151	36	Collapsed
1985	BSR	197	32	Still Profitable
1986	Jaguar	819	60	Acquired
1987	Amstrad	987	89	Still profitable
1988	Body Shop	225	89	Still profitable
1989	Blue Arrow	653	135	Collapsed

1.   Where a company has been top for more than one year, the next best company has been chosen in the subsequent year, e.g. Polly Peck was rated top in 1983, 84 and 85.

2.   Pre-tax profit as a percent of invested capital.

Table 2. Britain's Top Companies – *Management Today*

Table 2 lists the most profitable of Britain's top 250 companies each year from 1979-89. Of these 11 excellent companies, only five survived in their existing form to the end of the following year, 1990! Of these five survivors, only one could still be regarded as a strong performer. The majority had either collapsed or been acquired under depressed circumstances.

The explanation for this lack of robustness of these excellent companies is in the trade-offs made. When management seeks extreme performance along one dimension, the trade-off against other goals becomes correspondingly extreme. Similarly, the conflict between stakeholders is amplified as one group expropriates the resources of others. The result is that excellent companies are prone to exceptional instability.

The Tolerance Zone

These ideas are represented in Figure 3. The firm has multiple objectives and as it pushes to extremes (or excellence) on one of these objectives it increases the likelihood of not meeting the constraints on others. There is an outer ring of disequilibrium which signals this danger zone. Similarly, there is a corresponding inner ring where the organization fails to match the minimum requirements. Between these two extremes is a tolerance zone defined as that development path which permits the minimum expectations of stakeholders to be satisfied and reconciled.

A central task of management is to broaden this tolerance zone. Where this zone is narrow or non-existent the firm has little room for manoeuvre as key stakeholders are dissatisfied with the returns being generated and wish to replace the current management. If inadequate shareholder value or return on investment causes the problem, management are likely to seek to boost it by cutting back on investment and divesting parts of the business. If management is dissatisfied with the growth performance of the firm they are likely to increase debt and incur higher risks in making acquisitions. In both situations short term constraints displace the firm's long run objectives. Short term profit is enhanced at the expense of long

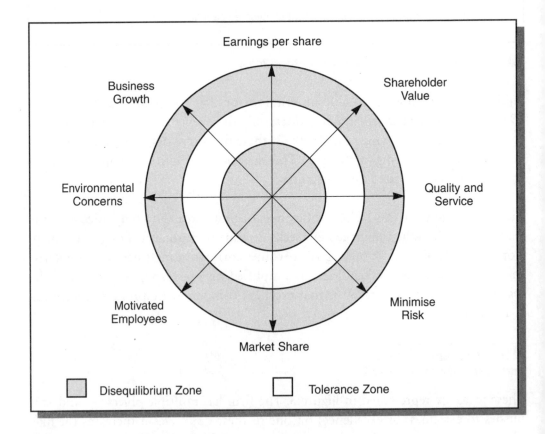

Figure 3. Corporate Objectives: Disequilibrium and Tolerance

run market share; immediate growth is accelerated by inflating the longer term risks borne by shareholders and creditors. In addition, the intensified focus on satisfying one stakeholder group increases the chances of a collision with other groups.

By broadening the tolerance zone management create more discretion for new initiatives. Because the minimum expectations of stakeholders are met, the pressures to sacrifice the long term for short term performance are curtailed. Management also have more scope to adjust to the negative events which threaten to trigger stakeholder dissatisfaction: new competition, environmental shocks or the militarization of a stakeholder group. Most important of all, a broader tolerance zone makes it possible to develop a set of objectives and business strategies which are perceived to be in the mutual interest of all the stakeholders. Participants are then bound together in supporting the continued success and long run development of the organization.

Managing the Tolerance Zone

The task of management is to develop a strategy which will meet the objectives of the stakeholders in the organization. A high performance organization is one which is able to achieve this consistently. As we have seen, the problem is that stakeholder objectives conflict with one another. In practice this conflict is disguised by lags in response to changing priorities. For example, it is possible to boost earnings quickly by curtailing the brand investment while the costs of this policy in terms of erosion of market share are not felt for a number of years. On the other hand, it has been argued that stakeholders are normally not aggressive in their objectives and that management should usually be in a position to treat their expectations as constraints and to reconcile their interests.

Management should actively reinforce the mutual interest of stakeholders and so broaden the tolerance zone. Western managers (especially in the US and Britain) have been much less adept at this than their Far Eastern competitors. The popular notion of 'excellence' or seeking to 'top the league' in a single performance measure has been a particularly damaging phenomenon in the West. As we have seen, seeking to maximize on one measure means minimising on others. Further, since each measure has special value to one group of stakeholders, excellence means expropriating resources of some stakeholders to enhance the rewards to a favoured group. Not surprisingly, those companies that have withstood the test of time: Unilever, Marks & Spencer, Proctor and Gamble, Boeing, Mercedes Benz, Siemens, Ciba Geigy or Nestle are not outstanding on any single measure of performance. Rather than see high performance as maximising on a single goal, they see performance as achieving a satisfactory level of results across a set of goals which are competitive both between groups and over time.

Building a sense of *mission* based upon mutual interest is a positive means of reconciling objectives. A mission statement is the formal representation of what should be the organization's cultural values. The core of the mission is an agreement on who the key stakeholders in the firm are and what objectives they have a right to see satisfied. To be convincing, all the stakeholders should of course participate in developing the agreed mission of the business. More difficult is making the mission statement the visible cultural reference for the quantitative objectives the organization establishes, the strategy it develops, and the decisions managers subsequently take.

This task will inevitably require the organization supporting the statement of mission with a comprehensive programme of cultural change aimed at building a community of interest amongst stakeholders. Two types of socialization programmes can be distinguished – these can be termed 'internal' and 'extensive'. A considerable behavioural literature has developed on the former.[28,29] *Internal socialization* focuses on developing a community of interest among two groups of stakeholders – employees and managers. It encourages mutual respect, bottom up management, better communications and effective adaptation to a changing competitive environment.

Internal socialization, however, is at best only a partial solution and indeed may be counterproductive if it creates a collusion of interest among these two groups at the expense of other stakeholders such as shareholders, customers, creditors or suppliers. *Extensive socialization* extends the programme to these groups. This has been most fully developed in Japan where the major companies have developed comprehensive informal networks (Zaibatsu) between their firm and its suppliers, distributors, creditors, shareholders and other groups. Internal and external stakeholders are bound together by complex and continually evolving ties of mutual benefit and commercial interest. Each participant is locked into a very long term or even permanent relationship based upon interwoven business links. All parties know that they gain from the continued development of the firm. The firm operates in such a broad tolerance zone that even environmental shocks or poor performance fail to trigger ownership changes.

An alternative approach to extensive socialization which has probably more to offer British and US firms is the German *Aufsichsrat* model. Here, the formal structure of the company's supervisory board represents the internal and external stakeholders and provides a mechanism for developing an agreed set of compatible goals and a means of monitoring the activities of managers. This contrasts with the American and British models where top management have successfully kept off the board competing stakeholder interests. Even non-executives have been appointed because they do not represent an interest group. It is hardly surprising that in these countries, boards have been subject to the most criticism of favouring the interests of managers with the consequent instability such a bias inevitably brings. In Germany and other parts of Europe where supervisory boards have been adopted, there is considerable evidence that this mechanism has dampened expectations on the part of individual stakeholders and increased the robustness of firms.

A final contrast in the behaviour of Western and Japanese firms is in the role of external communications. British and American firms have been poor at articulating their company's mission and vision to their stakeholders. While it is common to see Japanese and German companies advertising their long term mission in mass media, British and US managers have assumed that short term performance is a sufficient statement. The problem with failing to communicate long term objectives and strategy is that stakeholders assume that management do not have any. Consequently, short term performance is used as an indication of long term potential. The result is that temporary poor performance can unnecessarily erode shareholder value and lead to a collapse of confidence among other stakeholder groups. Managers themselves must bear a substantial part of the responsibility for the short termism which is endemic in both Britain and the US.

Summary and Conclusions

High performance is not about exceptional achievement on one or two measures but gaining satisfactory results along a broad set of criteria, each of which partly competes and conflicts with others over time. For this reason, consistent long term businesses rarely feature at the top of popular performance 'league tables'.

Businesses often focus on one or sometimes two performance criteria such as earnings per share or growth. But this is not sustainable over the long term. Focusing on one goal conflicts with other important goals. Since each goal maps into one stakeholder group it also means resources are reallocated towards one group. If an organization fails to meet the legitimate long term interests of its key stakeholders the organization decays. Sometimes this occurs quickly, for example, when outsiders stage a takeover of the business by offering current shareholders enhanced value. Alternatively, it can be slow as when customers withdraw their support because they feel their needs are not being properly met.

In practice, reconciling the interests of stakeholders should not be difficult as they are generally 'satisficers' rather than maximizers. Managements' main concern should be watching for performance and environmental changes which can trigger active stakeholder disgruntlement. More positively, the firm can seek to broaden its tolerance zone by actively seeking to dampen excessive expectations. This requires developing a culture which respects and integrates the interests of the diverse stakeholders. Businesses that achieve consistent long run performance build a sense of mission which reflects these mutual interests and have a board of directors which oversees the conduct of its managers to achieve such consistency. Finally, the board needs to communicate its long run mission to the outside world.

Firms that set objectives and measure performance in this way can reduce the pressures to act short term. Like most leading Japanese and German businesses, they can convince stakeholders that they have a genuine long term strategy which reconciles the interests of the different stakeholder groups.

References

1. Hayes, R. H. and W. J. Abernathy, 'Managing our Way to Economic Decline', *Harvard Business Review*, 58, July-August 1980, pp.67-77.
2. Hamel, G. and C. K, Prahalad, 'Strategic Intent', *Harvard Business Review*, 67, May-June, 1989.
3. Kagono, T., *Strategic vs Evolutionary Management: A US - Japan Comparison of Strategy and Organization,* Amsterdam: North Holland, 1985.
4. Altman, E. 1. .*Corporate Financial Distress,* New York: Wiley, 1982.
5. Hambrick, D. C. and R. A. D'Abeni, 'Large Corporate Failures as Downward Spirals'. *Administrative Science Quarterley,* 33, 1988, pp. 1-23.
6. Levine, C. H., 'Organizational Decline and Cut Back Management', *Public Administration Review*, 38, 1978, pp. 316-325.
7. Goold, M. and A. Campbell, Strategies and Styles: *The Role of the Centre in Managing Diversified Corporations,* Oxford, Blackwell, 1987.

8. Buzzell, R. D. and B. T. Gale, *The PIMS Principles: Linking Strategy to Performance*, New York: Macmillan, 1987.
9. Rappaport, A., *Creating Shareholder Value*, New York: Macmillan, 1986, p.l9.
10. See e.g., Morishima, M., *Why has Japan Succeeded?*, Cambridge Mass: Cambridge University Press, 1982.
11. Prestowitz, C. V., *Trading Places*, New York: Free Press, 1988.
12. Tsurumi.Y., *Multinational Management: Business Strategy and Government Policy*, Cambridge Mass: Ballinger Press, 1984.
13. Van Wolferen, K., *The Enigma of Japanese Power*, Cambridge Mass: MIT Press, 1989.
14. Doyle, P., V. Wong and J. Saunders, 'Competition in Global Markets', *Journal of International Business Studies*, October 1991.
15. See Note 2 above.
16. Marsh, P., *Short Termism on Trial*, London: Institutional Fund Managers Association, 1990.
17. Brealey, R. A. and S. C. Myers, *Principles of Corporate Finance*, New York: McGraw Hill, 1988.
18. McCauley, R. N. and S. A. Zimmer, 'Explaining International Differences in the Cost of Capital', *FRBNY Quarterly Review*, Summer 1989.
19. Fallon, 1., *The Brothers: The Rise and Rise of Saatchi and Saatchi*, London: Hutchinson, 1988.
20. Baumol, W. J., *Economic Theory and Operations Analysis*, Englewood Cliffs: Prentice Hall, 1961.
21. Williamson, 0. E., 'A Model of Rational Managerial Behaviour', in R. M. Cyert and J. G. March, *A Behavioural Theory of the Firm*, Englewood Cliffs: Prentice Hall, 1963.
22. *Financial Times*, 'Clues that Warn of Collapse', 26, May 1991, p.III.
23. See also, Pratten, C., *Company Failure*, ICA; London, 1991.
24. Porter, M. E., 'From Competitive Advantage to Corporate Strategy', *Harvard Business Review*, May-June 1987.
25. Jones, J. P., *What's in a Name: Advertising and the Concept of Brands*, Lexington Mass.: Lexington Books, 1986.
26. See especially, Cyert, R. M. and J. G. March, *A Behavioural Theory of the Firm*, Englewood Cliffs: NJ.: Prentice Hall, 1963.
27. Peters, T. J. and R. H. Waterman, I*n Search of Excellence: Lessons from America's Best Run Companies*, New York: Harper and Row, 1982.
28. See e.g., Pascale, R. T. and A. G. Athos, *The Art of Japanese Management*, New York: Simon & Schuster, 1981.
29. See e.g., Ouchi, W. B., *Theory Z*, Reading, Mass.: Addison-Wesley, 1981.

On Objectives

By *John Peters*

From *Management Decision*, 31 (6): 28-30. 1993, © MCB University Press Ltd, 1993.
Reprinted with permission.

An objective is the result that we want from the game we are playing in. It is the harbour we are sailing towards, the point we are aiming for on the map. It is why we are pursuing our strategy and our plans of action.

Quantification

There are three golden rules about objectives. The first is that an objective should wherever possible be quantified. This allows you to measure progress towards it so you know when you have arrived.

"To achieve 6 per cent share of the target market within twelve months of launching this product" would be an objective where progress can be measured.

Try measuring "To achieve a substantial market share as soon as possible". It depends what you mean by "substantial" and by "as soon as possible". This kind of objective may be all right for a very small business, where the strategist and the implementers are the same people, or they are in direct contact. But even in a one-person business, does it give any cues for action? Probably not. For "as soon as possible" can stretch away endlessly into the distance.

Plans too easily fall into the realm of dreams. It is a little like the light-hearted poster on some office walls; "Tomorrow I'll get organized". Plans are only of use if they degenerate into action.

Quantification helps plans degenerate into action, for it allows you to work backwards to steps and trigger points. If we're looking for 6 per cent market share after 12 months, what does that mean after three months? After six months? What does it mean a week on Friday? What does it mean tomorrow? What, indeed, does it mean now?

"What do I have to do to make that happen" is one of the most powerful questions managers can ask themselves. Ask it, then ask it again, then again. "Six per cent in 12 months. What do I have to do to make that happen? Gain at least two large customers contracting for at least £100 000 worth of business each this year. And what do I have to do to make that happen?"

And so on, until you get to a series of action points; book a half page advertisement in the *Weekly Trader* today before lunchtime; telephone my five most likely customers today for an appointment to see the MD, etc.

A half-page advertisement today before lunch seems a long way from the elegance of 6 per cent share in 12 months; but 6 per cent share in 12 months is a dream waiting to happen. It will not happen without action. Your plans must degenerate into action.

Realism

The second golden rule of objectives is that they must be realistic and achievable. Unrealistic objectives will either be mentally revised downwards by the audience, or will be taken literally, aimed for, missed, and then provoke feelings of failure and reduced morale. If they are simply not believed and are revised downwards by their receivers, it would have been as well to have set real ones in the first place.

To those who say that you just might hit an unrealistic target I would say that if you can hit it, it isn't unrealistically high. It might be tough and stretching, and prompt people on to greater creative efforts, which brings us on to...

Testing and Stretching

The third golden rule is that objectives should be set high enough to test and stretch people. Low objectives will not provoke any ingenuity in working towards them, or pride in their achievement.

They may in fact be positively damaging, as people will tend to perform to their own self-derived levels of performance. In other words, a £50 000 target salesperson will expect to sell around the £50 000 mark. If this figure has for some reason been reached in just six months, research studies have indicated that, by and large, the salesperson will not go on to sell £100 000 worth of products, but will sell instead at or less than what they would "normally" sell in the next half year – say an extra £20 000.

And next year, he or she will do the usual £50 000 again. That is, unless their self-image changes, and they now think of themselves as a £100 000 salesperson, in which case, magically (or not really so magically) they will go on to their new target, and do it again next year.

So the key challenge for those setting objectives and targets is to make them stretching enough to encourage high performance, but not put them out of reach.

Department and Organizational Objectives

We usually think of objectives as a hierarchy, coming down from corporate level to business unit to department. That means, for example, a corporate objective to increase the share price by 10 per cent over the next 12 months will be supported by a whole series of strategies from the corporate viewpoint – launch a successful new brand which achieves 10 per cent market share and 90 per cent consumer awareness in a year; cut the operating budget by 10 per cent; declare 10 per cent more dividend than last year; yet the whole organization registered to the ISO 9000 quality standard, and so on.

From a department or business unit viewpoint, these corporate level strategies become their operating objectives. If you are in the marketing department of the British subsidiary of a US multinational, US stock market value would be way beyond your level of influence, *except* in achieving your own objectives, in that they *supported* a super-ordinate objective of improving overall stock market valuation. And in turn you might have strategies to achieve your own departmental objectives which come down, eventually, to your secretary rearranging the filing system to cut down on paper production in the department.

What does filing many miles away have to do with the US stock market?

Only that the 10 per cent increase in share value won't happen by thinking about it, or writing an objective down on paper. Well, it might, but that would be pure luck. It can only be managed to happen by a series of actions which support the objective.

And as the actions which happen in a large organization over a year number thousands or millions, it is difficult to make sure that they all support the corporate plan.

But imagine if they all did!

Confusing Objectives, Strategies and Tactics

Although one person's objective can be another person's strategy, and so on, it is important to keep your eye at an individual business unit level on which is which. Our US multinational isn't trying to gain 90 per cent customer awareness of the name of their new product for any other reason than to contribute towards their share value perception. The reasons behind strategies govern how they are approached. For example ...

APC Ltd was an organization with a problem, although the problem was a not unpleasant one, being caused by its own success. For APC had a large and growing product line, and a large and growing production operation, but the production operation couldn't seem to keep pace with the products.

The problem was this. APC produced some 400 separate items in the course of a year, and each item's average time in production was 13 weeks; a quarter of a year. That meant that, at any one time, an average of 100 items, or one-quarter of the entire annual output, was in production.

To handle this range of products in the system, the production manager had taken on more and more staff to deal with bottlenecks. But in freeing one bottleneck, another one was created; and wasn't that the one he took on two more staff members to deal with just three months ago? There was simply too much in the system. And the problem was getting worse. Average time in production had crept up from ten weeks to 13 weeks even though there were proportionally more staff per product than ever before. And products were still being added. At this rate, production was heading towards a gridlock, with everything bottlenecked and at a standstill.

Then one of the directors of the organization had a brainwave. Actual production time on each item was only a matter of two or three days; they spent all the rest of the time waiting in queues for the next process. The longer it takes, she reasoned, the more items in the system at any one time, therefore the longer it will take, therefore ... gridlock.

But what if we got smart enough to get the production time down to five weeks? That would still mean, on three days actual work, products would be spending most of their time in queues, so it wouldn't be asking for unrealistically high levels of efficiency. What it would mean is that instead of 100 items and rising in the system at any one time, there would be only an average of about 40. And the fewer we have, the shorter the queues, the faster the process, the fewer we have ... and so on. A virtuous circle rather than a vicious one. It would require some nifty scheduling and some smart application, but, after all, that was why the production manager had been hired in the first place.

The *objective* became to freeze, then reduce, the overhead budget of the production operation by 40 per cent in 12 months. It could be done! The strategy was simply to get smart enough to take 13 weeks down to five weeks.

What happened? The production manager swallowed hard a few times, but was reassured that he would be given all the brainpower the organization could muster, and that his status or prestige would not be reduced if he had less staff. He was even given a pay rise just to demonstrate that everyone had complete confidence in him, even though he had doubled the overhead and slowed production time by 100 per cent.

Then the organization got very excited about five weeks production time. Taking 40 per cent off the operating budget of the production operation in the next 12 months wasn't exactly anything you could beat a drum about, or indeed something that anyone wanted to think too hard about, just in case it had unpleasant overtones.

But a five-weeks production cycle. Well, that was a different thing. Everyone could relate to that. It was tangible. You could see, or think you saw, the products moving along that little bit faster. There were lots of meetings about it. It became an opportunity for banter over coffee – "You down to five weeks yet, George?" "Ah, you just wait and see. My Grand Plan's nearly ready".

And then, somehow, somewhere along the way, the objective got lost altogether. The five-week production cycle plan took weeks, and then months, to be produced through its endless discussions and iterations. And the objective just got lost somewhere.

It was a little like the troubles in Northern Ireland – everyone can see what the activity is, but for most people the original question has been long lost. What *are* the IRA wanting? What *are* the troops doing there? No one remembers.

No-one at APC remembered 40 per cent off the operating budget – for the objective had become the five-week production cycle. The strategy had metamorphosed into the objective.

Have you guessed the punchline? Of course, the "objective" of the five-week production cycle was at last achieved. The production manager got another raise.

And the strategy to achieve it? Why, of course, to spend fiercely on the latest bells-and-whistles equipment, to hire yet more new staff and to subcontract around a third of the workload. And although by then no one had noticed, far from reducing the operating budget, it had been increased by around 50 per cent. The means had become the end.

This is a true story, and it happened in one of the most sophisticated and successful organizations I have ever come across. It can happen very easily!

Ends and Means

And so (see Table 1) the fourth, and most important Golden Rule is – don't let the means become confused with the ends. Don't mix up strategy and objectives. Strategies can be beguiling, but remember why you are pursuing them.

Objectives tell you where you are going. They are the result you want from the game.

Strategies tell you how to get there. (Copyright MCB University Press Ltd 1993)

1.	Objectives should be quantified wherever possible.
2.	Objectives should be realistic and attainable.
3.	Objectives should normally by stretching, i.e. not too easy to achieve.
4.	Don't confuse objectives and strategies.

Table 1. The Golden Rules

Strategic downsizing

By *David C. Band* and *Charles M. Tustin*
From *Management Decision*, 33 (8). 1995, © MCB University Press Ltd, 1995.
Reprinted with permission.

David C. Band Senior Lecturer at the Advanced Business Programme, University of Otago, Dunedin, New Zealand.
Charles M. Tustin Senior Lecturer at the Advanced Business Programme, University of Otago, Dunedin, New Zealand.

Introduction

Downsizing is one tactic within a corporate strategy for shifting the organizational structure from what it is now to what it has to be in order to sustain competitive edge and satisfy customers' needs. Little attention, however, has been given to the strategic aspects of downsizing that confront an organization, or the process of planning to ensure a successful downsize.

The main aim of this article is consequently to address those issues which should be considered when deciding to downsize, and when planning the downsizing once the decision is made. The actual implementation and evaluation of a downsizing programme then follows quite naturally from the previous two phases in the strategic downsizing model proposed in Figure 1: Sequence of steps to ensure a successful downsizing strategy.

We begin by distinguishing between downsizing and layoffs, and highlight the short-and long-term differences between these activities. This distinction leads naturally to an overview of the strategic reasons for downsizing, whether downsizing is usually the first or last thing management has done to retain the company's competitive edge, and which of the two it *should* be. Against the background of a company's overall strategy, we go on to consider all the factors that need to be

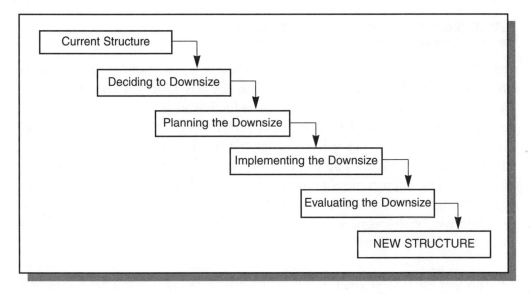

Figure 1. Sequence of Steps to Ensure a Successful Downsizing Strategy

taken into account when deciding whether or not to downsize and when formulating the downsizing plan. The end result is two checklists that will allow a manager to determine the overall effect of a strategic downsize. From this, he/she can:

- Gain an insight into the downsizing effects that will determine the economic welfare of the company and thus of the shareholders.
- Limit the adverse effects on those who leave and those who stay.
- Ensure that the desired strategic outcome is achieved. We also show, however, that downsizing is typically the result of a lack of strategic rightsizing – that is, the process of continually evaluating and adapting human resource requirements for the future through better management, rather than through reactive hiring and firing.

In addition, the article illustrates the effects of downsizing on the people who leave and those who remain with the organization. It provides examples of companies that have minimized the adverse effects on both groups by "accentuating the positive". Once a company has determined that its workforce must be trimmed, how should management go about it? We consider the roles played by management and employees, and the desirable effects on shareholders and customers for which firms should aim. To illustrate our case, we examine two examples from the computer industry: one a major organization, the other a small software publishing business.

Strategic downsizing versus layoffs

The difference between downsizing and layoffs is a reflection of the operating environment in which each might occur and the way in which each is handled. The common overt effect of each is a net reduction in headcount and usually a net labour cost reduction. The covert aspects are more critical to the strategic well-being of the company and will ultimately determine its long-run profitability, quality of service/product, and employee satisfaction levels. Downsizing offers a host of strategic opportunities to an organization, whereas layoffs often result in negative long-term effects. These differences and the covert aspects of headcount reduction will be discussed at each stage of the article and culminate in a strategic comparison of the two.

Strategic downsizing can happen during growth as well as decline, whereas layoffs are a function of decline.[1] Reducing headcount is one of the objectives of both functions, but the way each is achieved is distinctly different. Downsizing has the additional dimension that it plans for the future, whereas a layoff is usually an immediate remedy for an immediate problem.

Reducing labour cost need not involve reducing headcount, as shown by those organizations which have reduced work hours and pay rates (such as Ford[2]). The tools available to management for use in layoff situations are limited to those shown in Table 1: Comparison of the focus and organizational effect of downsizing and layoff tools, while managers using well-planned strategic downsizing techniques have many more options. Downsizing is also more powerful in changing organizational culture and can be implemented as quickly as layoffs, provided the appropriate prior planning has been carried out (cited in[3]). IBM's experience has shown that proper planning in preparation for downsizing can mean flexibility with regard to the timing of its implementation. IBM UK planned to reduce staff over an 18-month period but, in fact, accelerated it to eight months in response to worsening economic performance, while still maintaining its downsizing objectives without resorting to laying off.[4] Downsizing is also a surgical elimination of redundant work processes, while layoffs are typically instigated across the board for *short-term* benefits. Train's example of UPC in a case analysis gives rise to this judgement through Emmanuel Kampouris' commentary. Kampouris goes on to say that, if management can downsize by "stripping away all the non-value adding activities", it will be better off than if it merely laid off across the board, as was the original directive from the CEO to his general manager.[5]

Tool	Downsizing/Layoff	Organizational Effect
Focus — Headcount reduction		
Natural attrition	Downsizing/Layoff	Reduce headcount
Early retirement		Cost reduction
Support start-ups		Initiate cultural transition
Redundancy		Short- or long-term focus
Focus — Cost reduction/Avoid layoffs		
Reduced pay	Downsizing	Cost reduction
Reduced hours		Initiate cultural transition
Redeployment		Short- or long-term focus
Focus — Organizational redesign		
Eliminate functions	Downsizing/Layoff	Cost reduction
Unit rationalization		Long-term focus
Flatten hierarchy		Reduce headcount
		Productivity focused
Focus — Organizational redesign		
Job sharing	Downsizing	Team building
Alter work methods		Productivity focused
Flexible work practices		1-2 years time frame
Focus — Culture change		
Retraining	Downsizing	Team building
Reskilling		Productivity focused
Shift in responsibility		Long-term focus
Continuous improvement		Short/long-term time frame
Continuous downsizing (rightsizing)		

Table 1. Comparison of the Focus and Organizational Effect of Downsizing and Layoff Tools

Why downsize?

Interestingly, Cameron *et al.* find that the most effective downsizing strategies were across the board vertically (through all levels) yet selective for the *long-term* benefit. They state that one of the companies in their survey even considered that downsizing could directly lead to rising employment in the company, as efficiency gains were realized when non-productive job functions were eliminated.[1]

We believe that the driving force in downsizing must be part of an overall strategy:

- to position the company for the long term; and
- immediately to raise and maintain the overall productivity per employee.

Our argument is that strategic downsizing will achieve this, while staccato reactive layoffs will not.

There is a natural conflict in the process of strategically downsizing: the short-term remedy versus long-term human resource planning. Reactive moves by companies to ease financial pressures by laying off workers are very familiar, but are these companies thinking strategically? We recognize that these reactive moves are unavoidable when the financial pressures are so great that across-the-board cost-cutting has to include personnel reductions, but would prior strategic considera-tion have provided an alternative for such companies? Possible alternatives might include re-skilling and redeployment. These can be achieved only with a thorough consideration of the future position of the company, so that it can adjust or "downsize", before it has no option but to "lay off".

However, Faltermayer[2] questions whether some of the notable layoffs of recent times were even necessary (e.g. Ford Motor Co. in the early 1980s). He quotes Frank Popoff, CEO of Dow Chemical, as stating "Layoffs are horribly expensive and destructive of shareholder value". Along with Dow, Ford and 3M turned in high losses in recent times, but shunned using layoffs as a tool for reducing cost, citing as their reasons: skill loss, high cost of rehire, and survivor trauma. Instead they looked to reduced pay, reduced work hours, early retirement and being lean to start with. In Ford's case, it kept recent dismissals to a minimum, having remained slim after the plant closures and redundancies of the early 1980s.

A recent report released by Deloitte Touche Tohmatsu's Human Resources Group (July, 1993) shows that in New Zealand the "main impetus for downsizing has been the desire to save on costs, with other motivations being changes sought in the company's direction or culture, and the need to adjust to reduced demand for products or services".[3] The key word here is adjust, which indicates that there is advance thought leading to the downsizing decision.

Deciding to downsize

We turn now to the issues that should be taken into account before making the decision to downsize. The following checklist forms the basis of the planning phase, discussed later, but is also essential to highlight areas that influence the original decision. Issues to consider when deciding to downsize include:

- Define and analyse the company's competitive position (effect on company's strategy, culture, stakeholders).
- Determine the appropriate workforce structure to sustain competitive position
- Conduct a skills needs analysis.
- Match existing skills of workforce to skills needed.
- Evaluate current HRM practices.
- Identify critical HR areas of concern.
- Determine alternatives to address critical HR issues (for example, training, redeployment, multi-skilling, layoffs, downsizing, freezing recruitment, performance management, etc.).
- Consider positive and negative effects of the alternatives (including planning and implementation issues, and costs and benefits).

The need to downsize should be an outcome of management's planning for the optimal utilization of its human resources. Indeed, after careful consideration of all alternatives available to achieve this objective, a company might well decide not to downsize but to opt for a more appropriate course of action.

Once a company's competitive position has been analysed and defined, the most appropriate structure for its workforce can be determined to strengthen or defend that competitive position. Once that structure is defined by management, the shift from what the structure is now, to what it needs to be, can be considered. Defining how the shift is to occur and how long it is to take must be part of the overall corporate strategy. This entails employing, not vague long-term planning, but specific targetable measures of change. As Imberman states, "...unless the starting point of this [downsizing] journey is identified with great precision, and unless things are being done right today, using a five-year plan as a map to the Promised Land will lead only to limbo".[6]

Efficiencies achieved in other corporate functions such as operations management may have changed the number of tasks required to complete a job and therefore may have reduced the number of required labour units. A more flexible, multi-skilled workforce, which the current skill base may not reflect, might be needed and could induce the need for downsizing as a complementary strategy. The need to downsize is not always obvious to those companies for whom the need is greatest. Industries with a high content of labour in their product costings will be more thoroughly aware of the impact of low productivity on their competitive position than will those which have a lower labour content. Manufacturers build cost systems around "labour dollars" and, depending on union involvement, can remain flexible to their labour requirements by utilizing part-time workers.

However, businesses with high proportions of professional personnel and high material costs might not easily be able to identify the inefficiencies or causes of low productivity other than in terms of overall employee performance. This is especially true of young companies that have known only rapid growth. Some of these companies find it difficult to rightsize their workforce in tune with their strategic labour requirements and, in a recession, look to remain competitive through alternate means of cost reduction or productivity improvement, which may not be as strategically effective as downsizing. In David Enfield's words, "Any company considering downsizing as a solution to its strategic concerns should first think through what its strategic concerns are and then fit downsizing into that context".[5]

The reasons for downsizing need to be clearly defined by management. The process must be integrated with the company's strategic plans, culture and other corporate functions: finance, operations and especially marketing (with its customer knowledge). The company's objectives and goals, both long term and short term, must determine the structure of the workforce required. The process cannot be driven by short-term cost-cutting needs, unless the existence of the company is threatened. In this case, the company is in survival mode and the most likely outcome will be expensive layoffs. Implicit in the recommended sequence is the principle that management should not allow the business to get into the position of having to defend its competitive edge through layoffs.

Using the checklist above will assist a company in its strategic endeavours. The final issue in this checklist, namely a consideration of the positive and negative effects of the alternatives identified, and particularly of downsizing, is extremely important and is discussed as follows.

The effects of downsizing — good and bad

Stayers versus survivors

If the planners and implementers of the downsizing exercise have not considered the effects on morale and productivity of those who remain, then the potential positive outcomes may be negated at stage one. The survivors are truly survivors only if the human resource restructure is nothing more than a "layoff", while those who remain after strategic downsizing should be well-informed "stayers". Whereas survivors breathe a sigh of relief (one that can last for months) and assume the air of pallbearers in mourning, stayers take up their evolving roles with a sense of purpose and acknowledge that they *have been chosen* to "stay" rather than be *asked to* "leave".

Managerial survivor sickness

"As corporations restructure, they are forcing managers through one of the most harrowing stress tests in business history".[7] The possible effects of downsizing on the remaining line managers, senior staff and other executives are commonly not considered when deciding to downsize. Recent evidence[7] clearly illustrates that surviving managers report survivor sickness symptoms as varied as lethargy, feelings of emptiness, little job satisfaction, decreasing levels of creativity, questioning the value of tasks, guilt, harder working, fatigue, resentment, moroseness, extreme cautiousness, and contempt. The result is that organizations frequently have to contend with key staff members not working at optimal levels, with negative effects not only on productivity but also on employee morale, loyalty and commitment.

Being aware of the likelihood of, and the problems accompanying, managerial survivor sickness can assist those involved in the decision-making process to plan accordingly. Indeed, the costs associated with the problems might well exceed the benefits of the downsizing strategy in the long term should appropriate programmes not be put in place to support surviving managers.

Skills analysis preventing skill loss

If the downsize includes a request for applications from those who wish to leave, then there is a threat that the organization may lose some of those skills which it should retain in the new structure. The corporate strategy that leads to a decision to downsize should include a skills needs analysis which should in turn be followed by a review of the staff who have the critical skills. Once those key personnel have been identified, they can be encouraged not to leave. Their loss to rival companies must be prevented and appropriate incentives to ensure their retention need to be in place. This reflects the need for an effective appraisal system to be able to identify those with the desired skills and those who are candidates for

---

Case Study 1: IBM UK Limited

Profits had fallen owing to price reductions in hardware of 25 per cent per year, and the strategic decision was made to reduce the ratio of support workers to front-line workers from 1,22 to 0,53. Labour turnover had dropped from 10 per cent in 1972 to 2 per cent in 1991. This equates to 1 200 departures by choice in 1972 versus 340 in 1991. Headcount reductions of 2 639 (15 per cent) were achieved from a total workforce of 17 548, of which only 2,3 per cent was accounted for by natural labour turnover.

A process was undertaken of preparing generous packages for the early retirers and voluntary redundancies that were adequate enticements but did not encourage essential skill holders to apply. Communication was started early by briefing the top 159 managers and providing them with cascade materials.

Spin-off businesses were started for young employees who could then sub-contract back to IBM as required, and develop their own customer base.

The personnel group provided leadership and planning, but the whole exercise was carried out by line management working in concert with finance and other support departments.

Age, sex and skill profiling were used to ensure that the company retained the desired workforce profile.

The cost averaged two years' pay per person removed, but the removal of managers earning over £40 000, plus benefits, added another 37 per cent to the cost. The recovery period was expected to be 18-20 months.

The company maintained its image of "no redundancy" by providing appropriate incentives to encourage people to apply to leave. Only some staff with essential skills were actively denied the package.

---

departure. IBM UK had such a system and was able to identify those people who should go or stay[4] (see Case Study 1). IBM found that the effect on morale of those who were refused redundancy application was negligible, presumably because the retention compensation was negotiated to ensure satisfaction.

It is beyond the scope of this article to stipulate what an appropriate appraisal system is, but for downsizing purposes it must be one that answers the question: Which staff have the skills we require for the future structure and strategy of the company? The issue of who is in control of the process, and who should implement it, is discussed in a separate section below.

The costs of downsizing and compensation

A recent survey of some of America's largest companies, which suffered losses in 1991, showed that they all shunned layoffs because of their cost.[8] The overriding conclusion was that the companies had learned from their prior layoff experiences and were better advised to stay lean through the recovery periods. This gives strength to the view that management should not allow a company actually to get to the position of having to downsize, but should rather maintain a rightsizing strategy. In most circumstances, the cost of rightsizing will be less than the cost of downsizing.

The nature of the business cycle may determine the type of human resource management practices being followed. Those companies in a prosperous phase may foster human resource policies that do not focus on productivity and efficiency. This in turn can make the company sluggish and ill-prepared to face the demands of any ensuing decline phase. This reinforces the point that downsizing can be planned for and that, if the organization is kept lean during the good times, it will be better positioned to adapt quickly to downward trends in its markets, which is preferable to having to downsize. This is the concept of rightsizing.

Frenkel and Shaw's case analysis of the Value Hotel chain[9] showed that an uncontrolled and *ad hoc* recruitment policy resulted in overstaffing and the inability to control morale and productivity as a recession hit. Management had not defined long-term, or even medium-term, human resource needs, and had been operating several hotels from a stand-off corporate position with little idea of the operations or customer base of each. The result was an inefficient operation faced with financial constraints that required major surgery to the workforce. Motivation hit a low and central control was lost. Retention of skilled staff dropped and the overriding moral of the case was the necessity to combine the human resource function with both operations and finance, in considering the company's exposure in the event of the market turning sour – which it did.

Fieldman and Leana observed that treatment of blue- and white-collar workers differed on two sites they investigated. Blue-collars were given longer notice while white-collar workers received higher payouts.[10] The logic behind this was that the white-collar workers probably had access to sensitive information and therefore had to be denied further access – which limited their immediate productivity. Therefore, they went quickly but were compensated accordingly. In New Zealand, longer notice is becoming an accepted means of compensation in lieu of short notice and high payout. This practice adds credibility to management's position and is indicative of a cost-effective and more compassionate approach to redundancy.

The following phase in our strategic downsizing model highlights the crucial importance of thorough planning to avoid the downside of the downsize.

Planning the downsize

A checklist of criteria is provided here that should be considered before strategic downsizing occurs, in order to minimize dissatisfaction among those who leave and those who remain with the organization. Issues to consider when planning the downsize include:

- What is the focus of the downsizing strategy?
- What tools should be used?
- Who should implement/manage the downsizing process?
- What compensation will leavers receive and when will they receive it?
- What supportive programmes will be put in place for leavers?
- What supportive programmes will be put in place for stayers at *ALL* levels?
- To what extent will employee representatives be involved in the planning process?
- What information should be divulged to stakeholders?
- When should information be divulged to stakeholders?
- How are the leavers to be identified?
- When should the leavers go?
- How and when should the leavers be advised?
- How and when will the stayers' jobs be reorganized to reflect the new structure?
- What training will be necessary and who will conduct it?

What should be appreciated during this planning phase is that the *perceived fairness* of the downsizing strategy and its concomitant *changed work conditions* are paramount in reducing negative feelings in the survivors of any layoff.[11] This precept – that the *process* of downsizing and the changing environment will critically affect the stayers and should deliberately be planned for – is central to what follows.

Procedural justice and fairness

Not only must the process of redeployment or redundancy actually be fair, it must be seen to be fair. It is not simply a legal requirement to satisfy those who leave (be fair), but the process is also a potential source of motivation for the stayers (be seen to be fair).

Exactly how the leavers were notified has a bearing on morale following the downsize. In organizations in which continued contact between the stayers and leavers is likely, either socially or professionally, the method of advising the leavers will be known to all. Letters mailed out to all employees, following a meeting to announce layoffs, with either a "stay at home" or "come to work" notice, do nothing for morale. This method is typical of those businesses not strategically downsizing but simply taking the least effort, hard-hit approach to workforce reduction. Examples of this in New Zealand include Beaminc, with its removal of the entire corporate office, and Coverbolt Industries' wholesale downscaling of employees and management. Both these companies faced severe financial pressures, but, having created the new structures, are now moving forward in the development of their staff within these structures – taking care not to let the excesses of the past catch up with them again.

During downsizing, there should be other measures of cost reduction simultaneously in place to lend credibility to the overall cost reduction strategy. Stayers are more likely to perceive the downsize as being "fair" if they feel that the staff reduction was not the only means employed to reduce costs.[8] If the downsize is driven by technological change or changing market conditions, such as international competition in a deregulating market, then expenditure may be occurring in other areas at the apparent expense of human resources. If the reasons for the shift in expenditure and associated staff reductions are not transparent to the workforce prior to implementing the downsize, then a sense of injustice may be felt by the stayers.

Focuses and tools of a downsizing strategy

There are four key focuses of a downsizing strategy: headcount reduction, cost reduction, organizational redesign and culture change. The model set out in Table 1: Comparison of the focus and organizational effect of downsizing and layoff tools, incorporates the appropriate tools for each focus. Each focus can complement the overall strategy, depending on the characteristics of that strategy. Table 1: Comparison of the focus and organizational effect of downsizing and layoff tools, also indicates the difference between downsizing and layoff options. These focuses are not mutually exclusive, but rather dictate the process of downsizing and the strategy required. Some or all can be implemented, depending on the pressure to reform and the timeframe dictated by the corporate strategy.

Along with planning, communication and investment in retained staff, speed of implementation will greatly contribute to the effectiveness of the downsize. This, along with the evidence from companies such as IBM, implies that while clear timeframes need to be set, they must also be flexible enough to meet the short-term requirements of the company, should the process have to be hastened. With the advent of radical re-engineering and a greater focus on innovative change, while the overall strategy can dictate rapid periods of change and job elimination, it cannot sacrifice employee commitment to continuous improvement and process evolution. Cameron *et al.* found that the most successful downsizers implemented a variety of downsizing strategies, focusing on immediate measurable changes in productivity and unmeasurable changes in the way activities were carried out.[1]

There are several ways of implementing each strategy, and these are listed under "Tools" in column one of Table 1: Comparison of the focus and organizational effect of downsizing and layoff tools . Only those within the company can make this choice, because they are the ones who know the workforce and the shape of the industry. The objective should be to reduce the headcount with the smallest number of enforced redundancies (and enforced retentions for that matter), in order to raise per head productivity.

Who should initiate and manage the downsize — HR manager or line management?

The extent of involvement of a personnel department will depend on the size of the company and where the key information is held – with line management or with the personnel department. The process needs to be owned by one of the members of the overall strategy planning team, in order to give the downsize credibility. This person should drive the process while the line managers should be accountable for implementation. Ideally, this same person would have been responsible for the skills needs analysis. With regard to layoffs in New Zealand companies, this person has typically been the CEO. Two other examples include

Paul Allaire of Xerox Corporation, who pushed down the change to line management, but retained ownership himself,[12] and Sir Leonard Peach, who, as HR director, drove the process but assisted line management in implementing the IBM UK downsize.

The variety of organizational structures and differing attitudes towards the role of personnel departments and HR managers indicates that there is no universal method for determining who should run and implement the process. A guiding precept, however, is that responsibility for driving the process must remain as high as possible in the organization. The implementation must be left to those line managers who have to live with the stayers and who best know the employees and their jobs.

Communication

Effective communication with all employees before, during and after the downsize will help to reduce its negative effects by fostering a sense of opportunity rather than relief. Communication should include credible notice of the need for the downsize and of the fact that it is the result of considered, far-sighted planning rather than the result of "managerial greed or incompetence"[13] – i.e. without the downsize the organization will not survive.[5] Where possible, all employees should be given considerable advance notice in order to achieve co-operative behaviour and maintain productivity.[1] Being the first in an industry to downsize does not help promote perceived fairness unless the focus of the communication is to emphasize that the initiative is aimed at maintaining or improving the organization's competitive position.

Wood describes a two-tier process in communicating the information to district managers in the National and Provincial Building Society.[14] First, the district managers were actively involved in a general discussion aimed at assessing performance, perception, consensus and consultation. The second stage was a private interview establishing buy-in for those who would remain and options for those who would leave. As discussed earlier, achieving the buy-in of employees earlier rather than later can provide constructive methods of reducing the headcount while ensuring that those who remain are motivated and productive.

The payoffs of advance notice and transparent communication are twofold. First, the stayers will feel that the leavers were given appropriate time to find new employment, and therefore they are less likely to suffer "survivor guilt". Second, the productivity of those who are leaving does not drop off as quickly as might be expected with less notice.[1,13]

Market signals and advance notice

A possible downside to advance notice is that the signals sent to the market may not be beneficial to the company. Ginter *et al.* discuss the effect of acquisition on a company and liken it to the death phase of an organization's life-cycle.[15] The restructure of an organization after a merger or acquisition will often involve a degree of downsizing because of role duplication, cost-elimination or asset stripping. In these instances, the need to protect the public image of the company may forbid transparent communication to the employees in order to maximize the return (or minimize the cost) to the shareholders. While management are aware of the impending consequences for some employees, they are not able to give advance notice of those consequences, because the market will hear the "noise" created and the share value may be affected. (The reverse of this, of course, occurs when the market reacts very favourably to attempts to eliminate cost. In these cases, an early signal of the intention to downsize might well have a positive effect on share price.)

While the article by Ginter *et al.* highlights the negative aspects of a merger without constructive advice, Marks and Mirvis provide constructive post-merger advice on how to build up new teams in an environment of some mistrust and scepticism.[8] These can be difficult circumstances but ones that typify management's paradox when confronted with shareholder/employee compromises. Senior managers' own positions may be threatened if the takeover is hostile, further magnifying their personal dilemmas. This is not to suggest that management should ever take its strategic eye off the shareholder in favour of the employee, but that it should assess the potential for damage through alienating either party, and then act accordingly.

It should be noted that there was very favourable reaction from share market investors and analysts when Telecom New Zealand's CEO, Dr Deane, announced redundancies. The National Business Review stated: "The sharemarket gave both thumbs up to the news that staff would be reduced by 5 200 to a wafer thin, highly efficient, 7 500 over four years ...".[16,17] Telecom's action and the reception from the market also serve to highlight the distinction between downsizing action and layoff effect, because Telecom:

- was in a growth phase, not a survival situation;
- had planned the downsize to flow over a four-year period, not an immediate addition of 5 200 to the dole queue;
- was using the tools available to the strategic downsizer that cannot be used in layoff situations:
- planned early retirement, job sharing, reduced hours;
- had recently achieved higher levels of service and profitability, to the benefit of the customer and the shareholder, respectively; and
- was using downsizing as part of its overall corporate strategy, not a "quick fix" short-term remedy.

But what if employees and management have actually been at odds over issues relating to terms of employment prior to the downsize? This is not an unusual circumstance. Examples include companies in the freezing industry in New Zealand in the late 1980s and early 1990s, when union pressure for higher wages forced layoffs in a subsequent year due to the non-competitiveness created by higher labour costs and inflexible work classifications. Whether this could be deemed "strategic downsizing" is debatable – communication ahead of the termination notices in this instance might simply have been an inducement to down tools and further reduce productivity. It may therefore not be strategic to give advance notice of redundancies to an already partially alienated workforce.

It is also interesting to note the interpretation by the media of IBM's downsizing activity in 1993. Reuters reported a US$2 billion charge against redundancies in 1993 to "... pay for slashing its workforce by almost 50 000 people". A share trader was quoted as saying: "How many times have they done this in the last year?".[18] This underscores how critical is the communication of the process if damaging public reaction is to be avoided. This particular article did not report the pay-back period, nor the potential benefits to IBM's competitive position.

Changing work conditions

A proper analysis of the skills needed in the restructured organization will generate job specifications, against which existing employees can be matched. By way of contrast, let us consider the effects of a typical unplanned layoff scenario. In the absence of time to prepare a job needs analysis, the survivors are left carrying the workloads of their ex-colleagues. Specialist skills may have "walked out the door" and tasks that used to take short periods might now take much longer as those recently made responsible for them discover how they should be carried out.

The alternative for the overworked and undertrained employee is not to do the extra work. Before long, a frustration escalation spiral begins. If the need for the layoffs was to reduce cost in order to survive, then the objective must have been to raise the productivity of those who remained. The result, in the face of lowered morale and higher workload, is that more work is done less well by fewer staff. It is likely that the customer will be seriously affected and business could be lost unless all other competitors are facing similar circumstances[19] (the InfoLight Case Study provides an illustration).

The only potential upside in this situation is that short-term gains might be achieved if there is a threat that even the survivors' jobs are under scrutiny. Coercion then becomes the driving force. Often this is acceptable in smaller companies where management "lay it on the line" and the need for the layoffs can be credibly attributed to factors outside management's control – including larger players entering the market or general economic decline. Not surprisingly, a little insecurity can keep a workforce on its toes. The central point, however, is that, if the influencing factors can be forecast (i.e. management can be seen to have made the best attempt rather than ignoring the signals and hoping for the best), then there is an alternative to sudden layoff – strategic downsizing.

Motivation

Changes in sources of employee motivation go hand in hand with changes in the nature of the job. If work burdens increase without relative increases in compensation, resentment towards the more for less attitude can reasonably be expected to rise. Intrinsic motivation may evaporate, especially for middle management, who may have found their autonomy reduced. This occurs when there has been an overall downgrading of positions, effecting not only a salary or wage reduction but a responsibility demotion as well. The process of bumping, whereby senior personnel are put into what was their subordinates' role, reduces incentive and affects the individual's career path. Proper skills analysis will identify those whom the organization really cannot support and develop, and who would be insulted if offered a lower position.

The temptation to offer such a position (out of perceived loyalty) in a tight labour market may be more attractive than the hard task of counselling the person who

Case Study 2 — InfoLight International Limited

InfoLight grew through the 1980s from a start up partnership of two to a company of 200. Its selling, product support and service skills were the key success factors for this company and the ones that gave it a competitive edge in a developing industry. However, as its key software product became a commodity, the company was forced to reduce price and increase service levels. Cost reduction was sought by utilizing alternative channels of distribution and forcing down production costs of the printed materials.

Throughout this period, the company maintained a "no redundancy" policy for the personnel who had been with the company the longest (an admirable policy v loyalty). The most recently recruited employees were made redundant as a last resort and existing employees assumed new and lower level tasks to fill the gaps. Strategically, this was not sound. Management subsequently admitted that they should have downsized the workforce and removed the "old faithfuls" who could not cope with the rapid growth of the company. Had they done so, InfoLight today might be in a more competitive position than its current one, which sees it suffering from the effects of previous management and proprietor actions.

Manuals are being returned when they fall apart after six months. This keeps the customer service department busy reissuing them. The company is laying off as it consolidates with its US parent. The process has been given the name of "rationalization" but in fact resembles "death throes". Morale is currently low because communication of any strategy is poor and staff do not know who will be next, but the least productive employees are now being made redundant.

In short, during its period of rapid growth, the company had not given consideration to the skills needed to position it for the future. The technology outgrew the original partners and they did not shape the workforce by taking on the right skills at the right time. InfoLight is now reduced to bundling its product with other packages in "own name" parcels in order to remain competitive.

It is an example of a company which needed to downsize strategically at the start of the decline in its industry but which, on recognising the warning signals, elected to cut costs rather than aim to raise productivity.

really has to go. This serves neither party well and the strategic downsizer will have considered the outplacement services needed to support such an individual. Appeasing the manager's conscience at the expense of the employee's career development is not a strategic solution. Instead it defers the departure to a later date and can seriously damage the self-esteem of the demoted employee. However, mitigating strategic circumstances might include the opportunity for the employee to learn a wider variety of tasks while taking a pay cut, with the proviso that the appropriate benefits will be gained when the business turns around, if in fact the downsize is due to market conditions.

Imberman defines three basic tasks that "need to be done" to revitalize managers after a white-collar downsizing.[6]. Step 3 of the process involves retraining in order to allow the overburdened remaining managers to cope with their new roles. He emphasizes training in risk taking and accepting responsibility in the newly restructured and slimmed down organization. The primary objective is to retain and increase motivation to improve productivity. Because the downsizing strategy should be an integral part of the corporate strategy, it is possible to implement other motivation schemes at the time of the downsize. Some companies, for example, combine the downsize with quality award presentations in a "Build with pride week" activity.[1]

Consistency with culture

Organizations such as Lincoln Electric have a "full employment" culture that has ensured redeployment of employees whose job functions have been eliminated. This promotes a "recruitment from within" focus which may be compromised if the current corporate strategy equates downsizing with redundancy. A company can successfully and significantly downsize in line with strategic needs, without seriously compromising a full employment culture. Forward planning allows the use of natural attrition, early retirement and voluntary redundancy (with appropriate incentives) to take care of staff reductions. Other companies see changes in numbers and skill sets as a way to change the culture, especially if it includes major changes to middle and upper management. These companies, however, may then have to deal with the survivors' stronger feelings of unfairness.

Other issues of culture influence the decision criteria used -- last in first out, seniority, across the board versus selective, or divisional based on a unit's profitability. If a company is known to be an aggressive manager of staff, primarily looking to individual profit performance as a reason for retaining staff, then it would be no surprise to employees if consistently poor performances resulted in layoffs or redeployment. An example of this might be the financial services sector, in which dealer positions require high performance to achieve good results.

Employee involvement

Employee involvement is one of the best recipes for gaining employee commitment. Cameron *et al.* found that if employees believed that:

* the downsize was necessary for survival;
* personal employment was guaranteed for a certain period of time; and
* managers could be trusted and would be fair,

then employees were the most adept at finding ways to eliminate the fat and improve efficiency and would plan ways to implement the necessary changes.[1] The analysis process was shown to be bottom-up, while the top-down contribution was: motivation, mandate, and monitoring to help implement it. In New Zealand, the CEO of Coverbolt had shopfloor employees asking him what took so long to make the workforce reductions in non-productive areas. The employees were actively involved in advocating the staff reductions.

Implementation and evaluation

By considering all the influencing factors on the decision and plan to downsize, management should have already formed a framework for its implementation which complements the corporate strategy. In evaluating after the downsize, management must ask: "Have we achieved the structure required? Has the required structure changed since we started?" If the answer to the second question is "yes", then: "Are we flexible enough to cope with the change?" If not, then management needs to review the implementation and adapt the strategy. Downsizing is not, however, a reiterative business operation. If it has not achieved a radical change in the way a business operates, then it was not well constructed or was unnecessary in the first place. Alternatively, it may not have been radical enough. An attempt to make a downsizing process effective through a "second bite" is almost certainly doomed to failure.

Conclusion

The objective of downsizing should be to raise productivity per head. Strategic downsizing can achieve this -- layoffs cannot. It is possible to plan to reduce a workforce. In the absence of severe financial and environmental factors, which usually dictate an immediate layoff, downsizing can be carried out with the full commitment of the workforce to the long-term benefit of the company.

The key areas in the implementation are communication, employee involvement and proper preparation. If the downsize is to be successful and strengthen the company's competitive position, it must succeed first time in order to gain credibility with customers, suppliers, investors and, most importantly, the stayers.

References

1. Cameron, K.S., Freeman, S.J. and Mishra, A.K., "Best practices in white-collar downsizing: managing contradictions", *Academy of Management Executive*, Vol. 5 No. 3 , 1991, pp. 57-73.
2. Faltermayer, E., "Is this layoff necessary?"'. *Fortune*, 1 June 1992, pp. 53-63.
3. Forsythe, S., "Report on downsizing in New Zealand", *Otago Daily Times*, 6 July 1993.
4. Peach, L., "Parting by mutual agreement: IBM's transition to manpower cuts". *Personnel Management*, Vol. 24 No. 3, 1992, pp. 40-3.
5. Train, A.S., "The case of the downsizing decision", *Harvard Business Review* , Vol. 69 No. 2, 1991, pp. 14-30.
6. Imberman, W., " Managers and downsizing", *Business Horizons*, Vol. 32 No. 5, 1989, pp. 28-33
7. Smith, L,, "Burned-out bosses". *Fortune*, 25 July, 1994, pp. 108-13.
8. Marks, M. and Mirvis, P. , "Rebuilding after the merger: dealing with survivor sickness", *Organizational Dynamics*, Vol. 21 No. 2, 1992, pp. 18-32.
9. Frenkel, S. and Shaw, M. , "Employee relations and organizational growth and decline: a case study". *Journal of Industrial Relations* , Vol. 33, 1991, pp. 196-219.
10. Fieldman, D. and Leana, C. , "Managing layoffs: experiences at the Challenger disaster site and the Pittsburgh steel mills", *Organizational Dynamics*, Vol. 18, 1989, pp. 52-64.
11. Brockner, J., " Managing the effects of layoffs on survivors", *California Management Review*, Vol. 34 No. 2 , 1992, pp. 9-28.
12. Howard, R., "The CEO as organizational architect: an interview with PaulAllaire ", *Harvard Business Review*, Vol. 70 No. 5, 1992, pp. 107-21.
13. Brockner, J., Tyler, T. and Cooper-Schneider, R., "The influence of prior commitment to an institution on reactions to perceived unfairness: the higher they are the harder they fall", *Administrative Science Quarterly*, Vol. 37, 1992, pp. 241-61.
14. Wood, J., "How organizations can survive redundancy", *Personnel Management*, Vol. 22, 1990, pp. 38-41.
15. Ginter, P.M., Duncan, W.J. , Swayne, L.E. and Shelter, A.G., " When merger means death: organizational euthanasia and strategic choice ", *Organizational Dynamics*, Vol. 20 No. 3, 1992, pp. 21-33.
16. Ferdinand, F., " Telecom puts away rainy day profits as staff get drenched", *National Business Review*. 19 February 1993 , p. 4.

17. Brettkelly, S., " Telecom staff cuts costly, claims clear", *National Business Review*, 5 March 1993, p. 3.
18. *Otago Daily Times*, 14 July 1993, p 18.
19. McKinley, W., " Decreasing organizational size: to untangle or not to untangle? ", Academy of *Management Review*, Vol. 17, 1992, pp. 112-23.

Competence and Strategic Paradox

By *John L. Thompson*, University of Huddersfield, Huddersfield, UK
From *Management Decision* 36/4, 1998, pp. 274-284, © MCB University Press Ltd
1998. Reprinted with permission.

Looking at organizational decision and choices in the 1990s, it is tempting to conclude that we live in an era of focus and downsizing. The time of the conglomerate has passed. Downsizing can always be justified to improve efficiency, but only if it is really rightsizing to prepare a strong base for renewed growth. Focus, however, is a reflection of the way many organizations are choosing to deal with a series of issues they face, for which there are no black and white, right and wrong answers, and all of which interact with each other systematically. Moreover, focus is fashionable and diversity is not. This paper uses these often paradoxical issues to examine the complexity of strategy and explain why the search for winning strategic positions comprises a series of inter-dependent choices.

Introduction

It is certainly possible to argue that we do not know how to run our companies. If we did, fewer of them would go bust! Clearly some do succeed, grow and prosper; others survive but no more; and a fair number fail every year. Genuine failure may well end up in liquidation; relative failure or under-achievement can be overcome with new management and a new approach – or a new owner. Few organizations, then, can succeed without change – both continuous and gradual improvement and periodic major changes of strategy, structure and/or style. None will succeed without understanding – and satisfying – their markets, almost certainly in dynamic and changing circumstances.

From time to time new fads become popular and organizations everywhere take them on board. New gurus offer new solutions. Total quality management in the 1980s is one example; business process re-engineering in the 1990s is another. Valuable as these can be, they help at best. They are only partial solutions. Similarly, benchmarking both competitors and good or best practice anywhere, can be truly useful. It always has been. However, finding out what others do is only the start; the payoff comes from the learning and the actions which follow.

This paper builds on several earlier papers by the author, in particular arguments in Thompson and Richardson (1996). Here it was proposed that strategic success is dependent on an appropriate mix of strategic competences, a mix which is particular to an individual company and a mix which changes in a dynamic environment. Content competences are required for corporate and competitive success at any time; to sustain this success, change management competences must support the content; in turn, to understand success and the need to change, the organization needs competence in awareness and learning. Finding, changing and sustaining an effective competence mix is a key role of the strategic leader.

The discussion in this paper is built around the popular focus-diversification debate, a key manifestation of corporate strategy and content competence. This debate reflects our tendency often to think more about the "what" of strategy as opposed to the "how". Strategy is really about thinking and about creatively finding new positions and new opportunities for adding value. A particular strategic choice will succeed for some organizations but not for others. Understanding why this is, and the wider strategic position, is essential.

Strategic leadership and strategy

Figure 1 develops ideas in Kets de Vries (1996) where he argues that effective leaders perform charismatic and architectural roles to ensure the organization has a clear and understood vision and direction, supported by an appropriate organization structure and management control and reward systems, to ensure that employees are empowered and committed. In this way all key stakeholders can be satisfied. To achieve this – and in turn to establish the necessary strategic competences for the organization – choices have to be made along a number of dimensions. In this paper we explore these dimensions, which we present as a series of issues or dilemmas, each of which impacts on the others in a systemic, holistic way. We argue that strategy is the key to an organization's competitiveness, future and prosperity. By this we really mean strategic competence – translated into an ability to think and behave strategically with all that this implies for the corporate activity portfolio, the essential competitive advantage for each product and service, and organization structures and styles through which new strategic ideas are created and implemented.

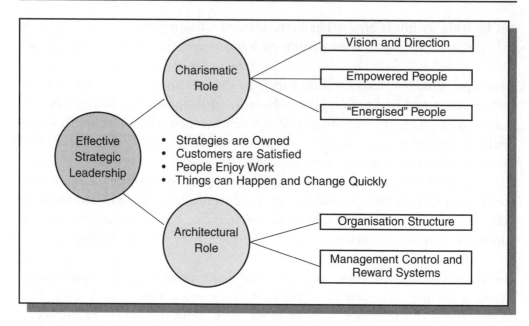

Figure 1. Effective Strategic Leadership

Strategy is about choices: choosing what to do and what not to do. Choosing strategies, both corporate and competitive, and choosing the ways in which they are to be implemented. When company performance deteriorates, changes to strategies, structures and/or management styles can be anticipated. However, it is equally important for currently successful companies to introduce changes while they are still successful and before environmental and competitive changes force them into a reactive mode. The interventions and changes may, and indeed should, be thought through carefully, be timely, appropriate, feasible and desirable. This relies on a clear understanding of the situation, appreciating where and why an organization is currently doing well or badly. It requires a clear understanding of which strategic competences really make a difference. As we have said, we may not know this. Consequently the "choice" may simply be an adoption of the latest idea or fad. It may be no more than a switch of emphasis on a single dimension:

> On some topics, management fashion swings like a pendulum: between centralization and decentralization, outsourcing and insourcing, focus and spread. Conglomerates have been out of fashion for years. It is therefore a fair bet that they are coming back (*Financial Times*, 28 August 1997).

When this happens we may not be concentrating on the issues which really matter and actually are in need of change. Moreover we may change one element and fail to consider the implications of this change on other issues – such that the overall situation deteriorates rather than improves. Peters and Waterman (1982) commented that any intelligent approach to organizing has seven features ... namely strategy, structure, systems, staff, skills, style and shared values (culture). These all interact holistically. Success clearly depends on a mix of factors, not just one.

Strategy, then, is not an exact science. There are no clear and definitive answers to the questions: what should an organization be doing and how should it be managing its activities? These are issues of judgement. Some organizations succeed with a particular strategy and approach; others which pursue the same strategy and approach fail. Grant (1997), for example, has shown how the leading oil companies have become successful and powerful by concentrating on different key competences, not the same ones. Exxon is highly skilled at financial management, BP at new field exploration and development, Mobil at refining and lubricants, and Royal Dutch Shell at managing a decentralized global empire with headquarters in two countries.

Simply copying observable practices from successful organizations is not the answer as all businesses face unique circumstances. Nevertheless we certainly can learn from the success and failure of various organizations.

Strategic growth and change

Hurst (1995) has shown how new organizations, especially those that are truly entrepreneurial, begin with a clear vision and purpose. Normally the founder will adopt a hands-on, centralized control approach. As the organization grows, the strategy emerges with learning and adaptation. Alongside this, it is desirable if the strategic leader accepts that he/she has to delegate more and more responsibility and introduce decentralization – in order to make decisions and cope with the new demands and complexities. Unfortunately, these necessary changes can make the organization increasingly difficult to co-ordinate and control. Consequently it is typical for structures and roles to then become more and more formalized; when this happens, planning assumes greater significance. There may even be a return to greater centralization. Innovation may now be reduced considerably, and, paradoxically, performance and efficiency are likely to improve. Unfortunately, in a dynamic and competitive environment, this is likely to be short-lived if the organization becomes too dependent on existing paradigms and fails to introduce appropriate changes. Some form of crisis will then force it into

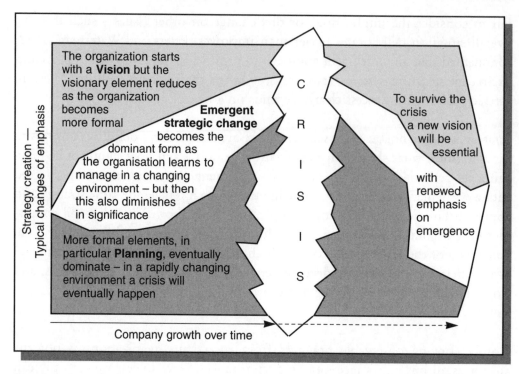

The organization starts with a **Vision** but the visionary element reduces as the organization becomes more formal

Emergent strategic change becomes the dominant form as the organisation learns to manage in a changing environment – but then this also diminishes in significance

More formal elements, in particular **Planning**, eventually dominate – in a rapidly changing environment a crisis will eventually happen

C
R
I
S
I
S

To survive the crisis a new vision will be essential

with renewed emphasis on emergence

Strategy creation – Typical changes of emphasis

Company growth over time

Figure 2. Strategic Change

a reactive mode; and to overcome this, a new vision – supported by innovative emergence – will again be required. This is illustrated in Figure 2.

Hurst further argues that where organizations are in danger of becoming too rigid and change-averse, a crisis should be created forcibly to overcome the inertia and entropy and restore vitality. This could possibly be accomplished by a change of leadership. The challenge for any strategic leader, therefore, is to strike an effective balance between the three elements of strategy creation: vision, emergence (with learning and experience) and planning. If this is achieved, there will be "order" inside the organization but not rigid control that prevents change – both continuous, emergent change and discontinuous change.

Strategic competence

Strategy is the ability of an organization to think and behave strategically. It involves paradigms (perspectives on how and where to compete – as a whole and with respect to every product and service in the activity portfolio), issues of positioning in relation to identifiable competitors and markets, and the ability to change. Positions will change as competing organizations continuously adopt new ploys and tactics in an attempt to steal an advantage, albeit a temporary one. Perspective changes imply discontinuity and a change of paradigm. This can reflect changing customer needs, demands and expectations; equally it can be promoted by truly innovatory breakthroughs which change the rules of competition. Southwest Air, for example, has grown into a very profitable low-cost US airline by being different. It sells all its tickets direct: seats are not pre-assigned; and routes avoid the hub-and-spoke pattern adopted by all the large airlines. Starbucks, which primarily sells premium coffees from small bars, has opened up a new market opportunity for coffee; rival organizations have extended the American market, and the format has been adopted in an increasing number of UK cities.

Simply, organizations must always be able to react to competitive pressures while looking for opportunities to proactively influence or affect their environment. These points are illustrated in Figure 3.

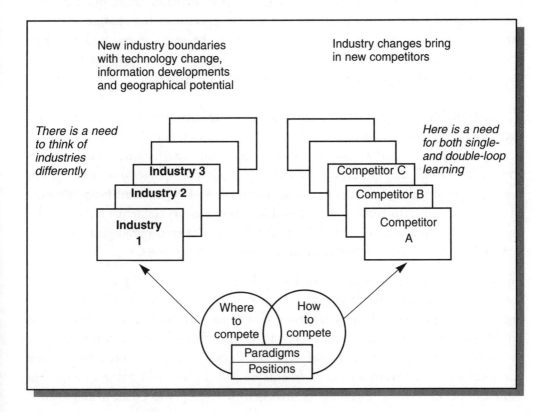

Figure 3. Strategy: Paradigm and Position

Truly strategic organizations are able to embrace innovation and entrepreneurship. They find and exploit manageable opportunities. Visionary leadership – at all levels of management – and flexibility are essential aspects. Planning and analysis provide essential support to the organization's efforts, but for some new ideas, no amount of analysis can predict the ultimate success. Sony's Walkman and the introduction of chilled fresh foods by Marks & Spencer are testimony to this argument. Because the prospects for new ideas are uncertain, and because an organization can never be sure when a rival might introduce an innovatory new development, current success must be seen as temporary. While current success might depend on existing perspectives and paradigms, sustained success depends on an ability to change them. As environments become increasingly global and dynamic, the relative fragility of current success must increase. For these reasons it is essential that organizations see themselves as living systems that must learn and evolve by looking for both opportunities and threats in relation to all the strategic issues they must deal with. Changes in fashions and fads can provide new product and service opportunities – so too can research-led technology developments. New ideas from management gurus or from benchmarking practices and achievements in other organizations can also trigger ideas for change. External threats in the form of competitive changes must always be monitored for their potential impact. Identified internal weaknesses from effective performance measurement systems – can stimulate change to drive improvement.

Unquestionably managing and promoting continuous improvement around existing paradigms (single-loop learning) and discontinuous, double-loop, change to new paradigms, simultaneously, is difficult and challenging. They imply approaches which are culturally different and use knowledge and information bases which are also different (see e.g. Thompson, 1996). Single-loop learning focuses on short-term time horizons and incorporates an element of crisis fighting; double-loop learning demands that existing strategic paradigms are questioned and challenged – possibly creating crises in the process.

There may well be creative tensions. We all know how easy it can be for different generations of a family to clash. Organizations must simultaneously learn by looking backwards (often a behaviour trait of old people), look around for threats (middle-age behaviour) and look forward in a search for new opportunities and the potential to be different (most typical of young people). Time, energy and resources must be invested in experiments and changes which bring quick – but limited – benefits; they must also be invested in attempts to create a new future, with no guarantees of success. Successful athletes have a will to win today, and a

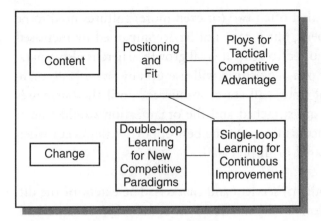

Figure 4. Strategy: Content and Change

will to keep training to prepare for future competition when new standards of performance may be needed.

As we can see in Figure 4, the idea is to manage the change process to establish and sustain an effective fit between the company, its products and services, and its markets and customers. To achieve this it will certainly have to improve and change its strategies. However, changing strategies often implies changes of structure and style. At the same time, changes to structure and style can enhance – or inhibit – the ability of the organization to manage this single- and double-loop change process.

Diversification or focus — a key corporate dilemma

It is now appropriate to look in greater detail at corporate strategic trends in the UK. The emphasis seems to be on "divest unrelated activities; acquire related ones". Restruc-turing to take out costs has been emphasized, but many organizations have simply downsized; they have not rightsized to create an organization with the necessary competences and motivation to stimulate renewal and new growth. In addition, a more recent trend has been share buy-backs, as company after company changes its gearing to make it less vulnerable to shareholder pressure. Really this is an admission that they cannot find desirable growth opportunities where any accumulated cash might be deployed and used for long-term growth and effectiveness.

Acquisition and diversification strategies are frequently linked together. Acquisitions (agreed corporate purchases), takeovers (hostile buys) and mergers (the joining of two organizations) fuel organizational growth and, quite often, the necessary capital is available from the city if the organization does not have sufficient reserves. With such strategies, organizations are likely to be able to grow much more quickly than by investing in organic growth to build existing activities and businesses. While organic growth is always going to be important, there is often a dearth of inspirational ideas.

The downside of acquisitions is that often two (or even more) cultures need to be integrated. Growth in size happens, but it may not be accompanied by increased profitability and the synergy required to generate real growth. There is also a paradox of timing and opportunity. An acquisition will use up any spare cash, managerial expertise and managerial time – all scarce resources. Until the businesses have been integrated, resources are stretched and the organization would find it difficult to deal with a further acquisition. Do the best opportunities occur when the organization is ideally prepared or ill prepared?

Diversification implies new products, services and markets. The extent of the differences imply the diversification is either related in some way, or unrelated. Where new technologies, new skills, new resources, new distribution channels and new markets are all implied, the learning challenge is considerable – together with the inherent uncertainty. But related diversification, perhaps by the acquisition of an existing competitor, can provoke interest from the competition authorities in individual countries or the EC – which can result in it being stopped. Whatever the strategy, in the end its relative success or failure depends on the ability of the managers involved to generate greater returns from the assets, possibly implying restructuring and some asset sales, and certainly requiring that any anticipated synergy is delivered. This in turn demands that too high a price is not paid for the acquisition in the first place.

At different times, different strategies and approaches enjoy greater or lesser favour. Strategies which are popular today may be unfashionable next year; when this happens those pursuing unfashionable strategies are subjected to considerable scrutiny from the media and from analysts.

The systematic cross-border acquisitions of Rowntree and Perrier by Nestle have contributed to the growth of a successful international foods business. There are some links between the products, with opportunities for sharing and learning. This strategic approach continues to be fashionable. Very recently, for example, the Zurich Group (Swiss financial services) has merged with BAT (originally British American Tobacco, which had already diversified into insurance and other financial services). The tobacco interests will subsequently be floated off separately. Similarly Reed Elsevier (joint UK and Netherlands) has merged with the Dutch company Wolters Kluwer to create the world's largest scientific and professional publishing business.

In contrast, in the mid-late 1990s, conglomerate diversification – building a corporation with unrelated acquisitions – is much less fashionable than it was a decade ago. There are strong arguments in favour of this change of popularity, but, nevertheless, it can still be a successful strategy if it is supported with appropriate implementation skills – and it may well become more fashionable again in the future.

To explore this issue in greater detail, we briefly track the strategic development of a number of organizations, including four leading acquisitive UK diversified conglomerates, BTR, Hanson, Williams and Tomkins. At different times all four companies have been very successful, typically using a "hit squad" approach by a small team of turnaround specialists who are expert in evaluating recent acquisitions, setting demanding (financial) targets, rewarding success and dismissing managers who cannot perform. Hanson in particular grew dramatically in the 1980s with this approach and was renowned for its expertize at selling off selected parts of the acquired businesses piecemeal to earn back the purchase price, while still retaining strong, profitable businesses. More recently, however, BTR and Williams have pursued more focused strategies while Tomkins remains truly diversified. Hanson has been broken up. First, several of its American businesses were floated off as US Industries, and then the remaining activities were split into four and shares in each given to existing shareholders. These comprised: Millennium Chemicals, Imperial Tobacco, The Energy Group and Hanson (building materials).

For acquisitive diversifiers such as these, two major challenges are the ability to find and fund a suitable acquisition at the appropriate time and stage of corporate development – as the organization grows, the size of acquisition which will make any real difference also increases – and then finding opportunities to release or add value. Diversified conglomerates have frequently concentrated on mature industries where the right competitive strategy can bring high rewards but where there is only limited growth potential. In the 1980s such under-performing companies were available, but in the 1990s productivity improvements everywhere have reduced the likelihood – and, moreover, institutional investors believe that they can unlock the value the acquirers used to release.

BTR grew strongly in the 1980s under the strategic leadership of Sir Owen Green. By the early 1990s the company was diversified into control systems (water meters and valves), polymers* (conveyor belts and hoses, and including factories in Taiwan), electrical products (Hawker Siddeley motors as well as Newey and Eyre), construction (Tilcon*, Graham Builders Merchants*, Pilkington Tiles* and aggregate businesses in America), transportation (railway equipment), packaging (Rockware Glass), paper technology and consumer products (Dunlop Slazenger* and Pretty Polly lingerie). The companies marked with a * have now been sold to other parent companies or to their existing managers; and packaging and building materials are available for sale.

Alan Jackson succeeded Sir Owen Green as chief executive in 1991 (Green remained as Chairman for some time afterwards) and instituted a strategy of withdrawal from non-manufacturing interests. Jackson's successor, Ian Strachan, has continued the strategy and declared BTR will become a focused engineering group based on four core activities: automotive components, power drives, control systems and other specialist engineering products. At the same time there has been a number of related acquisitions. Strachan has advised institutional investors that he believes that BTR's days as an acquisitive conglomerate are over and that organic growth in its core strengths is now a priority. Nevertheless, while BTR outperformed the Financial Times share indices for many years, this has certainly not been the case recently. BTR has fallen from favour and investors are waiting for the promises from the new strategy to be delivered.

Tomkins grew out of a buckle manufacturing business based in Walsall; acquired businesses included Smith and Wesson handguns, lawnmowers, bicycles (in the USA) and a range of different industrial products. The chief executive, Greg Hutchings, is ex-Hanson. In 1992 Tomkins acquired Ranks Hovis McDougall (the milling and baking business which owns the Bisto, Paxo and Mr. Kipling brands), beating off a rival bid from Hanson. Four years later, after successfully absorbing RHM, Tomkins bought the American company, Gates Rubber, the world's largest manufacturer of power transmission belts and industrial hoses. RHM cost £93,5 million; Gates was roughly the same. In 1997 a US manufacturer of windscreen wipers, Stant, was bought to bolt-on to Gates. There have been no major divestments.

Tomkins has also built up surplus cash and used it to buy back shares. Further suitable and timely acquisitions have not been found and there are only limited opportunities for investment in its mature businesses.

Williams Holdings was built by accountants Nigel Rudd (a deal-maker) and Brian McGowan (acknowledged to be good at handling City institutions). Williams grew during the 1980s from a Midlands base in foundries. McGowan left in 1993; Rudd remains as strategic leader. The acquisition strategy in the 1980s was based largely on good opportunities for restructuring, but Williams quickly realized the value of established brand names and concentrated on businesses where it could exploit its brand management skills.

Through the 1980s and early 1990s the acquisitions included: Fairey Engineering, Rawlplug, Polycell, Crown Berger paints, Smallbone (kitchen units), Amdega (conservatories), Dreamland (electric blankets), Kidde (from Hanson – aerospace and fire extinguishers), Yale (locks) and Valor (locks and heating). Several of these have since been sold as Williams chose to focus on three business areas: building products (including DIY), fire protection and security (locks). Other UK fire equipment companies were added to the portfolio: Angus, Rockwell and a Thorn-EMI subsidiary. These were followed by related fire and locks acquisitions in Italy and America, and in 1996 Williams bought Sicli and Siddes, the largest fire protection company in France. In 1997 Williams turned its attention back to Chubb locks, a company it had attempted to acquire earlier.

Williams claims to be Britain's first "focused conglomerate" but some critics argue that focus requires more than the structural "bundling of a number of businesses into separate divisions". The fire and security businesses help offset the economic cycles of the construction and building industries, and Williams (with 12 percent of the world market) offers a wider range of fire protection products than any of its rivals. As fire regulations are tightened around the world, this industry also enjoys a high growth potential; it has yet to reach the maturity stage.

Meanwhile the US General Electric (GE) continues to prosper as one of the world's largest and most successful businesses. GE is unquestionably a global conglomerate, diversified into manufacturing (aircraft engines, defence electronics and household consumer goods) and services (ranging from NBC Television to GE Finance which provides capital for a wide range of activities, including the very high risk passenger aircraft leasing). On the whole, though, GE is not acquisitive on a regular basis; its success comes largely from its ability to foster sharing and learning amongst its disparate businesses, and, most significantly leverage its existing resources to create new forms of competitive advantage:

> Our intellectual capital is not US-based ... we aim to get the best ideas from everywhere. Each team puts up its best ideas and processes – constantly. That raises the bar. Our culture is designed around making a hero out of those who translate ideas from one place to another, who help somebody else. They get an award, they get praised and promoted. (Jack Welch, Chief Executive, C,K)

This philosophy, of course, is in stark contrast to the finance-driven holding company style of Hanson (in the past) and BTR, an approach which sees each business as a very independent activity. The GE philosophy has also been seen to be successful at another diversified American conglomerate, United Technologies, which comprises Otis, Carrier and Sikorski – respectively the world leaders for elevators, air conditioners and helicopters – Pratt and Whitney (jet engines), aerospace and automotive components:

> If one of the companies needs some new ideas, they should go and grab them from wherever is appropriate (George David, President and CEO, United Technologies).

Another diversified UK conglomerate, Wassall, has adopted a different approach. In 1994 Wassall bought the US company General Cable for £150 million. This company manufactures copper wire and cable products which are not essential for Wassall's long-term product interests. After successfully turning around an underperforming business, Wassall has recently floated off General Cable as an independent company worth £340 million. Wassall has chosen to return the original purchase price directly to its shareholders and retain just £190 million for further acquisitions with which it hopes to repeat the approach. With this strategy Wassall does not become dependent on finding ever-larger companies it can buy to turn around.

There is, of course, further evidence to support the preference for focus over diversity. In 1993, ICI split into two, leaving ICI (bulk chemicals) and Zeneca (higher value products such as pharmaceuticals) – two quite different businesses with different strategies, cultures and financial needs. Since 1993 Zeneca has prospered, but ICI continues to struggle in a competitive global industry. More recently ICI has further divested a number of businesses, bought related and bolt-on acquisitions from Unilever and swapped assets with Dont. W H Smith, once concentrated on books, magazines and stationery, is returning to this focus. Travel agency businesses and do-it-yourself outlets have already gone; its Waterstone's subsidiary is being floated off; and the Virgin Our Price specialist music and video stores are likely to be sold. Having developed a range of outlets in America, these are also being culled.

Focus, then, is unquestionably fashionable. Caulkin (1996) argues that if you have relatively poor management, focus makes absolute sense as focused companies are easier to manage. Unfortunately focus, *per se*, is unlikely to create new value. The dilemma with diversification lies in establishing clearly whether it is the corporate logic of the diversification strategy itself which is in question, or the inability of many companies to add value to a disparate range of activities and sustain real growth in some way Sadtler *et al.* (1997) defend the case for a clear focus, built around a defensible core of related activities, arguing that focus is now a more popular corporate strategy for a number of important reasons.

First, it allows greater control. Diversified conglomerates must decentralize to allow flexibility and this can imply a trade-off with central control unless the organization can truly share information and learn. Second, divesting unrelated businesses can provide the finance necessary to strengthen the core. Third, it often builds shareholder confidence, supporting the share price and making the organization less vulnerable to takeover. Fourth, in increasingly competitive markets and industries poor performance is harder to hide. Focus can ensure the weakest companies are divested and stronger businesses not held back because of the need to cross-subsidize.

For Sadtler the activity core is built around similar critical success factors (what the businesses have to be good at) and similar improvement opportunities (what they are going to have to do in the future). A corporate centre must be able to add value to every constituent business; every business in the portfolio should add value by contributing to the success of the whole organization. Detailed criteria can be readily and sensibly established to justify what should and what should not be in the core. The factors embrace financial performance over a number of years, the company's stated mission, the relatedness of tasks and technologies, customer requirements and the opportunities for internal sharing.

On the other hand strategic leaders who have grown successful diversified businesses choose to disagree. Harold Geneen (1997), who died in 1997, is often credited as the founder of truly diversified conglomerates. Geneen's ITT at one time included telecommunications, hotels, baking, cosmetics and lightbulbs, book publishing and Avis Rent-a-Car. ITT has been comprehensively broken up – although Geneen's tight financial control style worked, when he retired there was no natural succession. However, Geneen continued to claim:

> To succeed in business it is essential to take risks. But they must be smart risks – researched, understood, survivable. The conglomerate is a good vehicle for identifying and exploiting them ... but ... running a conglomerate requires working harder than most people want to work and taking more risks than most people want to take.

Sir Owen Green (1994), ex-BTR, has defended conglomerates even more strongly:

> As soon as things go wrong, companies start talking about focus. Focus is the crutch of mediocre management ... if you are trained in the techniques

of management ... you should be able to apply them across a range of companies. Diversified companies possess both defensive qualities in a recession and a springboard for new ventures in more expansive times.

This argument is further borne out by the success of the US conglomerate, Textron which has outperformed the Wall Street stock index by 50 percent during the 1990s. Textron manufactures light aircraft (Cessna), helicopters (Bell), machine tools, automotive components, lawnmowers, watch straps and Shaeffer pens – as well as owning a consumer finance business. The company argues its balanced diversity (not being over-dependent on any one product) allows it to consistently improve its overall earnings through economic cycles. This case has always been used as an argument to defend diversity, while recognizing that with the wrong approach it can become dangerously short-termist. To succeed it needs a particular management style.

Summarizing this section of the paper ... most strategies can be made to work effectively and efficiently; the ultimate success of any strategy, though, lies in its implementation. Decisions concerning the implementation issues of structure and management style – as well as those affecting the competitiveness of each product or service in the portfolio – provide additional dilemmas which we now need to investigate further.

It should not be forgotten that concentrating our debate on this manifestation of corporate strategy can draw attention away from the real strategic issue – which is creating new values. Reinforcing earlier points, Hamel and Prahalad (1994) contend that today there is too much strategic convergence. High performance organizations reinvent industries and regenerate core strategies. They innovate around the theme of positioning.

Strategic choices

When contemplating future choices and directions, organizations will hope they can benefit from their past successes and experiences. Nevertheless, the future is rarely, if ever, the past projected forward, and, looking ahead, an organization is unlikely to be able to see the end from the beginning. The organization will need ideas, and it does not follow that the best ideas will always – if ever – come from those people with the most seniority and experience. There are, therefore, a number of clear challenges. First, embracing the contributions from both its experienced and youthful managers. Second, blending unity (clear direction and purpose) with diversity (the flexibility to introduce fresh ideas and changes quickly). This is sometimes stated as the ability of a large organization to behave like an archetypal small, entrepreneurial business – which implies size is a key issue. Large organizations can achieve a range of scale economies, and they should be able to enjoy critical mass in all their areas of interest; but size can threaten the essential ability to innovate, unless it is accompanied by an appropriate structure. Encouraging managers to be intrapreneurial means they must be empowered in a decentralized structure; as we saw earlier this can make day-to-day control more difficult. For these reasons we often see switches of emphasis as organizations grow. To stimulate growth, they decentralize; when control is threatened they centralize more until they re-establish stability. Stability may not foster innovation, and so they decentralize once more.

A key issue here is whether being bigger or being better is the driving philosophy. Some organizations and some strategic leaders strive to grow, and they may well favour acquisitions to achieve this. Their challenge is to create and exploit the elusive synergy from an acquisition. An alternative approach is to be more innovative, to seek to become better and more effective, to creatively find new positioning opportunities and to reinvent industries. Once successful, these companies will automatically grow. Both can succeed; relative failure lies in acquisition strategies which destroy rather than add new value.

These issues again imply creative tensions. Organizations must understand where and why current strategies are strong and successful – assuming they are, of course – and look for ways of consolidating this success in order to build on it. At the same time, it is dangerous to assume this success can be sustained without change. Renewal often comes from questioning the fragility of existing success and knowing when to abandon existing paradigms and positions. It can be argued that security will only be available to those who welcome insecurity. As we discussed earlier, complacently successful organizations might have to create some form of crisis situation in order to galvanize the actions needed for change and renewal in a dynamic environment. Timing is critical – this needs to happen while the organization is still able to be proactive and before it is forced onto the reactive defensive.

To achieve this, organizations must be simultaneously creative and analytical, and find a suitable balance. Developing ideas from Vandermerwe and Birley (1997), the strategic organization is able to blend vision and entrepreneurship with management (businesslike behaviour) and administration (for control) (see Figure 5). The entrepreneurial business has unreasonable convictions based on inadequate evidence (Tom Peters) but opportunism must be tempered with some caution to limit the risk-taking. As small, entrepreneurial businesses grow, they need to introduce sound control systems. A businesslike approach implies sound management principles such as managing the cash flow to ensure spending is supported by adequate earnings; equally, sound managers must not be constrained from being innovative. In recent years, with such changes as compulsory competitive tendering, we have seen public sector managers become increasingly businesslike and innovative.

At the heart of this issue is the organization's attitude to risk. In an ideal world managers would seek to maximize opportunity from the minimum risk – and not feel too constrained in their endeavours. A requirement to be entrepreneurial, to innovate, to take risks but make sure it never costs the company any money, will not work. Risk taking is essential, but it should be carefully measured risk; and managers must be suitably rewarded for taking the necessary risks. Correspondingly they need organizational support, especially if things go wrong, as inevitably they sometimes must.

In this context, it is useful to reflect for a moment on how we seek to develop managers. The MBA qualification, for example, is ubiquitous and popular, certainly with individuals if not with every organization. Some companies retain a scepticism because many MBA programmes concentrate more on analysis – management and control – than visionary and entrepreneurial themes.

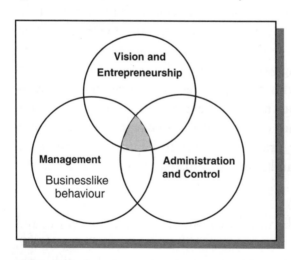

Innovation generally implies a search for opportunities to be different, which affects competitiveness and content competence. But is the innovation directed at achieving existing outcomes with fewer resources (a cost advantage) or finding new ways of adding value (a differentiation advantage)? As industries and markets become more and more international, with competitors in several countries, cost pressures undoubtedly grow.

Figure 5. The Strategic Approach to Management

But if we accept Hamel and Prahalad's (1994) argument that new competitors are a greater threat than international ones, differentiation is the critical element.

Another strategic trend of the 1990s, linked to the theme of focus, is vertical dis-integration – typically the outsourcing of non-core activities. This strategy allows organizations to both save money and limit the number of core competences they require, which helps explain its popularity. The Burton Group provides an ideal example. Once a leading manufacturer of men's clothing, Burton some while ago divested its factories to concentrate on retailing. More recently it has outsourced all its logistics. Also recently, it has decided to float off Debenhams, arguing that focused and branded high street units (Top Shop, Top Man, Dorothy Perkins and Principles as well as Burton) require different competences from multi-product department stores which include several specialist concessions. However, when this happens, an effective supply chain network is vital – and the process compe-tence of managing such a network for all-round mutual benefit, is critical. Many organizations are finding this is harder to achieve and sustain than it might first appear. It requires a strong dedication to service, value and fairness from every relationship. But is this natural? Is it not more typical for a supplier and buyer to each seek to negotiate the best personal deal rather than automatically think of mutual benefits? Again the strategy can seem justified, but it is tricky to imple-ment successfully.

Finally, to succeed, an organization must balance the often conflicting needs of its stakeholders; invariably this demands tradeoffs. Shareholders, suppliers, cus-tomers and employees must all be satisfied: increasingly social and ethical values should be incorporated to minimize the risk of damaging publicity. There is a cir-cular process at work. Unless an organization satisfies its stakeholders it will not be successful; unless it is successful and (where relevant) profitable, it will not be able to satisfy its stakeholders! People and information are critically important resources. However, investment in important information technology can some-times threaten jobs. People must be empowered and rewarded individually to fos-ter innovation; but to achieve synergy, it is essential they see themselves as "team players". The same theme applies to different businesses (if they are at all inter-dependent) in a multi-activity corporation.

Conclusion

It will be seen from the above analysis and arguments that while the strategic challenge may be clear – to create winning strategic positions and to sustain success with changes informed by awareness and learning – developing the competences to make this happen is difficult. Choices have to be made all the time. These choices frequently imply taking a stance on an issue such as focus or diversify, outsourcing or insourcing, centralization or decentralization. Individually each relevant issue may be clear; but systemically they all inter-link.

A paradox exists when something is contrary to perceived opinion. Strategy is full of paradoxes. There are no right and wrong answers concerning what organizations should or should not do. Clearly they have to make choices, and there will be good and bad decisions. But successful implementation is always essential and this means that we are looking at several issues and choices simultaneously, rarely at one in isolation. Hence, the appropriate competence mix is unique to an individual organization; and for this reason, so much depends on effective strategic leadership. As we have said, strategy is about choices – choosing what to do and what not to do. This requires thinking, awareness and vision. The answers cannot be found in books; similarly, it is rarely adequate to simply embrace the latest technique or guru-inspired idea. These can all make important contributions, as can benchmarking both competitors and recognized good practice, but only as a base.

References

Caulkin, S. (1996), "Focus is for wimps", *Management Today*, December.

Geneen, H. (1997), *The Synergy Myth*, St Martin's Press, New York, NY.

Grant, R.M. (1997), Presentation at a Strategic Planning Society conference. The presentation built on Cibin, R. and Grant, R.M. (1996), "Restructuring among the world's leading oil companies, 1980-92", *British Journal of Management*, Vol. 7, pp. 283-307.

Green, 0. (1994), Management Today, June, p. 40. Hamel, G. and Prahalad, C.K (1994), Competing for the Future, *Harvard Business School Press*, Boston, MA.

Hurst, D.K. (1995), *Crisis and Renewal: Meeting the Challenge of Organizational Change*, Harvard Business School Press, Boston, MA.

Kets de Vries, M. (1996), "Leaders who make a difference", *European Management Journal*, Vol. 14 No. 5, October.

Peters, T.J. and Waterman, R.H. Jr (1982), *In Search of Excellence: Lessons from America's Best Run Companies*, Harper & Row, New York, NY.

Sadtler, D., Campbell, A. and Koch, R. (1997), *Break Up! When Large Companies Are Worth More Dead Than Alive*, Capstone.

Thompson, J.L. (1996), "Strategic effectiveness and success – the learning challenge", *Management Decision*, Vol. 34 No. 7.

Thompson, J.L. and Richardson, B. (1996), "Strategic and competitive success – towards a model of the comprehensively competent organization", *Management Decision*, Vol. 34 No. 2.

Vandermerwe, S. and Birley, S. (1997), The Boss as a Force for Change, in Birley and Muzyka, D.F. (Eds), *Mastering Enterprise, Financial Times/ Pitman.